DOING LIFE DIFFERENTLY
in Thailand
Mel Pike

one woman ditching the daily grind, living solo and making memories

Published by Solo Sisters Publishing

Copyright © 2024 Melanie Pike

This is a work of non-fiction, inspired by real and historical events. However, some of the names of characters in this book have been changed out of respect for their privacy.

No part of this book may be reproduced, or stored in a retrieval system, or transmitted in any form or by any means, electronic, mechanical, photocopying, recording, or otherwise, without the express written permission of the author.

A catalogue record is available for this book from the National Library of Australia.

ISBN 978-0-9756185-0-9
First Edition Published 2024

For my wonderful Thai friends Pui, N'Bow, P'Sak, Kunya, Mickey and Khun Tuk. You're the reason I said that in all my wildest dreams I could never have imagined the people I've been lucky to meet, the places I've seen, the food I've eaten and the kindest hearts that have made me feel so welcome and helped me live so happily here.

And for Rosie Pearl, my chocolate Labrador gal, who sat just over my left shoulder on her green velvet armchair, keeping me company the whole time I sat at my keyboard. You never, ever missed an opportunity to be by my side. Your soft snoring and dozing provided comfort. Your endless patience while I was so absorbed in my writing has been noted and appreciated. Now it's time for more sniffaris (sniff safaris) together. Without a doubt, little choccy girl, you are my sunshine!

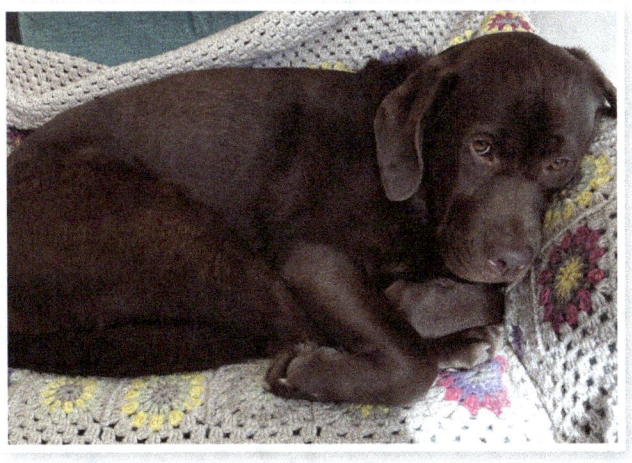

Foreword

I'm so pleased you have this book in your hands and can spend time with my inspiring friend Melanie Pike, one of the big-hearted people on the earth whom I first met on our Vietnam Gourmet Safari in 2016. We were travelling from Hanoi to Saigon enjoying so many delicious adventures spread across two weeks. Mel is one of those people who really lives in the moment, savours people and experiences, is huge fun AND loves food - so of course we hit it off. Her laugh is a classic!

While on this trip I was intrigued to hear her story and how this was her first trip away from her husband Joe who was suffering severe PTSD and depression after stints in Afghanistan and Iraq. He was struggling with life and often in a very dark place. She was very loving and hugely supportive of finding a way for his life to improve. Over the years she had moved mountains to help him get the right treatment and specialists.

We stayed in touch. I was so pleased when I heard her plan to give herself 'long-service leave from life' and spend five months in Thailand, a place she had a deep connection with. Many years ago, Mel spent twelve months going to high school in rural Thailand while she was an exchange student.

In 2023 off she went on her brave, challenging and hugely rewarding adventure. She felt sure Joe would be okay as now he thankfully has a great support team around him.

Working on improving her Thai language with its endless consonants, vowel combinations and tonal variations was hard, but wow did it open doors for Mel who wowed taxi drivers, nail artists, restaurateurs and shop owners with her linguistic skills. Such a compliment to the beautiful people of Thailand to speak their language.

Her daily Instagram posts from Phuket of her adventures while she was away - with the language and the food - were warm, charming and unique. While reading them I knew this was surely the basis of a book. An "Eat Pray Love" for the new times; something as genuine and authentic as Melanie herself. I suggested the idea and she ran with it.

Melanie carved her own path into the world of self-publishing and like everything in her life she found a way to make this book happen. She wrote it, found an editor, cover designer, and navigated a way to self-publish completely separate from the major publishing houses. In no time – whoosh, here it is.

I'm so proud of Melanie and all she has achieved. Life is not for sissies and to rise above and triumph and have produced this cracking good read that will make you hungry, smile and feel warm inside … that's gold!
I'm sure you'll enjoy reading this book.

You might also like to visit Mel's micro-business, Bright Blossom Bags www.brightblossombags.com . They sell vibrant colourful clutches and totes all made in Thailand. She's working together with her Thai friend, Pui and their business is built on kindness, laughter, knowledge sharing, respect and love. Women helping other women and paying it forward!

All success to you my friend.

Maeve O'Meara OAM

Introduction

I have a confession to make.

I'd allowed myself to buy into many of the common stereotypes surrounding Phuket (pronounced poo-ket) in Thailand. This was before I had even visited the place to see it for myself. I'd concluded that this city was all about the endless party vibe, the scantily clad bar girls and the overcrowded beaches; an island mecca for sex, particularly for the lost, lonely and desperate from all corners of the world.

Having been to Thailand many times I'd always avoided staying in Phuket, assuming that this wasn't the 'real' Thailand that I'd grown to know and love. This destination is a tourist magnet and I thought I'd progressed long ago from being just a tourist in this country.

I'm now delighted to say my misguided perceptions and unfounded presumptions about Phuket have been well and truly squashed. Sure, Phuket is a great place to party, and there are areas where you can go completely crazy and meet random strangers in various stages of undress dancing on top of bars if that's your desire. But you need to deliberately place yourself amongst it. In fact, the rich cultural experiences on offer far outweigh any of that. This amazing place and its people are friendly, welcoming and unique.

Before long you may even find that it has reached deep inside your heart and established a permanent spot there.

Phuket Island is separated from the mainland by a narrow sea channel and the 660-metre Sarasin Bridge connects it to Phang Nga province. If you ever feel like a drive to Bangkok, it's 840-odd kilometres away. Phuket is in the far south of Thailand, closer to Malaysia. It's a tourist hotspot with 14 million domestic and international visitors in 2023.

I grew up in Albury, New South Wales, Australia. It's located on the northern side of the Murray River with its twin city Wodonga being on the southern side in the state of Victoria. In my last year of high school, I decided I wanted to be an exchange student and live overseas for a year, hoping it would provide me with some sort of direction once I left school as I didn't really have any.

I applied to be an American Field Studies (AFS) exchange student. This program involved studying overseas for twelve months and having an intercultural adventure: living with a local family; attending a local school; absorbing another culture; often learning a new language and gaining life skills while making friends; and having a great time. When the letter arrived to say I had been chosen to participate in the program, I was full of excitement and anticipation. A whole year away, stepping into the unknown, seemed appealing. I originally selected Japan as my destination, only to be told that Japan wasn't available but Thailand was. This country girl knew nothing about Thailand apart from the fact that the food was spicy. Albury had recently acquired a Thai restaurant, which in itself was pretty unbelievable given the food choices in the 1980s in my town were limited to Chinese and Italian.

On 13 March 1989, aged seventeen, I said goodbye to my family and boarded a plane to Melbourne to connect with a flight to Bangkok. I don't need to reread the diary I kept back then to remember that I left home in a flood of tears. My dislike of goodbyes has stayed with me throughout my life.

I had exchanged several letters with my Thai host family and knew I was going to live in Kamphaeng Phet, a town some 350 kilometres north of Bangkok. For months I stumbled over the name of my town, until finally I got the pronunciation right: 'Gum-paeng-pet', not 'Cam-fang-fet'.

While deciding what to include in this book I found an old box of bits and pieces that I had kept from my exchange-student days. I came across the yearbook that the AFS Thailand exchange students from all over the world had made. We all contributed one page and wrote about how our year had played out. I was very curious to read what eighteen-year-old me had to say: *Thailand is truly a beautiful country, deep in history and tradition from ancient temples to hill tribe people. Thailand and its people have been good to me in my time spent here and I know I'll return one day to re-experience a bit of my year here again.*

Once my exchange year was over and I'd returned home to Albury, it wasn't long before I was ready for my next adventure. I moved to Melbourne, the capital of Victoria, a lively, artsy city with trams running down the middle of many of the inner-city streets, umpteen late-night cafés, Vic Market for fresh food and an eclectic mix of people and food choices from so many different countries. I felt very grown-up and capable as I carved out this new life for myself. I lived in the inner-city suburb of Richmond, worked at an upmarket food hall and coffee bar in South Yarra, and fell in love with all this city had to offer.

I eventually tired of the frantic pace of the coffee bar and making toasted focaccias. I started a business degree at Swinburne

University, while cleaning the homes of the rich to provide me with a minimal income. I met a man, not a wealthy one, whom I lived with for the next six years. I continued to study the Thai language on a Saturday morning in a class full of middle-aged men, most of whom had Thai wives or girlfriends. What a fun class it was, and our teacher was a posh Englishman who'd married a Thai lady, so we had access to a native speaker.

I travelled backwards and forwards to Thailand on holidays, to study at university and once for a short work stint as a Thai-speaking graduate at a major insurance company. Just as my career was taking off, my long-term relationship ended. All I wanted was to be close to my family and that meant moving to Sydney in New South Wales. For the next six years, drifting from job to job chasing the money, I was desperately trying to find something I enjoyed. I found myself working as a personal assistant to those in middle management in all sorts of industries. My weekends mostly revolved around where my Australian Rules football team, the Sydney Swans, were playing. The games were thrilling and we went as a family for many years.

Sometime in 2001, reading the paper during one of those football games, I saw an article about online dating. It was a new concept and seen at the time as an odd and somewhat embarrassing way to meet someone. I'd tried pubs, clubs, blind dates and desperate and dateless balls and knew I had nothing to lose. I went home that night and joined the online dating website, RSVP. I was flattered by the attention I received from complete strangers, but there was one man who impressed me with the written word. We exchanged multiple emails and then my internet provider went out of business. I came home from work one day to find a letter in my letterbox from this man. He'd managed to track me down.

For our first real-life date, I met Joe at Hoxton Park Airport. He was working as a commercial pilot and had flown himself from country New South Wales in a four-seat, single-engine Cessna 172 Skyhawk. (I let him add this bit because how would I know that!) Soon I was enjoying a joy flight over Sydney. My parents had always told me to be wary of getting into cars with strangers, but aeroplanes? Six years later he would become my husband.

I eventually went to live with him: first in country New South Wales, then in Darwin in the Northern Territory – the Outback, endless expanses of red earth, vast, starry night skies, crocodiles and swimming under waterfalls. Then Joe's job took him to Canberra, the Australian capital, nestled between Sydney and Melbourne. By this time my family had all moved to Hobart, the Tasmanian capital, 850 kilometres away. I wanted to be close to them, so Joe commuted between the two cities and we made it work. In Hobart, I became a Commonwealth public servant at the Australian Antarctic Division.

In 2008, things began to get difficult. I was in my late thirties when Joe deployed to Iraq and Afghanistan with the Australian Army. He was on the cusp of turning forty, slim and fit, an intelligent, articulate man who chose his words carefully and didn't suffer fools. He could turn his mind to most things and succeed. He was kind-hearted, considerate, quiet, loving, loyal and believed in making a difference. He valued his family and friends and wanted to make us all proud.

I will never truly know what Joe experienced in those wars. Yet by September 2009, when he had been home for less than a year, I was living with a man whom I barely recognised. He had become distant, hypervigilant, fragile, angry, incredibly emotional and depressed. He was having nightmares and night sweats, drinking excessively, totally shutdown and unable to get off the couch for weeks on end. This troubled man had broken into a million pieces. I was totally shut out.

Two years later, I celebrated my fortieth birthday in New York with Joe and my parents. The city I'd longed to visit delivered so much more than I'd believed was possible: Broadway shows; Magnolia Bakery cupcakes; and wandering for blocks and blocks amid this buzzy, iconic city. It was also a conflicting and sad time.

On our return, Joe went straight into intensive psychiatric treatment. We both knew something had to change. We had no idea what the road ahead would look like and maybe that was a blessing. The diagnosis was confirmed that he had PTSD and major depression. Meanwhile, the angry irrational outbursts continued in private and public over simple things or nothing at all. Despite my best efforts, I couldn't work out what would trigger him. My mate had become a ticking time bomb. I struggled to comprehend how our lives could've changed so dramatically. He was forgetful, frightened of the dark, easily startled, constantly fatigued, impatient, wary of strangers, antisocial, unable to function on a daily basis and often suicidal. A long list of medications was now his friend. He was a mere shadow of himself, often engulfed by shame and guilt.

As his capacity decreased, my responsibilities increased tenfold. My role changed from wife to carer.

Although this book isn't about my husband, I don't feel like I can ignore the impact those years had on me. They have undoubtedly shaped me into who I am today. The struggles we all face throughout our lives can be unspeakably cruel. Even now I wonder how we both survived those grim times. I learnt to live with a level of pressure I never knew existed. I became hypervigilant for situations that I knew he couldn't handle. There were arguments and tension between us. It was nothing short of life-changing. My health declined at times due to the immense and sustained stress. The relationship that should've been joyful and easy became complicated and hard.

We've often talked about how on earth we stayed together. To be honest, we don't know. We think it was due to our strong friendship and genuine love for one another, but even that has been beyond tested. The simple fun stuff can be a big deal and spontaneity is totally out of the question. Things I used to take for granted, like being able to calmly drive in traffic, go to new places to eat or asking Joe to drop into the supermarket for a few things, can all be a big deal and change the mood in an instant. And we still continue to muddle our way through life.

After more than a decade, white-knuckled on this emotional rollercoaster, I knew I needed to do something just for myself. I had no idea what that would be.

In 2022, just as the world began to open up again after the coronavirus pandemic, we were desperate for some time in the warm tropical waters of Thailand. This country had become a place Joe and I both enjoyed and we felt relaxed and happy whenever we visited. We seemed to find a level of peace there that eluded us at home. Despite the risks of international travel at that time, on a whim we booked a couple of weeks in Phuket, having previously dismissed it as somewhere we wouldn't want to stay. We couldn't wait to go.

When Joe and I arrived in Phuket, we found the people desperate for tourists to return to their island. The pandemic had been devastating as they relied so heavily on the tourist dollar to survive. The hit they'd taken confronted us everywhere we went. The sight of empty shops and deserted streets and the stories of survival from the locals were heartbreaking.

One afternoon, I was having a swim in the pool at our favourite hotel, The Sarojin in Khao Lak, an hour north from Phuket airport. The staff there have become like family to us. We were joking around together about me coming to live at the hotel and help them improve their English. I'd often chat with them using my limited and rusty Thai and we thought we could all benefit from some language lessons. That flippant conversation sparked an idea that I couldn't ignore. I knew I was ready to live in Thailand again for an extended period.

I was keen to soak up all that I love about the place and dive headfirst into the language. I'd saved a chunk of my long-service leave and started planning what a couple of months away might look like. Joe was totally onboard with my idea and made sure I followed through. I returned from that holiday and put my leave application in at work.

Joe and I have a theory that, once you've booked your flights, there's no turning back. I'd like to tell you I researched and plotted my time away, but the truth is I didn't. Location-wise I thought it would be best for me to be close to the language school I'd chosen, but I also wanted some time near the beach. That was about it for planning. Something I was sure about was that I wanted to escape any hint of my daily routine and erase the daily grind.

When I arrived I started capturing my days through photos and words which kind of morphed into a journal of sorts via my Instagram squares. The painfully practical side of me and my foggy brain (thanks to being fifty-two and in the haze of menopause) knew that if I didn't capture what I was doing each day in some form, I'd forget. It was as simple as that.

I wrote only for myself. I knew that afterwards I'd want to be able to recapture the sense of calm I felt as I sat on the beach alone, feet buried in the warm sand and staring at a golden sunset, or the taste of a ripe mango paired with sticky rice and smothered in coconut cream, or the feeling of the weightlessness of my body and the worries of the world around me evaporating as I floated in the warm, jade-coloured waters of the Andaman Sea. I wanted to be able to smile as I scrolled back through my photos, words and comments on Instagram. I tagged my posts #livinglikeathai. It never ever crossed my mind that my words would find their way into a book!

There was no polish to my writing. It was real and raw as I recorded the ebb and flow of my daily life, shared my thoughts, my sheer delight, my utter despair and sadness, as well as my interactions, hopes and, inadvertently, the lives of those I met.

Living vicariously through other people's travel adventures, whether through books, blogs or social media, has long been a favourite pastime of mine. Feeling part of someone's adventure through experiences generously shared would have me dreaming and scheming of doing the same. I'd imagine the excitement of stepping off the daily treadmill, packing away my everyday routine, travelling solo and letting life rise up to meet me. I never imagined that one day my travels might do that for others.

I'm writing this after having lived in Phuket for a whole 153 days. I still can't believe how fortunate I was to form genuine and lasting friendships with many wonderful people. Not only Thais but foreigners from all parts of the globe with whom I crossed paths and often found myself laughing.

The experiences that seemed to find me during my stay have given me immense joy. This book really came about by accident. After much encouragement by those who followed my Instagram posts, I decided to dip my toe into the unknow world of self-publishing.

You will meet some truly remarkable people in these pages, learn about them and their lives and hopefully gain a sense of the fascinating Thai culture, learn a bit of their language, have a laugh and come to understand why I have long referred to Thailand as 'my happy place'.

I've not necessarily set out to teach you anything here, only to share with you that doing life differently is possible. There's so much to be gained from travelling solo and just getting out there and giving it a go. For those who might have the desire to do something similar, trust yourself, dare to dream and the rewards will be yours for the taking. Don't live with regret – book that airline ticket or buy that caravan. Just make it happen.

I've found the relationships that have come my way have formed on a basis of mutual respect, understanding and laughter. My love and admiration for the Thai people and my happy place has deepened after this stay. I've had a print on my wall for more than twenty years which says: *Enjoy the little things in life. For one day you may look back and realise they were the big things.*

I hope you enjoy some of life's little things and the doing of life differently in the following pages.

Mel- Thailand 1989/90

22 February 2023
Hobart—Melbourne—Singapore / Kata Beach, Phuket

Five a.m. kisses from my fur girls, Jasmine, the super-smart black Labrador, and Rosie, the biggest cuddle-muffin chocolate Labrador. Oh and Joe, too. There's no looking back for me. I dread leaving my girls behind even if it's only for a short while. I'd tried to put this out of my mind in the days leading up to my departure. I'd repeatedly told them both how much I loved them and that it was okay for them to sleep on my side of the bed. I also knew they'd forgive me for being away, they always do. Thankfully there are now multiple ways of keeping in touch with husbands, but I'd given him the same messages as our girls. I love the anticipation of an international flight. I probably haven't done enough of them for them to become tedious. Even just getting yourself to the airport after all the prep and packing required for a lengthy time away is reason enough to high-five yourself. I'm now actually on my way.

These next four months all before me to do as I please is liberating and totally foreign. I've never had an extended break from my working life. I'd like to say that my departure from home has me on some sort of deliberate self-discovery path but that's not true. I just know I want to do life differently for a while, only be responsible for myself and improve my languishing Thai language skills. Nor do I want to think about what's for dinner each night (hello mental load – the invisible burden that women often carry when managing not only their own life but also those in their household).

It was 8 a.m. and, as I walked through duty-free, I was offered a G&T by a chatty man selling of all things Tasmanian gin. I gladly obliged. This simple act was, I believe, the start of doing things differently, although I was oblivious at the time. It was only when I reread my Instagram descriptions that this became obvious.

The flight to Singapore was seamless. I found myself thinking about what these next couple of months might hold while flicking through various movie options and watching the flight tracker. The flight time from Melbourne is around eight hours which I find goes quickly.

At Changi Airport, I went straight up the escalators to the Hainanese chicken hawker stall, not because I was necessarily hungry but rather because I wanted to check that it wasn't another Covid casualty. My favourite airport not only had its pretend hawker stalls back but also the umpteen luxury-end shops fully stocked and the browsing and buying public were back in numbers.

When flying from Singapore to Phuket, you no sooner sit down and you're on descent. Phuket has been the gateway through which we have most often entered southern Thailand during our past visits. The musty smell of the air conditioning that hits me as I leave the air bridge always signals that I've arrived in Thailand, as do the big smiles on the faces of the staff that are there to provide a warm welcome. I'd purchased a fast pass through immigration and customs that promised I'd be in a taxi and on my way in thirty minutes.

With my meet-and-greet lady waiting for me as I stepped off the plane, I was off and running with my Thai language. My aim is to use it as much as I possibly can, so there was no holding back. I find you can learn so much about people when you've got even a small amount of language here and probably anywhere you travel throughout the world. I found out where her hometown was, where she studied, how much she paid for rent a month and lots of other bits and pieces. Small talk is useful for me when I start speaking the language again. Such a great boost to my confidence if I can understand the conversation and be understood. She ushered me through immigration and straight through customs.

When my driver arrived curb side, I had my next opportunity to chat. Initially he thought I'd come to teach Thai kids English and couldn't quite believe I was here to learn their language. We talked about our favourite Thai food, how to tell the time in Thai, how much he loved his country and how good-hearted Thai people are. He also told me his Thai nickname. Thai names are impossibly long, but thankfully most people have a nickname or *cheu len*, which literally translates as 'play name'. When I came here as an exchange student, my Thai family gave me the name Sumalee: 'beautiful flower'. Thais love to know I have this name and will often call me by it.

The trip from the airport in the north of the island to Kata in the south took about an hour. After the quiet, orderly burbs of Hobart, the bustling, tourist-filled streets of Kata Beach can be quite a sharp shock. The bright lights were back on with restaurants packed, night markets open, locals smiling and street-food carts out and about selling everything from fresh tropical fruit to pad Thai. It was so heartening to see that the place had come alive again.

My brain was fried by the time I opened my hotel room

door. By the time my head hit the pillow, I could barely speak. I love seeing how far travel can take you in a day. I also like to know there's a shower and comfy bed waiting for me at the end of a twenty-hour day.

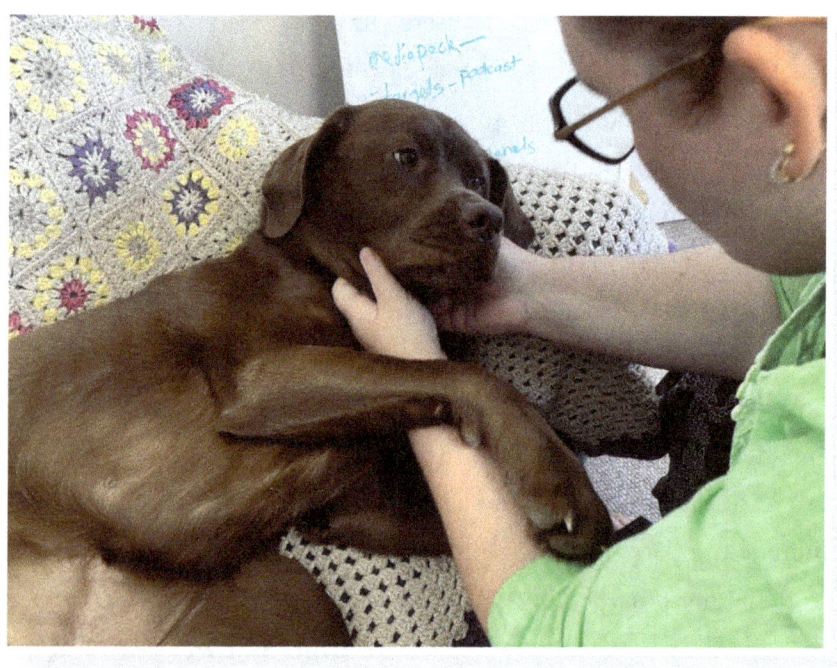

23 February

Kata Beach | Mani-Pedi | Uniforms

I learnt a new Thai phrase this morning. I now know how to say, 'I've locked my key in my room.' In the process I found that the helpful and sweet ladies at the reception desk of my hotel were keen for a chat and a laugh. I can't walk past them now without them saying 'key' (*koon jaer*). I'm staying at Kata Poolside Resort on Kata Road, the main street of Kata. It's nothing flash, probably a bit tired but perfect for me. Unpacking just involved taking piles of clothes still in their packing cells out of my suitcases and dumping them on the day bed. I figure that so long as I've got my pool and beach stuff out, I'll be fine.

    Down the lane from my hotel, I met a friendly roti maker. Looks like breakfast is sorted – fresh banana and mango made with a smile and a chat in Thai. We spoke about how hard it is to speak Thai, but she thinks English is harder. I told her I'd see her tomorrow and order in Thai again. The area around the hotel is full of thousands of microbusinesses. There's no welfare system or safety net for the unemployed over here. If you don't work, you don't eat. I've always greatly admired how Thai people find ways to employ themselves. They've found a market for tourists who can't or don't want to peel and cut the tropical fruit on offer, so they've done it for us.

In Hobart, not only are passionfruit expensive, they're also often shrivelled by the time they arrive in the shops. I can't imagine buying a tray of passionfruit at home. Here it's just over A$1 per tray of fruit, cut in half and served complete with a spoon. I rarely eat fresh pineapple at home. It's too tart and sour. Here it's addictive, sweet, cut in a pretty shape and readily available. The abundance and variety of cheap, fresh tropical fruit is one of the foodie highlights for me in Thailand. You choose how you eat it: as a smoothie, in a cocktail, in a roti, by the piece. What's not to love about that?

One of the first things I always do when I arrive in Thailand is head out for a foot scrub and mani-pedi. There are no fewer than twenty salons on the street outside my hotel. The biggest dilemma of my day was which one should I pick? Air conditioning and a clean front window won and in I went. There was a wait, but I had nowhere else I needed to be. I had a prime position for the best people watching I've had in ages, not only the passing street parade but also those coming into the salon: a steady stream of shapes, sizes, colours, nationalities and hair braids. We really are a weird lot, us humans.

The real action was outside. I lost count of the times I flinched as motorcycle-riding foreigners came within inches of crashing into one another. It's manic on the roads and my Thai vocabulary expanded once again. From my chatty beauty therapist I learnt the words for car crash, helmet, no helmet, blood and die. It's no surprise that Thailand has the highest incidence of road traffic deaths involving motorbikes in the world. Let's just say I'm walking everywhere.

A couple of hours in the salon not only gave me the smoothest feet and shiniest neon-pink-painted nails I've had in years but a few new friends. Tomorrow I'm going back for a massage. I think they'll be seeing a fair bit of me.

Salon staff often sit in a line in front of the massage shops as they coax the passing tourists to partake in the services they offer. They proudly wear salon uniforms in the brightest colours. This love of a uniform is very Thai. There's a practical side to this as it cuts down on the clothes they need to buy and wash. But they also like to look nice. Being neat and tidy in Thai society is very important and it starts when they are children. School children wear a uniform that hasn't changed in more than a century. The boys wear tan shorts and the girls knee-length, navy-blue pleated skirts. Everyone wears a crisp white shirt with their name and number embroidered in blue for public schools and red for private schools. I had the pleasure of wearing this uniform when I was here as an exchange student. Girls must not have their hair longer than a short bob and for boys it's short back and sides. I think they may have relaxed that rule for me as I had long curly hair that I pulled back in a ponytail.

You'll also see the police here in uniforms so tightly fitted you'll wonder how they managed to squeeze into them. Government officials wear uniforms more akin to military fatigues complete with fake gold buttons and often decorated with medals. I'm a bit partial to a uniform, too. Seeing the airline crew dressed smartly in crisp uniforms yesterday pleased me. Women wearing their hair in a tight French twist or a sharp bob, immaculate makeup and elegant jewellery complementing their look; men with neat, short hair that's freshly cut and the waft of expensive aftershave often lingering long after they've walked past. Asian airlines maintain their polished image very well.

In Thai society status and social hierarchy is strongly focused upon and uniforms do a great job of helping people work out where other people fit. This also influences the way they speak with one another. Respect is shown by using various gender-specific polite particles at the end of their sentences. For women they use *kha*; for men, *krap*. Many aspects of this society and the way it ticks are based on centuries-old traditions. I'm absolutely fascinated by this culture. My curiosity sees me asking lots of questions whenever I visit. As my knowledge of the language has improved, I've been able to gain a deeper understanding of their customs and traditions.

I took my freshly painted toes off to the beach where I was able to feel the sublime temperature of the water for the first time. I sat on the sand and watched the many tourists taking five-minute parasails out over the water and back. The speed boat begins to slow as it returns the thrill seeker back to the shore. The Thai person who accompanies the parasailer dangles from the frame of the parasail without wearing any form of harness. They solely rely on a group of about four men who run along the beach trying to grab their dangling legs. This is necessary to prevent the parasail from crashing heavily onto the beach. It's skilful but that's one activity that I'll be happy to watch from the shore. The atmosphere down at the beach was vibrant and lively. How could it not be when it was heaving with relaxed holidaymakers soaking up this beautiful place. Gosh, it feels good to be back here.

24 February
Kata | Fresh Food Market and a Massage

My body clock is still adjusting to my new time zone. This meant I was awake at 6 a.m. this morning, which was 9 a.m. at home. Last night, I googled a fresh food market I wanted to visit and thought I'd get up and have a walk to find it.

My love of fresh food markets is deep. While living in Melbourne I had a Saturday afternoon ritual of visiting the Queen Victoria Market, affectionately known as Vic Market. The abundance and variety of fresh produce had me eagerly returning each week with my trusty metal shopping trolley. I'd firstly fill it to the brim with fresh fruit and veggies, often buying in bulk to get a better price. I'd make my way into the meat and seafood hall: red meat from the Vietnamese butcher and fish from the Aussie fishmonger. I'd then go across into the hall with the continental delis. I can still smell that delicious mix of cheeses, olives, salamis, cold cuts, dips and other delicacies from the Italian, Greek and Polish delis. I'd select cheese cut from large wheels, several varieties of salami sliced up along with ham off the bone and small tubs of olives and dips. My bread and cake came from the German bakery. If I had enough money, I'd also buy fresh Italian pasta and Greek shortbreads. Once the shopping was done, I'd sit on an upside-down milk crate with other satisfied shoppers and eat warm jam doughnuts. There was nothing I didn't love about it. I still try and visit whenever I'm in Melbourne.

Google told me my local market was four minutes away but that must have been by motorcycle because I walked, in flip-flops, and thankfully I found it after more like thirty-four minutes. I needed to cross a very busy road. There was a pedestrian crossing, but that means nothing here. I've almost got my traffic-weaving confidence back again and I headed into the middle of the road. Unlike at home, no one here really wants to run you over. Well, that's what I was telling myself. But as a jumbo-sized bus approached, I was glad the driver stopped, allowing me to run to the other side.

Unfortunately, this market seemed quiet. Maybe it's more alive first thing in the morning. I wandered around looking at what was on offer and realised the seafood and meat probably wasn't being kept as cold as it should be. When I'd had enough of holding my breath and pinching my nose, I bought some fruit, wandered over to the drinks stall and ordered my mango smoothie in Thai. A group of Thai men sitting around were immediately on for the chat. 'How long have you lived here?' 'Why can you speak Thai?' 'Where are you from?' 'You're so clever!'

I sat down on a box and answered their questions. They were eating sticky rice with chicken satays and drinking beer. One had a whiskey. It seems I was sitting at the local pit-stop for the rogue motorbike taxi riders. None of them had a full set of teeth and their banter was funny until they asked me if I had a Thai boyfriend. That was my cue to leave my new friends, telling them that I didn't, but I had a husband and that they were very cheeky with their question. I can still hear them laughing as I wandered away.

I ventured out again at sunset, when I figured most of the tourists would be down on the beach taking selfies. I was heading for a massage armed with my Thai sentence for 'Can I have a massage, please?' (*kor newit noi kha*). I was greeted like a long-lost friend by my new salon friends from yesterday. They were curious to know where I'd been today (*wun nee by nai maa kha*), what I'd eaten (*wun nee gin arai kha*) and if I was well (*sabai dii mai kha*). All very standard greetings for Thais. I got my request out for a Thai massage, but had forgotten I needed to pick the particular areas of my body to focus on. So my new Thai words for today were neck (*kor*), shoulders (*lai*) and back (*lung*).

After being led up a few steep flights of stairs, I had my feet washed and stripped off for my massage. I'm not sure what I was thinking when I picked the Thai massage. The Thais massage with their elbows and knees and by standing or kneeling on you. The line between pleasure and pain is very thin and at times during my session it was decisively crossed. My brain recited my new words over and over while my body had every knot and ache stretched, kneaded and pummelled out of it. I was pleased when my hour was over. The various forms my body needed to comply with had left me a bit weary. After a much-needed cup of tea downstairs, I pulled myself together and went on my way, promising my salon friends I'd see them again soon.

After a shower I still felt slightly like I'd been run over, but I'm sure that tomorrow I'll be standing tall, shoulders back, though cursing myself for not picking the aromatherapy option.

25 February
Laundry | Sunbaking | Wai

Having not only slept well, but now rid of the pesky knots in my neck and shoulders, I wandered off with my bag of washing under my arm. I saw a handwritten laundry sign and an arrow pointing down a dirt side road. Turning off the main road, I walked into clouds of smoke. The locals were burning coconut husks to smoke fish. I chatted to the men doing the smoking and asked what sort of fish it was. They told me it was snapper and I asked them if it was delicious, *aroy mai,* another common topic of conversation with Thais. They assured me it was, even though what I could smell wasn't so delicious. A little further on in a cluster of small houses I found my washing lady, who offered to do two kilograms of washing and folding for 120 baht (A$5). I got to show off by not only speaking Thai but writing my name in Thai on the washing slip. Didn't that cause a stir!

Crossing the road, I headed to the beach. The jet skis were out, the paddle boards were out, the surf school crew were out and the female butt cheeks were out too. I'd hoped that trend might have waned as women wised up to the fact they're paying more for less bikini, butt no! I'm always amazed at the way holidaying foreigners here strip down to almost nothing, bake their bodies until they look brown and leathery and have no problem walking the beach practically naked. The beach is packed with people burning in the sun, no doubt believing that a tan gives them a healthy glow and leaves them looking like they've been on holidays. We've probably all been there.

Admittedly, having the warmth of the sun on your body can be incredibly energising, particularly if you've arrived from a cold climate. Coming from Australia where we have an alarmingly high incidence of skin cancer, it's impossible for me to deliberately lie out in the sun. The awareness campaign highlighting the risks of sun damage has clearly worked on me.

You'll rarely see a Thai do this. Thai people are generally shy and modest. They'd never wear a bikini down the street without covering up. They don't sunbake. They tend to wear long sleeves, pants and floppy hats when working outside to keep the sun off them. Thais don't want to be brown. You'll see some women with a white paste on their face in the name of beauty much like we wear foundation. Burmese women put a yellow paste on their cheeks for the same reason. My friends at the salon told me that they think the nail colour looks better with white skin and they'd love to be pale like me and not brown.

Looks like that fake tan I bought before coming away is going in the bin. Time to just be comfortable in my pale freckled skin because there will be no sunbaking for me. I'll be putting my SPF50 on and sitting in the shade whenever I can.

I had the worst sunburn of my life while snorkelling in Thailand and that will never ever happen again. I can still remember the excruciating pain of having to sit on a flight back to Australia with the backs of my legs blistered and burnt. Not something I intend to repeat. While we're talking about body bits, here's a little cultural insight. The head is the most sacred part of the body for

Thais and it's very rude to touch or pat someone on the head. The feet are at the other end of the spectrum. To point your foot at someone or push things around with your feet is seen as impolite. Shoes aren't worn inside. It's also not uncommon to see a big bowl of water with a ladle at the front door. This is so you can wash your feet before going inside. Thailand is also the spiritual home of flip-flops. No one wants to do up and undo laces multiple times a day.

Thais are extremely clean people having multiple showers or bathing in some form each day. The heat and humidity will do that. Some also sleep on the floor and sit on the floor to eat, so it's always swept and kept clean.

Thais don't ordinarily shake hands when they meet you. They *wai*, which involves placing your palms together in a prayer-like manner, with the tips of the thumbs at a level between the chin and eyebrows. The positioning of the hands can vary depending on who you are greeting and the level of respect being shown. It's one of the first things children are taught and it was something I learnt very early on when I first lived here. I was also encouraged to dip my head lower than those older than me when walking past them to show respect.

Each morning when we got dropped off at school by my Thai mother we would *wai* her as we said goodbye, no hugs and kisses. The maid who lived at our house always lowered her head when she walked past my Thai host parents. If she came into the room to speak to them, she would sit on the floor. It was all about status and respect. This aspect of the culture is still very evident in so many areas of Thai life. The *wai* is used when greeting and farewelling people, to show respect to elders, teachers, monks and others in positions of authority, thanking someone, apologising to someone, when visiting temples and receiving blessings.

Every time I handed money over to those I bought food from today, they would *wai* before taking it. It's nice to see this is still so much part of who they are.

26 February

Oranges or Mandarins / Cat Woman / Cannabis

I wandered to a taxi stand on the street outside my hotel and asked one of the drivers how much it would cost to go to Karon Beach, the next beach along from Kata. She told me 200 baht (A$8) and five minutes later I'd arrived. On the ride over, we discussed that I could speak Thai clearly. She said it felt cold as we'd had rain overnight – even though it was around 28 degrees Celsius – and that Thailand had changed for the worse and she wasn't happy about that. I reassured her that Thailand was not alone in this and that change was happening the world over. She took my money with a *wai*, saying it was her lucky day to start off with a fare of 200 baht.

It's hard not to compare and constantly convert the price of things back to what I'm familiar with at home. One hundred baht is about A$4.40. I use an app to do my conversions, but I keep A$4 in my head so I can quickly work out prices if I need to. It really is still very cheap and I'm told by the locals that Phuket is more expensive than other provinces around Thailand that don't have the tourism industry keeping them afloat. With the average wage in Thailand being between 16,000 baht (A$700) and 20,000 baht (A$900) a month, a minimum daily wage of 370 baht (A$15) and rent often costing about 10,000 baht (A$400) a month, there's not much left to live off.

Unlike at home, where the cost of living has increased substantially, I don't think prices here have risen that much since I first started coming to Thailand decades ago. It makes it a very affordable place for foreigners to live and holiday. The retirement market is growing each year and I can see why. Affordability and great weather seem to be at the top of the list for many and they're easily ticked off. The crazy growth in the sale of condos to foreigners is another indicator that you get good 'bang for your buck' here.

I strolled onto a stunning stretch of sand. This is a fantastic walking beach, being more than three kilometres long. You can't help but feel grateful when your day can start here. Tourists were out jogging, walking, swimming and sitting on the sand, beginning their day in the best possible way. The water was crystal clear and not the slightest bit cold as I dipped my feet in for the first time. I walked for a while and then had a refreshing swim. That first ocean swim of the day is really something to be savoured. For me it provides a level of calm, even more so when I float on my back. Absolute bliss.

Once I'd convinced myself to leave the water, I found a juice shop and sat down for an OJ. The oranges, tiny and sweet, taste like mandarins. The chief juice maker was still at the market, so I was told I had to wait six minutes. I told them I was happy to wait and the stall holder seemed surprised. There was nowhere I needed to be with my time now mine to do with as I please. I had a great opportunity to sit and listen to the chat around me. Seems to be my secret superpower over here, particularly when people say something about me and I answer in Thai. It never ceases to stun them.

After my fresh juice it was time for another taxi ride home.

The drivers were all lounging around in the shelter (*sala*) on the other side of the road, but were quick to move at the prospect of a fare.

I got another female driver and somehow we began talking about her love of cats. She has ten at home and a few fake fluffy ones on the dash of the car that let out a meow when pressed. By this stage, I was laughing hard as she drove and had the cats meowing at the same time. She told me she looks after sick and injured cats and goes to a shelter to assist as often as possible. Then she pulled out some cat snacks from inside her door because every taxi driver has cat snacks ready to go in their car. We laughed about the antics of her cats. The word for cat in Thai is *meaow*, but the word for dog isn't woof. This amuses me more than it probably should.

Reaching my drop-off spot, I fiddled around in my wallet for the fare. Cash is and always will be king here. I pulled out a 500 baht (A$21) note and told her 200 baht was for the trip and 300 baht was to feed the cats. Her eyes nearly popped out of her head. The sweet woman, she was so grateful. We parted wishing one another good luck and happy days and hoping we'd meet again.

Once the sting was out of the sun, I went to catch the sunset at Kata Beach and came back with weed. Just kidding. But I certainly could have if I wanted to. You see, last year Thailand legalised cannabis (*guncha*).

I'm still a bit perplexed by the decision considering their very hard stance on illicit drugs, but there's no shortage of cannabis shops now. There are cannabis cafés and lounges and cocktails with added extras and cookies and ice cream laced with it. They've added weed to just about everything. I can only imagine the number of people who spend most of their time here stoned.

There are restrictions and it's supposed to be used for

medical purposes only. Recreational smoking of a joint in public is still illegal, but rules in Thailand are made to be broken and certainly no one seems to be enforcing this one. In theory, the compound that creates the psychoactive effect of cannabis must be less than 0.2 per cent if used in medicine or food. I'm not sure who is doing the measuring of such things. Meanwhile, many tourists are in weed heaven. You can often smell it wafting around in the street.

There's been a fair bit of backlash from medical professionals particularly concerned about the younger generation of Thais using the drug inappropriately, so you now must be over twenty to buy it. The government believes the industry could be worth over three billion baht in the next five years, but the social problems might just outweigh any economic benefit.

I think I'll stick to sunrises and sunsets for my highs.

27 February
Street Stall Eating / Cha Yen

There are so many reasons to love Thai people but a particular favourite of mine is that they love to eat. They ask 'Have you eaten rice yet?' (*gin khao rue yang kha*) in the same way we say 'Hello, how are you?' They enjoy feeding you at every opportunity and you can't argue with that.

After my morning beach swims, I've been heading straight for the street food market for lunch. The road is lined with all sorts of food and drink choices and the smells alone make it impossible for me to walk past without trying something. Today I found a mother-and-daughter team making delicious stir-fry dishes using only a gas burner and wok. They have no electricity, just an icebox for refrigeration. I pulled up a plastic stool and watched them. The daughter takes the orders and cash while her mum works the wok. All the fresh veggies are pre-chopped beautifully, then it's just a matter of adding rice or noodles and the sauces, herbs and chilli. In five minutes, you have a seriously yummy meal. I could eat like this every day.

I got chatting to the daughter about all manner of things, including what she was eating, as it wasn't what they were selling. She had a local fish dish with quite a pungent smell. I enjoyed every mouthful of my stir-fry and finished up telling her I'd be back for more. Sadly they only work Friday to Sunday, so next Friday it is. Thais understand the need for people to be able to eat cheaply. My noodles were 80 baht (A$3.50), which many Thais would consider expensive, expecting to pay no more than half that. There is definitely a local price and a tourist price on many items.

Wandering back to my room, I stopped along the way to replenish a few supplies. I was ready to get out of the heat and enjoy some time lying on my bed in the cool of the air conditioning. I must've fallen asleep as it was around 5 p.m. when I looked at my phone. At least it was now cool enough for me to head out again.

I found a street I hadn't yet explored and was soon sitting up at a stall made from bamboo poles with a thatched roof. I ordered my favourite Thai cold tea drink, *cha yen*. This isn't like your ordinary black tea but is a terracotta colour with evaporated milk, condensed milk, sugar and lots of ice added to it. The secret to a really good *cha yen* seems to be in the steeping of the tea, the longer the better.

I had a great conversation in Thai with the lady making my tea while her kids ran around with fruit boxes on their heads. Their giggling was delightful. The stall also sold fruit and a young Russian man asked how much a mango cost. She told him the price was 35 baht (A$1.50) and he said it was expensive and walked off. This sparked a conversation with her friend who was helping cut up the fruit for her stall. She asked me if I thought her fruit was expensive. I told her what a mango costs in Australia, usually around three dollars, and how they're not half as delicious as they are here. I then asked to buy two of her mangoes and some baby pineapples. I said goodbye and crossed the street heading to the beach with my *cha yen,* my juicy mangoes and a bag of miniature pineapples complete with a bamboo skewer. I found myself a shady spot and set about demolishing my fruit.

28 February

Fish Spa | Nai Harn Beach | Long Sentences

There's no shortage of the weird and wonderful in Phuket. On one of my wanderings I came across the fish spa. You sit on the bench above the tank and dangle your feet in. The fish nibble on the skin on your feet and give you nice smooth feet, or so it goes. Not my kinda pedi, but it's a pity I didn't see anyone using one. It's a good reason to venture back at night when I might have more luck. I particularly love the sign warning you not to put your hand in the tank with these flesh-eating little fish. Seems toes are fair game but not fingers.

I went in search of a less-crowded beach today and took a fifteen-minute taxi ride to Nai Harn, a smaller, more secluded spot a bit further south from Kata. I soon found my sun lounge for the morning and got settled. The lounges cost 200 baht (A$8) and are worth every cent for the umbrella alone. My weather app told me the 'feels like air temperature' was around the high 40s Celsius, which is pretty crazy. The water seemed even more turquoise, if that's possible. It was also shimmering due to the cloudless sky and the brightest shining sun. Some beautiful whitewashed villas are built into the hillside and there is a pizza restaurant on the point.

The water temperature here is around 27 degrees year-round. In late February it can almost feel too warm. If you want to feel refreshed, a cold shower is probably better. I'll never complain about warm water to swim in, though, given where I live the average water temperature is around 14 degrees.

Wanting a break from human flesh and wobbly bottoms, I walked off the beach to have lunch. It felt like a spicy salad and roast chicken kind of day and I asked if they had sticky rice, which normally goes with this combination. They didn't, but said they'd go and get some from another shop. How lovely is that? I chatted with my waitress and engaged my brain and mouth to say in Thai, 'It's so kind of you to go and buy sticky rice for me. Thank you so much,' before I paid and left. Sometimes it comes together and sometimes I stumble all over the place like a child learning to walk. One thing is for sure, I'll keep trying. It was the longest sentence I've spoken in Thai so far. Who knows if it was right, but it must have been okay because I was invited back.

Back at the hotel, I spent the rest of the day in the cool of the air conditioning, napping and letting my mind wander. I've been here for a week and the change of scene and routine is totally agreeing with me. While planning to come away I thought a lot about how Joe would cope on his own. This has been a default position of mine for many years, as he has come to rely upon my support in many aspects of his life and I have also wanted to provide it.

Once PTSD became part of both our lives, me being available and close by if needed was necessary. We spoke at length about how we thought this time apart could work and also had a few sessions with our counsellor. I needed the reassurance that we had a plan in place and that we both felt comfortable. We've been incredibly fortunate to have a wonderful GP and treatment team surrounding Joe and that gave me great confidence while planning my trip.

Joe was at pains to reassure me he would be fine. In any case, he has the best caretakers anyone could ask for, Jasmine and Rosie. So far, so good.

1 March

Language Lessons | Tattoos | Ice Cream

I had an online Thai lesson this afternoon and I was so excited to talk with my teacher about all the opportunities I'd had so far to use my language skills. I've been doing these online lessons for a couple of months and I think they've helped. Thais often kindly tell me how clear my speaking is. It's not something that I'm overly conscious of but when I hear other foreigners, particularly Chinese people, speak the language, I have no idea what they're saying because of their accent. Each region of Thailand also has its own dialect. Once people switch to their local dialect, there's no way I can understand them and often nor can other Thais.

I'm trying to get my vocabulary and sentence structure moving along. I'm also working on my reading and writing. If you can read Thai, you have a far better chance of pronouncing the words correctly. The alphabet is based on the old Khmer script which dates from 611 AD. It has forty-four consonants and sixteen vowel symbols that combine into at least thirty-two vowel forms. And the Thais think English is hard. The language is also tonal, with five tones: low, middle, rising, falling and high. This can be tricky for foreigners as one word can mean different things depending on the tone. For example, the word *maa* can mean horse or dog or come.

After my lesson, my brain needed a break so I headed out for walk. As I wandered, I was asked by a Thai man if I wanted a tattoo. I had a tank top on and I've got plenty of clean real estate on my arms but that's how it will be staying. I couldn't help but think his trade would most likely pick up as the night went on and the cheap cocktails and Thai whiskey made many a foreigner a bit carefree. I can only imagine how many 'holiday tattoos' are done here and potentially regretted later. The tattoo craze that's taken on at home has always been here. Many men have tattoos, but previously most Thai women would never have considered them an option. From what I've seen so far, the younger Thai generation is changing that.

Having strolled past several ice cream stalls, I stopped at one outside my hotel. I was curious to see how they made their ice cream. They pour your selected flavour and a creamy, milky mixture onto a frozen metal slab. I'd chosen passionfruit. They chop it like crazy and scrape and chop and scrape and chop. Once it's all thoroughly mixed, they thinly spread it out again on the slab and carefully lift it with a metal scraper to create ice cream curls. This could well be very dangerous now that I've discovered it, but it was the perfect way to end this balmy tropical evening.

2 March

Old Phuket Town | Pink Eggs | Crying Tiger Pork

It was staggeringly hot today, a 'sweat running down the backs of my legs into my shoes' kinda hot. I'm not a huge fan of the heat. Many of my friends who know how partial I am to a cool crisp day can't work out how I will survive here and suddenly I was wondering the same. Usually if I have air conditioning, or a pool or beach nearby, I'm fine, but I had none of these this morning.

This was the first day since I arrived a week ago that I had to be somewhere at a specific time. I'd booked a food tour of Old Phuket Town and needed to get myself from Kata to the meeting point by 9 a.m. I had set my alarm. I ventured out of my room and to the end of my laneway (*soi*) to find the regular taxi drivers weren't there. This made me slightly uneasy as I wasn't exactly sure how long the trip would take. So up the street I walked to find a delightful driver who spoke to me in Thai for the whole thirty-plus minutes of our trip. He was a sixty-five-year-old local man and boy did we cover some ground. That gave my brain and my Thai vocabulary a great workout and I found him fascinating to listen to.

I easily found my tour guide waiting on the front steps of

the central market. I was excited to be doing this tour; as I've said, my love for a good fresh food market runs deep. There's always something interesting and unusual to see. Even while I was waiting for the others to join us, a motorbike pulled up with a stack of crates strapped to it. I couldn't work out what the golden blobs were that it was transporting. My guide told me they were hundreds of egg yolks. I hoped the strapping of the crates to the bike was secure.

The guide started our tour off by talking to our small group about the history of Phuket and how the food the people of Phuket enjoy today has been influenced by arrivals from other countries. She moved on to talk about the Baba or Peranakan culture. In the nineteenth century there was huge immigration from southern China into Phuket as people came to be part of the tin-mining industry. These new arrivals met and married the local Thais. Their male offspring were called *baba* and their female *nyonya*. The Chinese influence on the food can still be seen from the vegetables that are eaten to the dumplings and wontons.

We set off walking through the market tasting the local curry paste, chatting about the huge variety of freshly picked vegetables on offer and standing to watch fresh coconut milk being made by squeezing out the cream from the shredded coconut flesh. I was totally in my element browsing the offerings and chatting with the stallholders who start at 2 a.m. each day.

We ended up at a restaurant serving Burmese food. Fresh naan bread was coming straight out of the clay oven at the front of the shop. I knew this would be a great way to kill the curry paste taste that was lingering in my mouth. Placed in the middle of our table was a mild Burmese chicken curry, golden samosas, a dish made with tea-leaf oil and a cabbage dish with a stack of spices and chilli in it. We were encouraged to add little baked garlic cloves with their skin on to each mouthful of food we had. The blistered, chewy, hot naan bread was piled high on a plate and we all helped ourselves, tearing it into edible pieces.

The Burmese have been coming to Thailand for more than fifty years to work in the rubber plantations which are abundant in Phuket. They generally do the manual labour the Thais won't do for extremely low pay. They make up more than half of the country's migrant workforce. There are thought to be more than two million Burmese in Thailand, many of them working illegally. There's quite the community here and their contribution through their food is a definite bonus. There were Burmese families in the restaurant eating together, all with the distinctive yellow paste on their faces. Our guide assured me that this stuff they smear on is the fountain of youth. I'm now the owner of a pot of paste with no intention of using it!

On to our next stop, we wound our way through scruffy backstreets only a local would know, our guide greeting many of the shop owners as we passed by. Her passion about preserving the local food culture and sharing it far and wide was evident, and her knowledge and storytelling were extraordinary. It felt very much like we were being exposed to something special.

We sat down on small stools at another restaurant for crying tiger pork (*sua rong hai moo*). Thai folklore says that the marinade and dipping sauce of this dish is so spicy from all the fresh chilli that it would make even a tiger cry. The chilli was slightly above what I can handle but the flavour of the meat was incredible. The pork is marinated in a combination of soy, oyster and fish sauce with lots of chopped fresh chilli and garlic, plus sugar and crushed white peppercorns. It's grilled over coals which gives the meat a nice smoky flavour and a super-spicy dressing is used as a dipping sauce. Just add sticky rice and a salad made from fresh corn and shredded green mango with a lime, chilli, fish sauce and sugar dressing (*somtarm kow port*) and you have so many incredible taste sensations. I could feel my sinuses clear and my tastebuds tingle.

There was also a southern Thai curry, again big on the chilli, but I'd already reached my chilli quota for the day so I gave it a miss. Southern Thais love to tell you that not only do they like their weather hot, but they also like their curries spicy and full of chilli.

While we were sitting there, a man pulled up on a motorcycle and delivered some Thai sweets for us to try: sticky rice balls in warm coconut milk. They're called *bua loy*, or 'floating lotus', because the little rice dumplings look the same as the seeds found in the lotus flower. I'd eaten this many times before, but it was good to taste it again. Soon after, another motorbike arrived with a delivery of crepe-like sweets. The batter is made with rice and mung-bean flour and coconut milk, and they're cooked quickly in a wok making them crispy on the outside and chewy on the inside. It's a Phuket speciality that I was glad I got to try.

The buildings in this part of Phuket are beautiful, built in the distinct Sino-Portuguese style and painted in bright cheerful colours ranging from jade green to candy pink. The architecture of these buildings is best described as a blend of European and Chinese. Most are two or three storeys high, narrow but long with a ceramic-tiled roof, shuttered windows and the most exquisite patterned tiles on the tiny porch that butts onto the street. We walked past many of these building on the way to our next stop which was a noodle shop.

Rustic in decor and jam-packed with locals – we all know what that means. Here we had a lesson from our guide on how to season our noodles correctly, the secret being spicy chilli paste (*dtom yum*) stirred through the beef broth. This particular noodle shop uses a recipe passed down through the family from eighty years ago and it was very, very good.

Moving onto our final stop, our guide said we had to wait for the coffee maker, a Muslim man, to finish praying before we could expect our coffees to arrive. Five of us squeezed into the back of a tiny shop and before we knew it the table was covered in food. I couldn't get my head nor stomach around the pink egg that had turned into black jelly during the preserving process. This egg is the Thai variation of a century egg or thousand-year-old egg – an Asian tradition that involves preserving the egg for several weeks or months in a mixture of lime, clay, salt and rice hulls. This method of curing eggs dates back hundreds of years. Some of my tour mates were braver than me and reported it tasted just like an egg. It certainly didn't look just like an egg when it was opened. For me, some things are best eaten fresh.

Pandan roti, black-pepper biscuits, sticky rice rolls and rambutans (*ngo*) totally tipped us all over the foodie edge. But the best was still to come. The coffee man arrived and put on an impressive show as he began pouring the cold coffee from a reasonable height from one jug to the next without a drop being spilt. He'd created quite a decent amount of froth in his jugs and a crowd of people wanting to order this unique coffee soon gathered. Seems he's very well-known for his 'coffee show' and the crowd showed their appreciation with a rowdy round of applause.

I never tire of the way food can provide such a fascinating window into a place and its people, from times gone by to the present day. Today that window was wide open and shared in such a delicious and passionate way. It was soon time for me to get myself home for a cold shower and a swim – but no dinner.

3 March

Super Surf Bars / Night Hawkers

Every time I walk down to the beach and pass Super Surf Kata I have to stop. It just draws me in. This bar-restaurant-cum-beach club has a mini wave pool for people who want to surf. I'm told it's called 'flow surfing'. As the force of the water creating the wave is super strong, I laugh out loud watching the wobbly surfers try their hardest to stay on that board. More often than not they're off it in seconds and gracelessly spat out the back. Mind you, while I'm happy to sit and have a chuckle, I'm too much of a chicken to give it a go. I've seen groups of friends having the best time together and, as their alcohol consumption increases, their ability to stay on the board decreases rapidly.

Little did I know when I pulled up a stool today at around 3 p.m. that it was happy hour – two cocktails for the price of one! So who was I to say no? I sat sipping on my margarita, watching and laughing at the expense of those who stacked it early on. The kids were great as they're flexible and able to right themselves easily, but the adults had more trouble, some lasting barely a few seconds before toppling over. There's an attendant who passes a rope to the surfers which helps stabilise them. He gradually lengthens the rope, then lets go, and that's often the end of them as down they go. Just another lazy Thursday afternoon at Kata Beach.

Once I'd finished my second margarita, I slung my beach bag over my shoulder and headed back to my room. I was ready for an afternoon nap or a swim in the pool. I ended up doing both and then headed out again in search of food.

Every evening at dusk the streets in this area come alive with hawker stalls. They're nowhere to be seen during the heat of the day. But after sundown, out come their tables and wares, ready to sell stuff to tourists who've spent the day at the beach or touring the island. The hawkers sell an extraordinary range of bits and pieces, everything from fake watches and handbags to noisy toys, bowls made from coconut shells, artwork and jewellery. They stay open until late waiting for the cashed-up, souvenir-hunting, post-dinner crowd to arrive and spill out of the tuk-tuks whose flashing lights and blaring music contribute to the show.

Thankfully I'm beyond the souvenir stage and getting things home wondering what I was thinking at the time, but I still love to see what's on offer. This retail night shift intrigues me, especially as when I venture out for breakfast the next day, there's no sign it had even existed.

4 March

Power Cables / Imploding Footpaths / Mango & Sticky Rice

This wonderful country can often leave me puzzled. While out walking it's hard to ignore the tangled power cables you see on every pole. It's beyond me how anyone would ever know which wire to pick should there be an electrical problem to fix. I'm guessing that if a problem does occur a new cable is simply added, hence the cobweb. I looked a little closer today and could see the redundant ones dangling.

To display power cables so overtly was once seen as a sign of progress and independence, a demonstration of technological mastery. Times have changed, but as yet no one seems to have found an alternative to this tangled eyesore. The good news is that someone must know what's happening as everything works and blackouts are few and far between. It's so different from what I see walking around my neighbourhood at home or what would be deemed safe in Australia, but here we're doing life differently in so many ways.

Another very big difference to what I'm used to are the footpaths here or, actually, the lack thereof. If there is a footpath, the curb and guttering is often only on one side of the road. When it rains here it pours and flash floods are common. With such a huge volume of water and only one side of the road having drainage, the water has nowhere to go. Maybe one day curbs and guttering on both sides of the road will be the norm.

I've found it a very good idea to watch where I'm walking. Most pedestrians end up walking on the road to avoid tripping or falling on an imploded footpath. I do this all the time, because at least it's even and not full of gravel and wedges of concrete waiting to catch your ankle. I suppose it doesn't help that I wear flip-flops everywhere I go.

There's some construction going on up the road from my hotel. Nobody seems to think there's a problem walking among the welding, operating diggers and reversing trucks. There are no safety barriers or fluorescent witches' hats. We all just walk among the chaos as best we can. Yesterday one of the workers had his flip-flops on while welding; no steel-capped boots or safety glasses. They just get on with the job and nothing seems to bother them.

Passing a souvenir shop, a few things caught my eye. I'm in need of nothing, but the cute, colourful clutch bags, Thai silk and impressive wooden carvings drew me in. I got talking with the shop owner and asked him where the silk came from. I'd presumed Chiang Mai, a city in the north known for its handicrafts, but no, it came from Surin, one of Thailand's seventy-seven provinces, located in the region of Isaan in the lower northeast of the country.

Thirty years ago, Chiang Mai was renowned for the Thai silk it produced. I've always loved it and on an early trip I bought ten metres of raw Thai silk in a creamy champagne colour. It would be another ten or so years before this silk was made into my wedding gown. So special.

Nowadays, the charming shop owner explained, Chiang Mai

largely makes only cotton as it's more useful in the colder climate.

I was chatting with the shop owner about all sorts of things when I spotted a dog sleeping in his changing room, so of course I had to know about the pup. He was found on the beach during Covid when people could hardly feed themselves, let alone their animals. He now lives with this kind man. Then a cat wandered in and had a feed from a little bowl of kibble at my feet. Another cat came out from behind a clothing rack and ate from a bowl close to the entrance of the shop.

Further questioning revealed the immense kindness this man shows to these homeless animals. He feeds them because no one else does. During the day he fills the bowls with food and water so stray cats and dogs can wander in and out as they please. When he closes his shop at night, he puts the bowls out for any animals that might happen to pass by. A food stop for the homeless, hungry and helpless animals of Kata. I love this with all my heart.

I finished my retail therapy. Seems I couldn't resist buying a few bright, cheerful little clutch bags. I did indeed need something to put my phone, glasses, sunglasses and lip balm in when I'm out and about and these floral and neon beauties would be perfect. Just as I was saying goodbye, the man reached behind his counter and gave me three tiny brass elephants as good luck charms while I'm in his country.

Unbelievably, it has taken me more than a week to seek out my favourite dish here: sticky rice and mango (khao niaow ma muang). Now that I've found it in another market, which happens to be very close to my accommodation, it could be seriously dangerous – 100 baht (A$4) gets me a decent-sized container full of sweet ripe mango and sticky rice cooked in coconut milk and sugar. A small amount of fresh coconut milk with a bit of salt and sugar added is drizzled over the top and crisp, crunchy mung beans finish the dish off. It's incredibly addictive.

Mangoes are used in so many dishes here and not all mangoes are created equal. Top of the range are the sweetest golden ones called nam dork mai, which literally translates as 'water flower'. This one accompanies sticky rice and has a delicious floral smell to it when ripe. At the other end of the flavour spectrum are the tart, fragrant green ones called khieo sawoei, which are used in spicy salads, or thinly sliced and dipped into salt and chilli powder or fish sauce cooked with sugar and dried shrimp. It's all about balancing the sweet, sour, salty, spicy and creamy qualities of the dishes. The Thais have definitely mastered this in their cuisine.

The other day when I was talking to my favourite fruit seller, there were foreigners buying her fruit and they asked her to wash the fruit with the skin on. A bit like washing bananas. I asked her in Thai, 'Why are they asking you to wash the fruit?' Or so I thought, but what I actually said was, 'Why is the fruit having a bath?' So now I know there's one word used for washing people and another for washing things like fruit. Laughing and learning every single day.

5 March

Motorbikes Versus Walking

Thais often ask if I ride a motorbike. Today in my online Thai language lesson I learnt the words for 'too risky' (underlai mark). I already knew the words for 'I'm afraid of having an accident and dying' (chun glua rot chon lae seea cheewit). That has become my standard response when I'm asked now and it's always received with a knowing nod of the head and words like 'good idea'. You can rent motorbikes and scooters so cheaply and they're available everywhere. Seems every second house has a couple out the front with a 'FOR RENT' sign on them.

There's definitely an appeal to getting around so easily, but I've never been tempted. I figure I don't ride one at home so why would I here? I don't know how I'd go in the chaos of the traffic. It's mainly the other tourists you need to watch, as they have no idea what they're doing. I'm very happy to walk and not have the worry or hassle of a bike. I've come here to rest and recharge, not to recover from gravel rash or worse.

Living here as a teenager I rode on the back of friends' motorbikes. They all rode them to school. There seemed to be no minimum age for driving one, and the locals literally grow up on the backs of them. As we wore skirts to school we had to sit side-saddle, no helmet, of course. Every day here I see people riding without helmets on. I'd hoped this dangerous habit might have disappeared since my schooldays, but it seems not.

Not having a vehicle at my disposal for four months doesn't worry me. The little red tuk-tuks are readily available and cheap if I can't be bothered to walk and the taxis around town include a free language lesson and cultural insights as part of the service. The local bus costs 40 baht and stops everywhere, but I can walk faster so I haven't tried that yet. This gal will be keeping her feet firmly on the ground and her stress levels low. I've enjoyed finding so many different places by walking the streets, seeing so much that I would otherwise miss.

6 March
Jai Yen Yen | Work-Life Balance

I found a delicious pad Thai street stall today. It had me sorted for lunch. I stood on the footpath and watched from afar as the stall owner cooked for hungry beachgoers while her kids laughed and played beside her on a mat – the ultimate in juggling work and kids. She was multitasking like you wouldn't believe, particularly when things got a bit rowdy with the kids. The words *jai yen yen*, 'calm down', could be heard often. The kids were happy and having fun. No screens, no asking for stuff, just playing on the road next to their mum.

There's no formal family daycare program here and it would be far too expensive for this lady to send her kids to anyway. So they come to work with her. It just goes without saying. It won't be long before she'll have them chopping veggies or helping in another way so the family can earn more money. Everyone is expected to pitch in and help as soon as they can. Culturally this is how Thai families work.

It's not uncommon for Thai people to live where they work. They will often have a shop selling something or providing a service on the ground floor and they might live at the back of the shop or above it. This saves having to pay double rent for a business location and a home. Thais are used to making the most of the space they have and combining home with work. You could say that they've been 'working from home' long before Covid made it a thing.

In the eighties, when I was an exchange student here, I lived with a doctor and his family. We lived above his clinic, so every day I could see patients waiting to see him, some of whom he'd treat on-site. He also dispensed medication, which is the way things work here. You go to the doctor and come away with the medicine as well. My Thai host father worked late into the night treating patients, only shutting his doors around 10 p.m. He told me that when he first started his clinic, before his kids came along, he also ran a small hospital where our bedrooms were.

There were four levels in the house. The top level was a rooftop, where the washing was hung out to dry. We all slept on the third level, ate and watched TV on the second level, and on the ground floor, close by the clinic, there was a kitchen, a laundry and a small bedroom for the maid. We lived right on one of the main streets and there was no garden or front yard. You literally stepped out onto the footpath. My Thai family still live in the same house, but the father is now retired.

Last night I was talking to my friends in the beauty salon about their working week. They work from 10 a.m. to 11 p.m., six days a week. The public holidays are in April for Thai New Year. They only take a few days off because they don't get paid if they don't work. It really makes me appreciate where I live and the working conditions I enjoy at home. My working hours and days off go without saying and I'm not required to work outside my core hours. We're constantly encouraged these days to strive for some level of work–life balance, to focus on our lives outside work. I don't think I've ever heard my Thai friends refer to a work–life balance.

They work so they can live.

7 March
Chalong / Paddle-Boarding Hound

I took myself off on a little mystery tour this morning. I plan to stay in Chalong, another area of Phuket, after April. It's in the same area as the language school I plan on attending for a couple of months. I wanted to see if what I'd booked on the internet was what I was expecting. I also wanted to scope out the neighbourhood.

Some of my best and most interesting conversations have been with taxi drivers. Today certainly didn't disappoint. My driver was a young man supporting two families on one wage and doing his best to keep them all fed and afloat. So many Thais are still struggling after the pandemic, but he told me how everyone shared food and rice so they could survive during that difficult time.

That doesn't surprise me as Thais are great at making food stretch. I think it's called 'just add more rice'. You constantly see people sitting in groups and sharing whatever little they have. Often there will be four or five different dishes to choose from on the table. A spoonful of each is a lovely way to eat. There are no heaping plates full of one type of food for yourself. Nor do you sit in front of the TV. Eating is often very communal and brings people together. They enjoy it even more if they ask you to eat with them and you say yes.

The taxi driver dropped me at my location and offered to come and pick me up again 'because,' he said, 'you're not a serious person'. I think he meant I liked a joke and a laugh, so we exchanged WhatsApp numbers. I wandered around my potential new hood, mainly scoping out where I'd eat, of course. I came across an older lady frying bananas on the roadside and asked her if they were delicious. 'Here, try one,' she said, handing me a fried banana. 'And you tell me if you think they're delicious.' They were. I took eight pieces for 20 baht (A$0.85), and lots of little crumbly bits because they're the bomb, and I was on my way again.

The area seemed very clean and tidy compared to Kata. There was a big supermarket next door to the accommodation I'd booked with everything from Australia in it and plenty of fast-food options within the shopping centre. I opted to get out of the heat and found an air-conditioned cafe to sit in and ponder if this area was Thai enough for me. I'm here to be out talking to Thai people, eating among them, and eating their food while sitting in open-air tin sheds with thatched roofs. I'm guessing this area was once like this. I feel I may need to reassess. I have absolutely no desire to be going to the supermarket to buy groceries as that has daily grind written all over it. I'm pleased I did my recce as it has reinforced how much I'm ready to 'do life differently'.

My friendly taxi driver – who'd told me his name was Khun Tdon – sent his dad to collect me. His dad had Tdon on video call so I knew I wasn't getting in a car with some random stranger (which I probably would've anyway), so he was kind to me once again.

Later I walked down to the beach for a swim and a sunset. Not a cloud in the sky and the golden glow of the sun as it sank down below the horizon made the water shimmer. Right before we lost sight of the sun it turned pink and so did the water. Just magic.

I also saw a very clever paddle-boarding beach hound. I watched him for ages. He carried the leg strap down for his owner, barking with excitement as they got closer to the water. When they paddled away from shore he sat down on the board enjoying the sunset like the rest of us. I'm not sure he knows just how lucky he is. My fur girls Rosie and Jasmine would love the swimming here too.

It left me thinking about how important our canine friends are in our lives. Jasmine is not only a much-loved member of our family but also a certified assistance dog for Joe. She was in training from the day she was born, being desensitised to the world around her so she could become the calm, steady and reliable companion that she is today. I have watched her loyally stand beside Joe during periods of high anxiety and hypervigilance for him. She senses the mood change and will ask for a pat or lie on his feet.

She adores her job, almost revels in it. She loves nothing more than to hear Joe say, 'Jasmine, in the car', even if she's snoring on the couch. She never misses an opportunity to be by his side. She's undoubtedly responsible for getting him back into the community and giving him that part of his life back.

8 March

Makha Bucha Day / Broom & Feather-Duster Seller

As I walked to drop off my washing this morning, I noticed many Thais placing food and offerings at the spirit houses that can be seen everywhere around town. *San phra phum* is the Thai for spirit house with *san* meaning 'shrine' and *phra phum* meaning 'spirit', 'god' or 'angel'. These colourful little doll-like houses are believed to be home to the protector spirits that inhabit the land they are on and look after their property and assets. The spirit houses sit on a pole high enough to be respectful but within reach of those paying their respects. You often see Thai people making offerings of special food as well as drinks, fruit, flowers, incense and candles.

 I could smell burning incense lingering in the air, a smell that I immediately associate with being in this country that I love. I asked the sweet lady who does my washing what was happening but couldn't quite understand what she said so I came home and looked it up.

 It's Makha Bucha Day, one of the three most sacred days in the Buddhist calendar. The Buddhist calendar traditionally used in Thailand is a lunar one, and the third lunar month is known as 'Makha'. This comes from the word *magha* in Pali, the sacred language of the religious texts of the Theravada strand of Buddhism. Meanwhile, *bucha* is a Thai word, once again deriving from the Pali language, from the word *puja*, which means 'to venerate' or 'to honour'. Therefore, Makha Bucha is a day for honouring the third lunar month. Specifically, it refers to Buddha and the teachings that he delivered on the full-moon day.

Buddhism is by far the most common religion in Thailand, with roughly 94 per cent of the population being Buddhist. It plays a central part in the lives of many and shapes and influences Thai society. During all the years I've been visiting here, no one has ever pushed me to go to a temple or tried to share their religious beliefs with me. It's very much left to the individual to follow what you feel comfortable with. I find the gentle nature of Thai people to be calming as they will generally avoid confrontation, come from a place of respect and are very aware of making merit (*tam boon*) through their actions and behaviour towards others. Of course, there are those who don't live this way, but I haven't yet come across them.

I had a swim in the hotel pool when I got back from dropping off my laundry as my T-shirt was already sweat-stained and smelly with the high humidity. I took the opportunity to lie and read my book while I was the only one at the pool. The peace and quiet kept me there for longer than I had anticipated.

The afternoon rolled around and I headed out again, coming across a broom and feather-duster seller on his bike, all loaded up and ready to do business. There's no carpet here, only wooden or tiled floors inside most buildings, so brooms are used to keep the floors clean. I don't think I've ever seen a vacuum cleaner here. Floors are swept and mopped. The brooms have a handle made from bamboo and various grasses are used for the sweep. They're easy to use as they're light and do a great job.

I hope the seller did well today because I can't help but think this is a pretty hard way to make a baht. The mobile sellers generally sell on behalf of larger shops. They've been operating for generations, long before home delivery services and online shopping exploded. Each mobile street-seller has a different-sounding horn so you know who is coming before they arrive. The broom-and-feather-duster shop on wheels has been allocated the circus clown's *beep-beep*. I did wonder how many roosters were needed to make the feather dusters but, given the hour that they start to crow in the morning and the frequency with which they continue, I reckon there'd be no shortage on offer.

9 March
Curve Balls / Meeting the Locals

I've now been here solo for about two weeks and I'm yet to feel lonely or alone. I enjoy my own company, actually I need it to recharge. This time has been perfect for me and I'm beginning to feel like some of the pressure and stress I've been coping with is finding somewhere else to be.

Just before Christmas I found out that my job was unexpectedly changing. As life often does, it threw me a curve ball and, instead of catching it, I purposely dropped it and ran. The urge to run – and fast – had presented itself and I wasn't going to ignore it this time. I actually had somewhere to run to with my trip already in place. It feels great to be able to do that, but as these situations often do, this has played on my mind. It's encouraging me to think more about my employment options.

There's also a ripple effect of living with and dealing with someone who suffers from PTSD and depression. It can never be underestimated. I've learnt the hard way that sustained high levels of stress don't tend to do anyone any favours. Walking on eggshells might keep the peace temporarily, but eventually the building resentment will combust. Slowing right down, getting quiet and prioritising my rest has proven to be the best therapy there is for me.

I took myself on a date to Karon tonight to try a restaurant I'd heard good things about. The name, Sabai Jai, 'Content Heart', seems very apt in many ways. I ordered the 'money bags', which are made from a wonton wrapper filled with a prawn mixture, each corner of the wrapper then gathered up and tied with a small piece of pandanus leaf. They're fried until crisp and served with a sweet chilli dipping sauce, and the crunch of the golden wrapper is what I like most. I then opted for a Penang curry with chicken and a mild level of spice; as with many Thai dishes, the intensity of the spice can be altered by adding more coconut milk. Penang curry is made from a base similar to that of red Thai curry, but it's a bit richer, sweeter and stronger in flavour. The reviews I'd read were spot on. This place makes very good food and the smiling staff will have me returning.

After dinner I went for a walk. It was a delightful 27 degrees at 9 p.m., and writing this now that I'm back in my room, I can't believe how many people I met and spoke with.

It all started with Khun Mon, a friendly taxi driver who took me to the restaurant. He couldn't get over me speaking Thai and peppered me with questions. He knows Tasmania, has seen it on TV and particularly likes foreigners who embrace his country. We're now friends on WhatsApp and he sent me a picture of his son.

Then there was the beautician who I had change the colour of my nail polish, a job that cost me four Australian dollars. We were chatting away when two young foreign women came into the salon and asked for a massage 'with the stuff the salon smells of'.

The Thai ladies couldn't work out the smell and thought it was massage oil. I told them, 'No, it's Tiger Balm.'

Suddenly one of the women said, 'Yes, it is!'

The Thai ladies thought I had psychic powers. 'Wow, how did you know?' they kept saying. Well, the place reeked of it. Maybe they don't smell it anymore.

After that was Mr Roni, the tailor. He was touting for business on the footpath and we got talking. He had beautiful fabrics on display in his shop, but I think fast fashion has killed his business. The days of having a dress or suit made in twenty-four hours might be behind us now. A tough way to earn a living. It was a great chat all the same.

Finally, there was another friendly taxi driver who drove me home, lamenting the fact that he'd studied English for so many years and still couldn't speak it properly. He was intrigued by me speaking Thai and had question after question about who taught me, how I learn and how long it had taken.

He then told me all about his life during the pandemic, which was heartbreaking. He just did his best to survive each day by going out fishing and sharing his catch with his friends. He told me there were days when he didn't eat as he had no money and how depressed he had become as the restrictions dragged on. I've since been told the suicide rate here at that time was incredibly high. Many just couldn't see an end in sight nor a way forward. At one point the suicide rate was more than those dying from Covid. As I got out of the taxi, I wished him good luck (*chork dee*) as I do all the taxi drivers and I really meant it. It's survival of the fittest out there for them, Covid or no Covid.

I relish 'time for self', but I also love a night of meeting random and interesting locals. There's certainly plenty of people looking to chat and connect. They're curious about all manner of things when they get someone who can and will talk back, Thai language or not.

10 March

Self-Care / Dissolving Inhibitions / Choosing the Beach

I've got to somehow keep my hair from going too feral in the heat. I have a head of reasonably thick curly hair that turns into a frizzball within minutes of the humidity hitting it. My hair already attracts attention with the Thais as they don't see many people with curly hair. As I'm swimming multiple times a day, I've been slathering on a hair mask and just pulling it back and putting a hat on. I don't think I'll be getting any fancier than that somehow. Even the thought of using a hairdryer makes my already hot skin prickle. My normal self-care routine comes to a screeching halt here as makeup of any kind dissolves or is wiped off as soon as those first beads of sweat hit my forehead. It's sunscreen all the way and maybe, if I'm feeling fancy, lip gloss. That will do me and works nicely with my simplified approach to life here.

I've noticed there are plenty of people wandering around with crazy-coloured braids and plaits and strands of neon-coloured threads woven through their hair. It's not just the kids getting this done as a holiday treat or so their mum won't have to tell them to brush their hair. Shockingly, there are middle-aged women, just like me, having fun with their tresses too. I can see the advantage of not having to do a single thing once it's braided. Having a bit of fluorescent green woven through your locks certainly serves to mix things up.

Isn't it funny how new locations, moods and atmospheres give you permission to just let it all go and do things differently? The inhibitions that we carry with us dissolve as the carefree holiday feelings kick in. Then our holiday is over and we try so desperately to hold onto that chilled and adventurous state of being. For me, that first grocery shop when I get home brings me back to reality with a thud. I couldn't be more thankful I don't need to think about that for quite some time.

I spent most of the day trying to decide where to stay for April, May and June. Having seen Chalong the other day, I have to say it's the daily sunset swims here in Kata, and dare I say the vibe, that has made me reconsider my choice. I'm also not convinced Chalong has enough street-side, tin-shed restaurants selling locally made Thai food for me to discover. There's no point in me sitting in an air-conditioned café; though this could be something I come to regret.

Where I had planned to stay in Chalong is not near the beach. I'd chosen that area for its proximity to the language school I was keen to attend. I wanted to be able to walk there and back. I figure if I can have daily sunsets and ocean swims then I'm in, particularly when Joe tells me he put the heater on at home today. I'm sure I'll find another way to get to school.

I love lists. I made one of the potential places to live around

Kata and Karon and asked my taxi driver friend Mon to take me to both neighbourhoods so I could look at the rooms available. Some owners were more helpful than others and some places got struck off as soon as we arrived based on location alone.

However, I found what I think will be a nice place back here in Kata. I spoke with the young reception staff in Thai and they willingly showed me the room I was interested in. It was a good size, air-conditioned and has pool access from the back door. It's close to the beach and the action, and all the little spots and people I've grown fond of in a very short space of time are just a short walk away.

Free Zumba was on in the park this afternoon down by the beach. The atmosphere was great with the music pumping. The smiles were wide and the instructor was full of energy encouraging his participants. The public spaces are plentiful and there are tons of places to exercise if you feel like it. That said, given the heat, swimming in the ocean is more appealing for me.

I've acquired a new beach accessory and it's not a bright pink G-string bikini, although there are lots of them for sale. It's my very own miniature sweepy brush. I can't tell you how handy it is to use on my feet as I come off the beach instead of walking home with sand between my toes. The ultimate accessory for any gal who intends to spend quality time at the beach.

11 March
Croc-Wearing Gardener / Fresh Seafood

I was sitting out on my ground-floor balcony at my modest hotel, having my morning fruit and reading, when along came the gardener. I greeted him as I do all the friendly staff here and received a warm greeting in reply. I then watched as he placed his ladder against the concrete wall that I look out on, the boundary fence between the hotel and the restaurant next door.

As he climbed the ladder, I noticed he was wearing Crocs. The wall is about three metres high and he walked along it like he would a footpath. He started trimming the vine that is poking above the wall. Steady on his feet, he trimmed as he crept along. Then he got to the end of the wall and I wondered how he would get down as his ladder was all the way back at the other end. Well, of course, that was no problem for him; he simply stood up without even a hint of a wobble and walked straight back along the slender top of the wall just like walking on a wide footpath . Maybe a whipper-snipper is overrated as are work boots and someone to hold your ladder, I thought. I was nervous watching him, but I shouldn't have been. Thais are very nimble and flexible people. I think it comes from sitting on the floor and squatting from a very early age. I struggle to get out of a bean bag these days, let alone walk along the top of a wall in Crocs like a cat along a fence.

Staying by the sea means that every second restaurant is selling fresh seafood, and by fresh I mean some are still swimming until you select them for dinner. There are large tanks full of live crayfish and crabs lining the street and nothing is too expensive. You can't get any fresher than this and you can eat fresh and local every day.

Around 5 p.m., big displays of the day's catch, buried in mountains of crushed ice, are placed at the front of the restaurants. The selection varies from day to day, but what remains unchanged is the constant stream of holidaymakers who love to pick a whole fish and have it barbecued on the spot. I always think of my dad when I see this, as I know how much he loves a whole fish any time we eat Thai. He'd be in heaven here. Seafood and an icy cold beer or three is the perfect combination for many after a big day out taking in the sights or lounging at the beach. The staff stand at the front of most restaurants funnelling people in and getting them excited about the fish that will be just right for them. It's a competitive business with an abundance of dining options to choose from.

As I'll be heading inland to Phuket Town tomorrow, this was my last sunset swim for a week or so. There was a smattering of clouds that turned a dusky pink just before we lost the sun for the day. It was beautiful to watch day turn into night, and I think Kata knew I needed a sunset to remember before heading off. Heaps of people tend to stick around after the sun disappears, which gives the beach a great atmosphere. Many want to squeeze as much out of the day as possible, and when you're on holidays, why wouldn't you? Couples, singles, friends, families and plenty of furry friends all seem to find it hard to leave at the end of the day. There are many expats living around this area and the beaches are dog-friendly.

Once the sting of the scorching sun has gone and the temperature drops, lying back on your towel and closing your eyes seems like the perfect thing to do. Time just stands still during these moments. See you again soon, Kata Beach. You've been exactly what my soul needed when I didn't even know what that was.

12 March

Moving On | Phuket Town | Apple's Carport Restaurant

As I wait for my friendly taxi driver to arrive and take me to my next hotel, my thoughts turn to what a perfect place this has been for my first sixteen days back in Thailand. There wasn't much available when I booked as it's the high season. I just wanted something close to the beach and with air conditioning. I got that and so much more. My hotel has been nothing fancy but the shower was clean, the bed big if a bit lumpy, the pool so refreshing to swim in and relax by when I couldn't be bothered walking to the beach, and there was enough space in my room for me to spread out. I've only woken up once during the night wondering where the hell I was. I've also been able to sit outside on my balcony and stare up into the sky and listen to the eighties hits booming out from the restaurant next door every afternoon. All those songs I haven't heard in forever. If I was at home and a neighbour did that I'd think how inconsiderate and probably shut my door, but here I'm embracing it because that's all part of doing life a bit differently for a while.

What has made my time extra special has been the two cheerful ladies on the reception desk, the young helpful bell boy with a wealth of local knowledge and my shy housemaid. I don't even know their names but that hasn't stopped us from chatting together each day in Thai, laughing so many times – mainly at me when I can't remember the Thai word I want to use or use the wrong one.

They have asked me every day where I was going, where I'd been, what I'd eaten, what I'd bought and if I was okay. It's their Thai way of being warm and welcoming. I have really appreciated feeling very much at home here. They've told me what app I need to book a taxi, what prices I should be paying when I go certain places, where to get a particular Thai chicken dish I wanted to eat, and always kept their little honesty fridge in the open-air reception area full of cool water. So many times, returning from my walks, I have headed straight to that fridge. I'm going to pop in and see them when I return to the area in April, but for now it's good luck and take care of yourself (*chork dii kha duu lae duu eng kha*). I'm off to my new hood in Phuket Town.

When I arrive, it's nothing like where I've been, which is exactly what I was hoping for. It feels like the burbs a bit more with no beach at the door, but I'm staying in a delightful boutique hotel, built in the Sino-Portuguese style, called Little Nyonya. I check in speaking only Thai. My confidence in using the language seems to have grown during the short time I've been here. I'm daring myself to give it a go every day.

As I mentioned when I went on my foodie tour, the Sino-Portuguese architecture is a favourite of mine. It's not only the architecture that I love but the incredibly vivid colours used on their facades very much appeals to me: musk pink next to banana yellow next to apple green. Most of these buildings have been restored, but you can still see the beautiful original decorative tiles and intricately carved wooden windows and doors on so many of them. Little Nyonya has a certain charm about it. I've already spotted a huge, ornate wooden door I'd happily have at my house.

Although it feels like I'm in the middle of nowhere, the biggest weekend market is next door and a few other spots I want to visit are not far away. This was another random pick from the Internet. So far, I'm happy with my haphazard way of selecting accommodation. Not overthinking things definitely has its advantages. It already seems so quiet here in comparison to the beach, which won't be a bad thing. There's a decent-sized pool which all the rooms face out onto. I'm again on the ground floor and can walk out of my room and straight onto the pool deck. I can already see myself spending plenty of time beside it or in it.

This spot will be home until Joe and our friends arrive next week for some holiday fun of their own. Our friends are just getting started on ticking places off their travel wish list. They've raised their family and are now ready to see the world.

After unpacking and settling into my hotel, I walked out and turned right straight onto an extremely busy main road with trucks, motorcycles and cars rushing past me. I very tentatively walked along the side of the road in flip-flops in 32-degree heat because there was no footpath. I'm still not sure why I did this, but I told myself once again that the Thais don't really want me to be a road statistic.

I eventually turned right again to get off the dusty, crazy, manic road and came to a market selling a few dinner snacks like satay sticks and noodles. One thing my time in Thailand has taught me is to never buy meat of any kind from the hawker stalls. They often have no refrigeration nor hygiene around flies so it's a no-go zone, but gosh it's hard as they smell so good. I did, however, get mango and sticky rice for half the price they charged in touristy

Kata. I kept on walking, looking for a place to sit and eat as it was now dinnertime, but had no luck. I decided to head back to my hotel via the backstreets. I'm hopeless with directions at home, but here I got my Google map up on my phone and followed that arrow. It took me down a very suburban-looking street. In the absence of lawns and gardens there were plenty of decorative potted planters and impressive ornate gates keeping us out and the owners' dogs in.

I came across a little restaurant in the front yard of a house. I asked the lady if she was open and she said yes, so I asked in Thai, 'What do you have that's good to eat?' Her husband told me to try the noodles with chicken and spicy paste (*dtom yum*), so I did. I took a seat in their carport, where I spotted the menu on a board on the wall. Unsurprisingly perhaps, given my passion for Thai food, I can read most food-related words in Thai. I've gladly given myself plenty of opportunities to practice not only reading them but saying them too. As it turned out, all my favourite dishes appeared on this lady's menu – I'd found the simple food that Thais eat every day and it's not pad Thai or green or red curry. This is exactly what I had been looking for in Kata, but understandably their offerings are more for the tourist crowd.

My noodles arrived and needed no seasoning. The broth was so flavoursome! I slurped them back at a pace in between talking to the lady who had by then introduced herself to me as Apple. At least that's easy to remember. She saw my sticky rice and mango and asked where I got it and how much it cost. I told her and also how expensive it was in Kata. I truly felt like a Thai housewife comparing food prices and great foodie finds with my neighbour. She said she was open from 10.30 a.m. to 8.30 p.m. every day. I told her I'd be back every day to eat from the top to the bottom of her home-cooked favourites menu.

I felt chuffed to have come across this place and proud of myself that I'd stopped and tried the food. Once again, I've found walking in my neighbourhood has uncovered otherwise hidden treats and treasures, and it's only Day One here.

13 March
Pool Time / Lego Man / Naka Market

I spent my whole morning in the pool or on the sun lounge under the umbrella. There's not a cloud in the brilliant blue sky and the peace and quiet couldn't suit me more. The rest I was craving before coming here is finding me. The dizzying pace and intensity of life seems to weigh heavily on so many of us. I find it's not until you completely opt out for a bit that your body and mind can exhale and begin to relinquish what once mattered. Years of putting others' needs before your own will do that to you. I know many people can relate to this. I feel as though the stress in my life is cumulative and almost invisible until it's not.

Eventually I scraped myself off the sun lounge, slipped a dress over my bikini and went up the road to find lunch. Out in the traffic-clogged street I walked warily, watching for motorbikes that zip up the outside lanes to avoid the traffic jams. I'd called into a very neat and tidy café on my way home yesterday from Apple's house and had a good *cha yen*, the icy milk tea that I love. Thankfully this café is only about a five-minute walk from my hotel, close enough for me to not feel hot and bothered when I arrive. I ordered *cha yen* again, and a Thai dish from a menu that had lots of Western food.

The young man I'd met yesterday came out to check on me

and chat. I had a feeling he had a story waiting to be told. His English is the best I've come across and he was extremely keen to speak it with me. I'm always happy to speak English with Thai people as some never dare to use their English skills. They're self-conscious and can be painfully shy. They desperately want to practice but let the opportunities slip by. I know exactly how that feels.

It turned out he used to work at a glossy, big-name hotel as a bartender and was mentored by a French guy. He was bartender of the year in 2008 at an international championship in LA. When the pandemic hit in 2020, he volunteered for redundancy as he figured his one wage paid for four of his team members to stay on. He had enough money to open a café a year ago and his family were able to help him. While the pandemic kept everyone at home, he made Lego figures with his free time, and they're displayed throughout his café. He makes the food himself and has certainly got the culinary skills. It seems he's very happy running his own show while caring for his elderly mother. I'm glad I took a chance again and wandered into his cafe yesterday. Such an interesting man out here in the burbs and still so proud of his achievements.

Having done a small amount of research on the Naka Market I was pleased when I found a hotel within walking distance. Starting at 4 p.m. on Saturday and Sunday, this place comes alive with the most tempting selection of Thai foods. When I arrived, I needed to do a couple of laps just to take it all in. I still couldn't decide what I wanted to buy so around I went again.

We like to think that we have a great range of food at home in Australia, but we've mainly relied upon cuisine from other countries for variety. The Thais have such a diverse variety of food that you really only find in their country, though there have been influences from the Chinese, Malaysian, Burmese and Indian cuisines, and various adaptations of Western food that have taken on a distinctly Thai twist, like deep-fried sandwiches! There were plenty of sweet snacks (*kanom*): golden sticky Thai sweets made mostly from egg yolks; small metal trays full of coconut custard; coconut-laced buns; doughnuts; and homemade rice cakes. There was meat from every animal, including the fried insects that seem to pull a large tourist crowd; many want the photo to prove they ate a bug. Trays of pre-made curry, fried everything, fish balls by the hundred, fruit made into delicious spicy salads, corn on a stick, French-type pastries, noodles of every kind cooked to your taste, freshly squeezed sugar-cane juice, aloe vera juice, fruit smoothies and on it went. Each stall specialised in one type of food and did it exceptionally well.

I bought a couple of my favourite Thai sweets. Crispy sweet rice cakes (*khao taen*), small rounds of sticky rice, dried and lightly fried and drizzled with cane sugar, are simple but moorish. My other favourites, *khanom buang*, are small disks of batter that are cooked on a hotplate until crisp but still able to be folded. Mine were filled with meringue and a sprinkle of freshly grated coconut. The temptations were endless, but I mainly enjoyed watching what others were eating and their curiosity around foods they'd never seen before. The tourists not only come for the incredible food, but also for the fakes and replicas: handbags of every designer label, shoes, T-shirts, perfume, makeup, watches – you name it. I also found where all our old jeans end up: cut off into shorts and sold here.

The heat under the tin roof, with a mass of frying food and sweating humans, had me looking for the exit after an hour or so. I had an urge for a cool lemon tea. I walked through the backstreets heading towards my friend Apple's place. There was a lovely warm welcome waiting. I told Apple that despite all the food at the market, I knew I'd get a better meal at her house. My much-anticipated *kaow mun gai* translates literally as 'chicken and rice cooked in chicken fat', but it's really rice cooked in a chicken stock with the poached chicken served on top, finished off with a delicious, slightly syrupy, spicy soy sauce and garnished with slices of fresh cucumber. You get a little bowl of chicken soup to drink alongside. Again, it's a super-simple meal but one I love. I could easily eat it a few times a week. Apple and I chatted, and I found out that she got one of her four kids to go and buy sticky rice and mango for her yesterday. Seems these kids come in handy.

It was getting dark and I was full of food so I thought I had better go, or risk tripping over while walking along the busy main road. I told Apple and her husband that I'd be back tomorrow night and wandered off feeling content and grateful for such delightful people being in this neighbourhood. When I eat out here, I prefer a roadside restaurant run by locals, where you know you're contributing directly to the livelihood of those who are making the food. They run on a shoestring and are so proud of their offerings, and rightly so.

14 March

Thai Boyfriend | 3D Museum | Phuket Sunday Street Market

The taxi apps are fantastic. The drivers are often at the front of the hotel before I get there. There's an abundance of taxis on the road. It turns out that not every driver does the right thing, however. This afternoon I wanted to go to the Phuket Sunday Walking Street Market, known locally as 'big market' (*lard yai*), a very well-known foodie haven. As the name suggests, it's only held on a Sunday, opening at 4 p.m., and is right in the middle of Phuket Town on Thalang Road. My plan was to visit early before the crowds arrived and come back for a swim in the pool to cool off.

Well, my taxi driver had another plan. He was sure that there wouldn't be anything for me to see before 6 p.m. When he's not driving or even when he is, this man is a tour guide and so he had every single brochure you could think of stuffed in the seat pockets of his car. Much to his disappointment, I'd done pretty much everything he suggested apart from the Phuket 3D Museum.

I gave in and agreed that he could drop me there and I'd then walk to the market.

As we drove towards the museum, he started asking if I had a Thai boyfriend. 'Why would I want one of them?' I replied. 'One husband is more than enough.' He persisted and said he'd pick me up tomorrow and take me to the Tiger Park. By this stage, I was feeling annoyed and told him in Thai, 'No, you won't. I'm busy.' Thank goodness, we soon arrived at the 3D Museum. But then as I got out of the taxi, he insisted on helping me buy my ticket. My patience was wearing very thin. I went in, thinking that if he was out the front when I came out, I'd be crossing the road to the police station. Lucky for him, he'd gone.

The 3D Museum was surprisingly very well done. I had no idea what to expect. Once called the Phuket Trickeye Museum, it's housed in a converted old cinema. There are more than a hundred 3D paintings covering the walls and each create a 3D illusion on a flat background. The tour guide showed me where to stand, then took my photo many times. The optical illusion places you in blockbuster-movie-like scenes such as standing on a broken bridge above rapids, walking on a tight rope and other clever scenarios. Sadly, my mood was off, but I'd come back and do it properly again. I was annoyed with myself that I'd let this random man change my plans. Lesson learned.

With the help of my phone to get my bearings, it didn't take me long to arrive at the market. Unlike the suburban Naka market, it was easy to see this was the hipsters' food market with a modern, young and funky vibe, along with an interesting mix of handicrafts, including sunglasses for dogs and the ubiquitous elephant souvenirs.

The whole street is closed off with stalls set up in the middle. Not wanting to miss a thing, I went up one side and down the other. There was entertainment from buskers. I stopped to listen to a young Thai girl singing English songs and she was great. Her mum was proudly encouraging her from the front row of seats as was the appreciative crowd.

With heaps of food that took my fancy, I could've easily gone on a buying frenzy, but seating was tricky, so I needed something in a bowl. I chose a shredded green mango salad (*yum mamuang*) with tiny dried prawns, small pieces of dried fish, crunchy peanuts and a punch of chilli. That combination of sour and salty made it an absolute taste sensation. It's the sort of salad I wish I could make at home, but green mangoes are non-existent in my part of the world.

I loved the lively, open-air market atmosphere, but once my arms had beads of sweat on them and the crowds started to swell, it was swimming-pool time for me. I called a taxi and thankfully got a different driver this time.

15 March

Local Living | Central Phuket Shopping Mall | Coconut Ice Cream

And just like that, I've turned into a local. My one job today was to get my washing done. Unlike in Kata, where practically every street corner has a shop doing laundry, I hadn't seen anything in Phuket Town. I asked Google to help me and found a place that would pick up and deliver, which sounded perfect. I put their number in WhatsApp and made contact.

In Kata I'd been paying 60 baht (A$2.50) per kilogram for a wash-and-fold next-day service. The new service I just found was a minimum four kilograms at 90 baht per kilogram and 800 baht for pickup and delivery; minimum 1,160 baht. That's a week's pay for some people here and, for this foreigner, a total rip-off. I'm well beyond the stage of not understanding what things should cost. Everyone must eat, but like most people I don't like to be taken for a ride. My brain started working out how many poached chicken with rice dishes (*khao mun gai*) I could buy from Apple for that. So it looks like I'll be washing my undies in my bathroom sink until I'm back around Kata.

You'll find Thais are understandably very conscious of the

price of things and every single baht counts. They're never afraid to say something is too expensive and haggle it down or move on. And now, nor am I.

This afternoon I grabbed a taxi and went about fifteen minutes up the road to check out Central Phuket, an enormous shopping centre spanning four floors and two sprawling buildings – the designer label building and the ordinary peeps building. I stuck with the everyday peeps side and didn't even get halfway around it. They section their shopping centres up by category here so all the banks are together, all the cosmetics brands, kids' stuff, technology etc., which is quite handy when you're not familiar with the layout.

I wandered aimlessly as there was nothing I needed. Soon enough I found myself in the food section and was surprised to see Coles, the Australian supermarket chain. I can honestly say I've never seen Coles look so beautifully stocked and full. There were long queues at KFC, definitely not what I come to Thailand for. One KFC drumstick is 50 baht so the whole meal is pretty pricey compared to the average daily wage here or my plate of chicken and rice.

It's interesting how some Thais strive for the Western lifestyle they see in movies and on the Internet. Whereas we tend to come over here to escape the trappings of our lives and Western ways. I know I'm very happy to leave it all behind and simplify the way I live for a while. We humans are hard to satisfy at times.

I got myself home after several failed attempts at booking a taxi. I'd unexpectedly hit a peak period. Then I headed around the corner to see Apple and have a late lunch. I told her I'd been to Central Phuket Festival shopping complex and the food wasn't delicious and I was back to enjoy hers. This made her smile. Working through the rice menu, I was up to crunchy pork with rice, which was great.

Apple introduced me to three of her four kids today as they're on school holidays. I got a very lovely hug from her sweet youngest son and a *wai* and *sawadee krup*.

While I was eating, I could hear in the distance a ringing bell. My ears knew immediately that this was the sound of the ice cream motorbike. It's a bit like hearing the sound of the Mr Whippy ice cream van as it slowly crept up your street, giving you enough time to beg your parents for money and run out the front of your house.

I quickly paid Apple, said goodbye and headed across the street to where the ice cream man was serving another lady. I said *sawadee kha* and he replied in Thai, 'Oh, you speak Thai very clearly, how come?' The lady he was serving said he could serve me first because I was standing in the sun, so I moved out of the sun and told her that I was happy to wait. Such kind and respectful people.

The ice cream is a simple coconut (*kati*) flavour, but what makes it particularly delicious are the balls of sticky rice that you can have with it. You can also have it served in a long white roll like a hot dog bun. It might sound weird, but don't judge until you try it. I guarantee it won't be your last. When it was my turn, the ice cream man said, 'You want the big size with lots, don't you?' He's a mind reader too, it seems.

Before he rode off, he asked me to taste my ice cream and tell him if it was delicious. He had the biggest smile on his face when I said, 'It is, but I knew it would be.' And off he went to find his next satisfied customer, leaving the sound of his ringing bell in his wake. There's no doubt this is how I'd rather shop and buy my food any day.

16 March

Excess Words / Hair Sparkles

I'm propped up in a café, the one where the *cha yen* is amazing and the owner loves Lego, doing my Thai language studies. It's easy to see why it's difficult for Thai people to speak English and for us to get the hang of Thai. For starters, our sentence structures are completely different. We say 'red car', they say 'car red'. They're also good at cutting words out without changing the meaning. For instance, we might say, 'Do you want to go out together?' They will say '*bai duay gun*' or 'go together', which has the same meaning but why say seven words when two will do? So you almost have to think like them before you can speak like them. The missing words are often obvious from the context of the conversation, but it can take a little getting used to.

My listening and comprehension has always been way better than my speaking, but slowly my speaking is catching up. It can feel like I have a delay button being pressed in my brain when I go to answer or speak Thai. Then, after a little while, when there's no pressure on me to deliver, I think, 'I knew how to say that, why didn't

I?' It just takes time, patience and the ability to laugh at yourself often and never give up.

I walked back to my room ready to take on the sparkles in my hair that I saw when I looked in the mirror this morning. I've come prepared for doing my own hair colour for the next couple of months, thanks to my thoughtful hairdresser at home, gorgeous Abbey. What could possibly go wrong?

I did see a salon at the mega-shopping centre, but I'm guessing as time goes on I might well care less and less about my hair. I don't plan to let the natural silver totally take over. I'm not ready to embrace the grey, but I might just relax my usual colouring cycle because nobody here will be looking at my regrowth, least of all me. The feeling of liberation that comes with this one simple act cannot be overstated.

I still haven't quite worked out why I can be so carefree while away, yet once I get home I slip back into the routine almost without thinking about it. It no doubt contributes to the feeling of 'the grind'. I'll put it down to often being on autopilot in my everyday life, which is a tad concerning given how we're told we're meant to be 'present' and 'in the moment' regardless of where we are in life. Might need to keep that in mind.

17 March
Sino-Portuguese Buildings / Pink Night Skies

This part of town, adorned with urban street art, is full of quirky cafes, artists, galleries, cultural landmarks and shophouses selling Thai ceramics, beautiful fabrics, handmade jewellery, bags and clothing. Records show that the tin-mining industry began in Phuket as long ago as 1528 AD. In 1583 a tin warehouse in the Thalang district was opened. Thalang Road, lined with elegant Sino-Portuguese shophouses, was the first street in Old Phuket Town. This was where most activities and commerce took place, with workers coming to the town to buy essentials, to eat or just to have fun. The whole area was rich in tin and continued to attract more and more miners. The city grew quickly over several years, and soon there was not one main street but five. This mining boom continued for a long time and it was only in 1973 that the Tourism Authority of Thailand confirmed its plan to pursue the development of the tourist industry. Gradually the mines closed and tourism took over.

As circumstances changed when the tin reserves dwindled and the transition to tourism commenced, many workers subsequently left the city and Old Phuket Town fell into neglect.

Thankfully there has been a shift with a younger generation breathing new life and vibrancy into many of the buildings and the area has regained its popularity as the place to be for locals and tourists alike. The old buildings have become a very big draw for many people who visit Phuket, providing the quintessential Instagram backdrop which so many are looking for these days. I would really like to join a walking group so I can find out more of the history of the significant landmarks in the area. I've got so many questions.

When I arrived at Apple's for dinner with her lovely family tonight, I got the biggest hug from the youngest, her seven-year-old son, who's always by my side as soon as I arrive. Although he says very little and is too shy to speak any English. I also got to meet their dog. 'Little' was having a wash and blow-dry and looked slightly spooked and terrified by the whole ordeal.

I ordered the egg noodles with pork, and the chilli did a great job of clearing my sinuses. The food Apple serves is so nourishing and satisfying. There were handfuls of vegetables in it and crunchy pork crackling on top. She's always busy doing something when I'm there, but tonight a friend called in and she sat and had a good gossip. Experience tells me Thai women love to do this, much like we do at home. Nothing like sitting and having a great download and laugh with a girlfriend. It made me smile to see her relaxing and obviously enjoying herself.

Afterwards I walked around to the small local market for sticky rice and mango, then ever so slowly walked back to my hotel. It was such a mild night with a striking hot-pink sky and I couldn't help but imagine how beautiful it would have been on the beach.

Each new day I'm feeling more and more like I'm lowering my shoulders and unclenching my jaw as I rest and relax. Doing life on my terms means I can take as much time as I need doing what I feel like doing. My foggy brain is creating space, not so cluttered with what can feel like a million different decisions, just to get through the day. There's no sense of expectation or urgency to anything I'm doing. When I feel like I've had enough, I just make another decision that suits me. It's definitely a different way of being and one that's agreeing with me.

I floated around in the pool alone tonight and felt a pleasant level of contentment and a mind that wasn't racing all over the place. That hasn't been in my life for some time.

18 March

Joys of foodpanda / What's For Dinner?

In a short space of time, foodpanda has become a very good friend of mine. It's one of the food delivery apps here and it's nothing short of brilliant. Tonight I felt like swimming late and staying in for dinner. I'd had a pool-and-sun-lounge day and didn't feel like getting out of my bikini any time soon. I'm getting very comfortable with going with the flow and chopping and changing my mind on a whim. I'm already wondering if any of this new way of being can stay with me when I get home. It's far too early in my stay to even be thinking about that, but I was. The absolute luxury, of course, is no one asking me or having to come up with 'What's for dinner?'

Talking with my mostly female friends at home, we all seem to be totally over the 'what's for dinner?' dilemma. I'm guessing you must reach a certain point in your life and just the thought of it makes you want to reach for the cheese and biscuits or boil an egg. I've tried prepackaged meals, frozen meals, menu planning, chef-designed recipes that I can select from for the week and have the ingredients delivered to me, and I still feel exhausted by it all. I can cook and don't mind it, but it's just so tedious and monotonous at times. It's little wonder that when I see that little pink panda from foodpanda heading towards me on the map on my phone, it makes me so incredibly happy.

Once I was out of the pool, I placed my order. By the time I was dry and changed, my phone was showing the little pink panda icon was arriving at my hotel. There's a vast food selection on the app. I'm currently only interested in Thai food, but you can get whatever you feel like. The delivery charges are never more than A$2 and each time I've used it my freshly cooked food has arrived in under thirty minutes. That's from when the order is received to the motorbike rider handing it to me. It's clearly the little things in life for me at the moment.

As we don't have much in terms of convenient, delicious fast-food delivery where I live at home in the burbs of Hobart, although I've ordered my groceries online forever, this is a total novelty for me. The other night using a different app called Grab I ordered big bottles of water that were otherwise too heavy for me to carry. You still can't drink the tap water here. My snacks and fruit and water were picked and packed and with me in thirty minutes. They even called to say one item wasn't available. Who does that?

With over 21 million motorbikes in Thailand and only ten million cars, the ability to get goods delivered quickly anywhere via motorbike is obvious. For some Thai people their motorbike is their primary source of cash and not just a means of transport. Many work very long days as demand for their speedy service is high.

My delivery driver was a friendly woman, whom I tipped well, as personally I can't imagine riding around day in day out delivering people their food for two dollars a delivery. They must cover fuel and maintenance on their bike, not to mention being out in the heat all day with a helmet on and weaving in and out of the heavy, traffic-choked streets. Another hard way to earn a living, but so appreciated by people like me watching the pink panda get closer and closer on the app map. The fact that it removes any planning and preparation around 'what's for dinner?' means I'm totally sold.

19 March

Street Smells / Real-Life Connections

I'm the kind of person who can be transported back to a time and place just by inhaling a particular smell. I find the perfume I wear when in Thailand always reminds me of being there once I'm home. The street smells here, however, can take your breath away. The use of a mask is not just for Covid at times. The lack of proper drainage leading to stagnant water and the never-ending tropical heat can create quite the stench.

And then there's the fruit… durian. You know it's bad when hotels have banned it. It smells like nothing you've smelt before, though someone described it as 'the flesh of some animal in the state of putrefaction', which I thought was pretty close. It's such a weird fruit; those who can get past the smell become quite addicted to the creamy texture of the flesh and absolutely love it. My Thai father was a big fan, but he always told me that you could not eat too much as it would increase your blood pressure. Scientists say it's a rare amino acid that gives it this funky smell. The Thais have a word that encompasses anything that smells revolting: they say *'men'*, and durian fits that category for me. I try not to insult Thais with my dislike of it, but I always politely decline it when it's offered. I figure it would be a total waste on me and the urge to spit it out might not go down too well. It's one of only a couple of things that I won't go near food-wise. Give me a mango or pineapple or practically any other fruit over this bad boy any day.

I felt like some fresh fruit this morning, so I placed my order on foodpanda. Sometimes I find myself scrolling through the menus to see what I could order if I wanted to. Maybe I have too much time on my hands? Anyway my guava, pineapple and mango arrived in twenty minutes, all peeled and ready to eat, complete with the Thai and Laotian packets of dipping salt, sugar and chilli. That's me sorted for the next three days.

My teacher for my online Thai language course lives in Phuket and today we met for the first time. I took a taxi to her apartment in Chalong and we went to Nai Harn Beach, south of Kata. She went for a run around a big man-made lake and I went swimming. How I've missed my ocean swims.

Afterwards we went for dinner and a chat. It was great to sit with her and find out more about her life. She is ten years younger than me and has spent a fair amount of time living in the US. She's really enjoying being back home in Thailand, although all her family don't live in Phuket. So many of my relationships with people are online these days, it just seems to be the way my world works. Many I may never meet. It was fantastic to meet with her and it reminds me that the human connection is important and still matters.

20 March

Unwinding | Nothing Changed | Picnic For One

Today is my last day at this lovely tranquil hotel. Although it's on one of the major roads heading north out of Phuket, Chao Fah Tawan Tok Road, you'd never know that there was constant heavy traffic out the front as you can't hear a thing. It has been my little oasis of serenity and calm.

I've felt very secure and content tucked away here. My room has been so cosy and comfortable, no lumpy mattress, and umpteen pillows that you sink into for a deep restful sleep. I've had some pleasant conversations with the staff each day and even worked out how to ask for a pool towel as opposed to a bathroom towel.

Unwinding from our ordinary lives doesn't just happen. How many times have you been on holidays and the day before it's time to leave you feel like you're finally relaxing? It takes time to release the pressure valve and, while doing so, it can feel unsettling. I'm so glad that I have time on my side to let this happen as slowly and deliberately as it needs to. I'm aware of what a luxury that is. When did our lives get so stupidly busy and full?

I've found my thoughts sometimes trawling back through the past decade. There were so many things that would suck up my time and a large chunk of my energy and I think I'm still trying to make sense of it all. We were not only fighting for my husband Joe's physical and mental health, but also for our entitlements that were so poorly administered and handled. I wrote to the ministers, senior public servants and those in positions of power who ran these government departments. I explained the detrimental impact their systems, processes, lack of compassion and common sense was having on us out in 'everyday land', but nothing changed.

I joined a ministerially appointed advisory group as the 'partner and family representative' to provide a lived experience. I shared my lived experience in all its grim detail, knowing that this was my chance to make a change. After five years doing that time and time again, I saw many decision makers in tears on hearing my story, but nothing changed. I confronted those who said they were trying to help but were only hindering: doctors, psychologists, psychiatrists, counsellors and ex-services organisations. I never settled for 'this is as good as it gets'. I always thought that there had to be something more that could and must be done.

I hit many brick walls and often headfirst. But the nagging question around what others out there were doing and how they were coping kept me going. What about the other wives, partners, sisters, brothers, parents, children, grandparents and family and friends? If it was so hard for us, what was it like for them? This played on my mind.

I became angry and despondent more times than any human should have to. I regret none of it, but I'm mighty glad this isn't still part of my life. Something did change and it was me deciding I had done all I could. I left my burning desire to be part of the change behind. I extracted myself from all my commitments that related to the veteran community. I knew I needed to move to a place where it was all about healing. I'm certain this time away now will help even more with that period of my life ever so slowly finding its final resting place.

Tonight for my last meal in this neighbourhood, I wanted to eat with Apple again, but when I walked around to her shop it was closed. Her kind husband told me she had hurt her back and must rest up. He told me she has been working too hard, which didn't surprise me. Those long hours cooking for everyone had caught up with her and, under her doctor's orders, she had to rest. I was concerned for Apple and asked that he pass on my best wishes to her and thank her for all the delicious meals she made for me.

With my dinner plans upended, I returned to the Naka Market. This being my second visit, I was very strategic at getting what I wanted and getting out of there. It was pumping again, full of locals and tourists, and the food in vast quantities ready for hungry tummies. I got myself a spicy papaya salad (*somtarm*) and told the lady making it how hot I wanted it. Thais measure the heat in their dishes by how many chillies are added and I asked for one. I'm lucky to do one most days; those tiny red chillies pack a big punch.

I also found my way to a shop selling dried caramelised pork bits, much like jerky, and while there I bought some sticky rice to eat with the meat. Then I stopped at the fried-catfish-with-green-mango-salad stall. The fish is fluffed and fried until it is crispy and golden in colour. The crispy crunch of the fish contrasts with the tangy and sour green mango salad –the textures and flavours combine very well together. Having a sweet tooth, I always need a little sweet something to end my meal. At home it's often a chocolate, but here the heat isn't a friend of chocolate, so I chose a small banana-leaf-lined tray with four mini coconut puddings in it. Perfect. This was a table picnic for one.

Thumbs up for all of it, although in the end my eyes may have been a touch too big for my belly. But I do like to have options. The whole thing cost 180 baht (A$8), and the only effort on my part was carrying it all home.

21 March

Karon | Table For Two

Joe has arrived and, in two days' time, our 'Team Phuket', as it has become known, will be complete when our super-excited friends get here. This won't be #livinglikeathai for the next seventeen nights, but we certainly will be living our very best holiday lives in Phuket. We booked this trip together in February 2022, when the pandemic was still in full swing, knowing we needed something to look forward to. We quite literally started counting down the days when we still had more than four hundred to go. It's hard to believe we're here now and doubtless we'll never start counting that far out again. It felt like forever. This is something I've been excitedly looking forward to sharing with our friends, and I feel like it will be a special time for all of us.

We're staying at the Mandarava Resort and Spa. This hotel, built into a hillside surrounded by lush tropical gardens, is tucked away from the hustle of Karon but within easy reach of the beach. The rooms, nestled within the gardens, give you a feeling of seclusion and privacy. With the hotel facing west there are heaps of stunning spots to enjoy the sunset looking out towards Karon Beach. I stumbled across this gem last year while we were in Phuket and decided to do a one-night stay to see if we liked it. There is very little to not like about this place.

We've unpacked like we're never leaving and enjoyed the pool in front of our room and a walk around town. We spent considerable time in the mini-mart looking at things we didn't need just to cool down. All four swim-up bars are open and happy hour with half-price cocktails is every day from 4 to 6 p.m., so no guessing where we will be at that time.

Even though we've talked on the phone each day I've been away, it's great to see Joe again. He has put together the most awesome itinerary. He's been responsible for activities and I've looked after food and pampering. Now we both just want to roll it out. Last night it was a table picnic for one; tonight it was a tiny local restaurant on the side of the road and a table for two. I'm pleased I've been able to give myself the last couple of weeks just to find my feet again and not feel guilty doing so. I feel reenergised and having the support of my husband has been important, as he knows how much I've needed this, probably more than I even knew.

Other people's holiday stories can be very annoying and slightly boring, so I'll leave it here and pick up once the fun and adventures for Team Phuket (TP) are over.

6 April

Team Phuket / Blu Pine Villa / Fruit Smoothies

You know you've had a great holiday if it comes to an end and you just want to do it all over *again*. This morning we said goodbye to our wonderful friends. The fifteen days of activities, sightseeing, food and good times could not have been more enjoyable. Joe and I haven't really holidayed with others before so it wasn't something we were used to. We know what we like doing, but as for how others holiday, we had no idea. There was only one rule on our TP holiday and it was, you do you, nothing was compulsory.

We wanted to introduce our friends to some Thai culture right from the beginning so we worked with the wonderful hotel staff who organised a group of Thai dancers and musicians as the dinner entertainment on the first night. I can still see the shock and amazement on our friends' faces as the elegant Thai dancers, dressed in beautiful traditional costume, came onto the pool deck where we were having a private dinner. We ended the night doing our best Thai dance moves together with the ladies.

There was a Thai cooking lesson with a visit to a local market to collect the ingredients; scuba diving and snorkelling; and a hilarious day at the Andamanda Water Park. Don't ever let anyone tell you these parks with crazy, scary waterslides are only for kids. We arrived when the gates opened and departed when they closed. In between we went on rides and slides where you could hear our screams across the park and our laughter wasn't far behind. I'm so glad we took plenty of videos as I'm sure there will be much reminiscing in the future.

We made sure our friends fed and got up close and personal with the residents of the Phuket Elephant Sanctuary, a peaceful forest home for rescued and retired elephants. There was a day spent sea kayaking into the caves and lagoons at Phang Nga Bay. A 'floating afternoon tea' arrived in our private pool with sweet snacks and bubbles; and we provided the girly chats. There were massages and mani-pedis, Big Buddha, Chalong Temple and Karon Viewpoint visits, jet skiing and lots of time lazing in the pool or around the pool bar, enjoying each other's company. We finished the holiday by ticking off a very big wish on our friends' bucket list: a surprise dinner on the beach as the sun set, with our feet in the sand, surrounded by twinkling fairy lights. Unforgettable.

Every morning when we met for breakfast we'd share our three favourite memories from the previous day. These all now live in a precious book put together by our friends with these words on the back cover: 'The best thing about memories is making them! Friends forever.'

I really enjoyed seeing Thailand, a place that I'm so familiar with, through the eyes of first-timers. Watching Thais provide the welcoming and generous hospitality they're well known for and delighting in those who appreciate their beautiful country was heartwarming.

Joe is staying on for a few more days and then I'll be flying solo again. After our friends left, we arrived back in Kata to my home for the next couple of months, Blu Pine Villa, a simple hotel surrounded by mountains. I'm already pleased I trusted my gut on this accommodation and location when I first saw it. We've been out and about scoping out my local hood and have pretty much found everything a gal could want or need. There is a fruit shop making fresh tropical-fruit smoothies, a friendly laundry lady, a mini-mart and plenty of massage parlours, all within a fifteen-minute walk.

Later that afternoon, we ate at Red Chair, a nearby restaurant recommended by the lady who had just given me a manicure. Our table was filled in a flash with crispy golden spring rolls, chicken satays with spicy peanut sauce, stir-fried chicken and cashews, spicy fresh corn salad and jasmine rice. We ended up eating it in a flash as well.

Now that we're back in Kata, I was keen to get down to the beach to catch the sunset and see if the throngs of tourists have left. April means it's officially low season, which lasts until October. The price of accommodation drops and there's a change in the weather with the rain coming, though the heaviest rainfall is not until September. It's also never really cold. The beach was still pretty packed, but the Thais are telling me many tourists have left already and more will be leaving soon. Selfishly I hope they're right.

It was quiet without our friends. At least we are still in paradise and not sitting on a plane wondering how those fifteen days went so quickly.

7 April
Kata Noi / Khun, Phii and Nong

Today it wasn't just hot but sizzling hot. So I made a purchase that I wish I'd made sooner, a handheld rechargeable fan. So handy for a bit of relief and I took it to the beach. This was a new beach for us, Kata Noi, meaning 'Little Kata'. It's smaller than Kata Beach, but we loved it. Sun lounges galore with umbrellas, fruit smoothies ten steps away and the beach so incredibly beautiful and inviting with picture-postcard translucent turquoise water.

Unsurprisingly, we were the only ones wearing a rash guard or 'rashie' as we call them at home. We both have long-sleeve rashies that give us the sun protection our fair skin needs while out swimming on a day like this. There were some very bright red people out there on the beach. Wait until they hit the shower tonight. *Ouch.*

Joe is trying to get his head around the different prefixes I use when I address Thai people. Thai society being based very much on status and respect, this comes through strongly in their language. When you first meet someone, you use the prefix *khun*, so they call me *Khun* Mel and I call Apple *Khun* Apple, for example. This is used for both men and women and shows respect to the person you're speaking to. It's polite and formal and for adults. A different word is used when speaking to children. As time goes by and you become friends with the person you can drop the *khun*, though only if they're a similar age to you. If you are an older person, you will be called *phii* plus your name; if younger, *nong*, so *Phii* Mel or *Nong* Mel. This replaces *khun* in both cases.

When they speak to foreigners they don't know in English, Thais will often call us madam or sir. They learn this at school. Back when I was living here in 1989, when the kids would see me outside school, they'd yell out, 'Hey you!' I thought this was rude at the time, though they never meant to offend because 'you' is almost the equivalent of *khun* and they just wanted to say hello. If they knew my name, they would yell that. It's also common for Thai people to address others using their occupation. For instance, my Thai father was a doctor so everyone called him *Mor* Nimitr, *mor* meaning doctor, and my Thai teacher is *Kruu* Noi, *kruu* meaning teacher.

I've had such a hard time getting my Thai friends to call me Mel. They will always err on the side of respect. I'm called madam in front of their kids. I've invited them to call me *Phii* Mel and even then, they've struggled. It's truly part of who they are.

I can understand this as for such a long time I would only feel comfortable calling Thai people *khun*, not wanting to offend in any way, but over time I've been able to understand the social structure a lot better. It's not so complicated when you get familiar with it. Listening to how Thais refer to one another is the best way to learn. Joe is going to stick with calling people *khun* for now which works very nicely all around.

8 April
Vitamin Sea / Triggerfish

There's little doubt in my mind about the benefits that the ocean provides. During this trip I find I'm gravitating towards it more than ever before. The truth is I've never been a big beachgoer. I didn't grow up near the sea, and although I live near the beach in Hobart, I've never swum in the water. It's just too cold. I certainly appreciate a walk along a lengthy stretch of sand, but I've probably done more bush walking than beach walking. Here, any chance to be at the beach or go for a swim, I don't hesitate. The fact that I've moved my long-stay accommodation from the inner city to be closer to the beach tells me something. All that 'vitamin sea' really is good for my soul.

Today we went out on a dive boat: snorkelling for me and scuba diving for Joe. We both look forward to doing this each time we visit. The Andaman Sea is truly a beautiful place to spend some time whether on the surface or under it.

The conditions were calm and smooth and I was keen to get my fins and mask on, jump in and have a look around. I've not yet been convinced to learn to dive. It's not being able to get back up to the surface on my own that I don't like. I'm sure I could overcome it, but I haven't pushed myself as I love just floating on the surface and seeing what I can see. It's simple and uncomplicated and provides one of the purest forms of relaxation for me. Once I'm out there swimming around in the pristine aquamarine water, watching the activity below me, nothing else matters.

We went to two snorkelling sites, Racha Yai, *yai* meaning big, and Racha Noi, *noi* meaning little. These islands are only about an hour out from Phuket and popular for day-trippers, but I've never felt swamped by others while there. I was the only one off our boat snorkelling. Once all the divers are in the water, it's happy days for me to jump in, swim off and see what I can see. It's quite shallow at both sites and the white sandy seabed seems to be an ideal hiding spot for some fish, which you only see when they flinch. I'm no fish expert and I always rely on the fish identifier once I get back on the boat to properly identify what I saw.

When I first jumped in, I was greeted by humbug damselfish, small, cute fish with black-and-white stripes that dart around in the water. There were schools of them everywhere. They always make me stop and stare, dazzled by their sheer numbers, often hundreds. Another I saw in large numbers was the yellowtail snapper, a silver fish with yellow fins and tail. I also saw a moray eel, but I just can't warm to them. I'm not sure if it's the gaping mouth, the fact that they look very snake-like or their sheer size, but I moved on pretty quickly.

As I got closer to the coral, one of my favourites was there, the triggerfish. There are forty species of them and without exception they're stunning. Their markings make them particularly striking with a combination of spots, stripes and an array of bright colours, especially blue, yellow, black, white and purple. I always marvel at the mood Mother Nature was in when deciding how these fish might look, the ultimate in pattern clashing.

I could hear them eating off the coral as their teeth pecked at it. Their jaws are powerful and they can crush food quickly. They're bottom dwellers and tend to eat crabs, worms and molluscs. I could see them using their fins to move the sand out of the way to find their food. They also shoot water out of their mouths to move sand and find a meal. They eat for most of their day. Little wonder I'm drawn to them! But they can be aggressive and territorial, and I've seen them battling it out with other fish, hunting them away. They've been known to bite humans should they interfere or get too close. Joe's had his own close encounter when he swam a little too near.

I saw so many different fish – nature's aquarium is an absolute wonderland. The hard coral provides a colourful home and landscape and plenty of opportunities for hide-and-seek for its residents. This area had plenty of purple sea stars, sea cucumbers and spiny sea urchins. It really is a treasure trove of colours and critters.

When I'm out in the ocean snorkelling, I'm never in a hurry. Time almost stands still. I just tootle around keeping an eye on the boat and an ear out for the blast of the air horn so I know when my time is up. It's fun being back on deck watching all the surface-marker buoys pop up to indicate that the divers are surfacing. The happy faces were everywhere today as the boat was filled with many first-time divers. It's never hard to strike up a conversation with people after they've been diving. Their enthusiasm and awe bubbles over when they share what they've been lucky enough to see. Joe dives with a camera these days so I get the pleasure of seeing what he has seen.

After a whole day out on or in the water, as we headed back the sun began to set and we relaxed together with a drink on the deck. Swimming in the sea, having the wind in your hair, the sun on your face and the taste of the salty sea spray on your lips feels like a day well spent. Joe and I cherish this time spent together doing something we both love.

10 April
Navel Oranges / Spot the Poser

Walking into our local smoothie shop this morning we found navel oranges imported from Australia. The lovely owner told us she ordered them for Thai New Year this week and they were expensive. They'll be eaten or juiced for this special occasion. Who knew the humble navel could be such a treat. I'll be sticking with my pineapple and passionfruit smoothie. I also felt like eating something refreshing and was pleased to find boxes of watermelon wedges and bags of baby pineapples sitting on ice.

Since moving back to Kata I've subconsciously begun to play the game of 'spot the poser'. Not a day goes by without me seeing a woman pouting, throwing her hair and head back, looking over her shoulder as she runs onto the beach, striking a pose on a sun lounge and adjusting her itsy-bitsy bikini so maximum flesh is on show. Some foreign women here seem totally obsessed with capturing the perfect pose and photo of themselves. It's astonishing and freaking me out a bit. This self-obsession has gone to the next level and I blame social media.

It was right on my doorstep the other day. Our next-door neighbours, a young Russian couple, passed us as we were returning to our room. She was wearing what looked like a tin-foil bikini that only just marginally covered her lady bits while the thong G-string meant her butt cheeks were out and proud. She had reflective sunglasses on, pink glossy lips and very long swishy hair. I'm all for body positivity, but this seemed to go beyond just being confident about who you are.

We went into our room, drew back our curtains and there she was sprawled out on a sun lounge directing her man to take photos of her with the sunlight reflecting off her bikini. Let's just say he didn't look overly impressed as he dragged on a cigarette, standing in the scorching sun.

After about ten minutes of her angrily rejecting every shot he'd taken (and you didn't need to speak the language to know what was being said), things took a turn. She tried the selfie, but wasn't happy. She gave him another chance, but was again unhappy with the result, and then she stormed off into the room. He followed. An almighty argument exploded as clearly her man just didn't get how important those shots were. Doors banged and he found himself locked out on the balcony with her screaming at him from inside. We were in the pool by this stage and not hiding our sniggers very well as he started tapping on the glass door to be let back in. I bet he'd just forgotten his cigarettes.

Later that evening we saw them on their hired motorcycle. She'd changed into her animal-print bikini and was filming herself on her phone as they rode off to the beach, maybe for 'Take two'.

11 April
Lotus Flowers

When I'm at home you'll often find me out in my garden. My front garden is full of flowers. From roses to rhododendrons, lavender to dahlias, there's always something blooming. Among the flowers are Japanese maple trees of all colours and leaf shapes. I've cultivated this garden over a number of years, adding to it slowly. I get just as much pleasure working in it as I do sitting in it. Absorbing the beauty and calm it provides on a warm summer's evening when the light remains long into the night is pure heaven.

My back garden is very different. In structured beds defined by creamy-coloured crushed-rock paths I have planted mainly Australian natives. My thinking was that this garden needed to be low-maintenance and pretty much take care of itself. My time would be stretched a little too far to fuss over both. Every September and October, the waratahs, long-stemmed bush flowers with a flashy red bloom and large, smooth waxy leaves, steal the show. This iconic native bloom also comes in pink and white. It's actually the pleasure they provide to those that I give them to that makes them extra special.

I think my love of gardens and gardening and all the goodness they can bring into your life is in the genes. My paternal grandfather was a gardener growing mostly flowers and vegetables. He was appointed head gardener for the grounds surrounding Australia's Old Parliament House in Canberra in 1966, and he cared for the famous rose garden with a team of people. My dad tells me that my grandfather always had a story to tell about which politicians requested bunches of roses for their lady friends. Both my parents love to garden and they've created stunning gardens over many years with a big focus on vegetable patches nowadays. You can always rely on my dad for a great haul of tomatoes, garlic, strawberries, snow peas, spinach, lettuce, zucchini, pumpkin, yellow beans and carrots. He seems to have an endless bounty of the freshest fruit and vegetables.

Here in Thailand, it's the lotus flower that I've always been attracted to, even before learning about what it represents. In Buddhist and Thai tradition, the *dawk bua* – *dawk* meaning 'flower' and *bua* meaning 'lotus' – is a symbol of purity, faithfulness and spiritual awakening. The flower itself emerges from the mud, constantly growing upwards towards the light and warmth, representative of the act of spiritual growth and reaching enlightenment. Buddhist lore says that the lotus flowers would bloom at the feet of the Buddha, and he also compared people's ability to understand dharma or Buddhist teachings to the four levels of the lotus:

- Lotus in the mud – someone who is unable to understand dharma
- Lotus under water – someone who would understand dharma if given enough time
- Lotus blooming on the water's surface – someone who would understand dharma with a bit of effort and study
- Lotus in full bloom above the water – someone who would understand dharma at their first hearing and

attain enlightenment

You often see lotus flowers growing in big deep ceramic pots outside houses to attract good fortune and luck, and in big expanses of water, either natural or man-made, where they really do shine and look magnificent en masse. At the tranquil gardens at The Sarojin, my favourite hotel in Khao Lak, you can tell so much thought has gone into the garden. The hard landscaping, consisting of multiple large ponds and water features, is softened with the abundance of lush-foliage plants. As you arrive at the hotel and are guided through the open foyer to the comfy lounges to check in, directly in front of you is a rectangular pond overflowing with lotus flowers. If the sun is shining, you're lured towards the pond by the vivid pink, purple and white flowers, often full of bees and floating above the waterline. I have a whole library of photos that I've taken there over many visits. I just can't help myself.

You always see Thais carrying a lotus flower, a candle and three incense sticks when at the temple and making merit. They fold the petals of the flower to make them look even more exquisite. These offerings are believed to attract good fortune into your life. The flower is incorporated into the murals and paintings on the inside walls of temples, and statues are often surrounded by them. The lotus flowers most common in Thailand also include water lilies. You'll see this flower symbol used regularly and in so many situations once you're aware of it.

Every part of the flower is used in cooking. The roots are sliced up and steeped in hot water to make a tea, stems added to creamy coconut soups and the petals and seeds are also eaten. Traditional Thai healers have used the lotus flower in medicines to treat coughs, control blood sugar, cure stomach ailments and mitigate inflammation. Whether used in cooking or to cure ailments, planted in a single ceramic pot or in a vast and peaceful water garden or used to represent virtues from spiritual growth to enlightenment, the lotus flower commands a prominent place within Thai traditions and everyday life. It will always be a favourite of mine.

12 April
Spicy Papaya Salad / Pizza

It felt like a barbecue chicken (*gai yang*) and spicy papaya salad (*somtarm*) and sticky rice (*khao nioew*) kinda day for me this lunchtime. There's a shop ten minutes up the road where they flatten the chook and roast it over coals, giving it the best smoky flavour. You can smell it before you see it. I asked for my papaya salad without chilli and felt like I needed to apologise for dumbing down their food, but the kind lady offered me dried shrimp instead. They're salty little flavour bombs and I could eat the salad without my eyes watering or the back of my throat burning. I think my tolerance for chilli has dipped, but it might return after I've been here for a while. When I first lived here, I couldn't have any chilli at all. By the time I left, I was adding my own from the small communal condiment containers found in the middle of most restaurant tables.

I'd taken my washing with me when we went out to eat. When I dropped it off, the laundry lady invited us to her Thai New Year celebrations tomorrow afternoon. They will be throwing water on everyone who passes by from the front of their house. The lady at the smoothie shop also invited us to come up to her shop and do the same. These lovely people just want to include you in their fun and share their culture with you. It's so nice.

This is the first Songkran Festival post-Covid, so we're told there will be no holding back on the water thrown or the beers and whiskey consumed. It's New Year, after all. Foreigners can be quite the target for some of the fun and games, but we'll wear our cossies and, with this heat, welcome the drenching.

After our sunset swim down at the beach, we both fancied pizza. There's an Italian restaurant directly outside the hotel so that made life very easy. They serve their red wine chilled, which seemed odd but was understandable given the weather. I haven't really been craving any particular Western food so far, but it was good to eat a pizza with freshly sliced pineapple on top and have a glass of wine.

We've been finishing our days off with a night swim in the pool and tonight we did the same. We chatted and laughed together and it's probably the most relaxed we've both been in quite some time.

13 April

Songkra / New Year Celebrations

Happy New Year! (*Sook Sun Wun Songkran*). I've already been well watered this morning and had many laughs as everyone gets into the water throwing. I was drenched a couple of times, mainly by crazy foreigners. The Thais are gentle and almost apologise while gently tipping water over you or your hands. But the tourists go out with massive plastic water guns, as if it's a game of paintball, or are on the back of trucks with huge, pressurised hoses, and pelt you with ice-cold water, totally missing the point of what this is all about. Although it's appreciated in this heat, it's a bit of a shock when it first hits you.

I've also been given the white paste treatment by a Thai lady. The paste is typically made from talcum powder, food colouring and water and can have a pleasant scent. Applying it to someone's face is a symbol of friendship and good wishes for the New Year. The paste can be various colours, but white represents purity.

It was fantastic to be out in the community joining in. I couldn't help but remember my first Songkran, which was in Chiang Mai in the north, thirty-four years ago. They celebrate for longer there, sometimes four days. My Thai family were very protective of me because they probably knew I'd be a bit of a target. I wrote in my diary then, *Wun Songkran was so much fun today. I enjoyed throwing water on people and having my face covered with white powder.* Seems not much has changed, though I don't remember the plastic water pistols that people use now.

So why is water so important during Thai New Year celebrations? I thought I knew this, but wanted to check so I looked it up. It was interesting to read the many versions of what Songkran is all about. What I share below is a mix of my own knowledge and first-hand experiences and what I've read.

I've always known that water plays a strong role in Thai culture. It not only symbolises fertility and refreshment, but also prosperity and purification. Thai people believe that water is spiritually purifying, that it cleanses you of any bad luck or grievances from the past year, and blesses you with fortune and happiness for the year ahead.

New Year is in April because this is the month after the harvest season, when traditionally the farmers would finally have their long resting period, and farmers still celebrate this way. Festivals are held during this long holiday and merit making, giving food to the monks, going to temples and doing fun activities with the family are the focus. Before the day of celebration, people traditionally clean their homes and prepare new clothes as well as food and desserts for monks and their neighbours.

Songkran has now developed into a kingdom-wide water fight. As with so many historical and cultural festivals, for some the emphasis has shifted from the spiritual and religious to enjoyment and joviality. The Thai government now wants to invite the world to their Songkran party, looking at ways to attract more tourists to come and see for themselves and participate in their celebration.

We ended our day of renewal and new beginnings fittingly

in our pool. It was lovely to see a local performing the ritual of slowly pouring water on the Buddha statue and the hands of an elderly man outside a local house this morning. Preserving the true meaning of this sacred and special time of the year, I feel, is still very important.

Being in Thailand now and celebrating a new year, new beginnings and letting go of the past somehow felt right.

14 April

Online Shopping / Microbusinesses

A few days ago, I tried buying some new flip-flops as that's pretty much the only footwear you need here. But the shops didn't have my size 40. And most of them sold by street vendors are plastic, which end up giving me blisters, so I set about finding something online. I wasn't sure how I'd go as the website I found selling what I wanted was in Thai. When I got a knock on my door yesterday afternoon and my parcel was handed over, I couldn't believe it. My new pretty flip-flops came from Bangkok via normal mail and were with me in three days and delivered on a public holiday. Sure leaves our postal system at home wanting. The good news is they fit and are so comfortable too. This could be a dangerous discovery. I'm pretty partial to a good online purchase.

These days I wake up and my mind turns immediately to a pineapple and passionfruit smoothie. It's such a fantastic way to start the day. When I arrived in the shop this morning I was the only one there and I got talking with Mickey, the lovely lady who owns it. I asked why her smoothies are so good and she told me it's because she's generous with her fruit portions. That I can vouch for.

It's so hard to tell how old most Thai women are and Mickey is no exception. She wears colourful clothes and has her long black hair back in a ponytail or in a messy bun most days. Her face is soft and friendly and she always has a warm smile. Mickey had a restaurant before the pandemic, but had to close like so many here did. She had to work out how to support her family during the crisis, so she started growing fruit and chilli on a patch of land where she lives and sold it online.

She markets her fruit as organic and she's able to supply her two shops with most of her own fruit. Her next step is to change her shop roof, which is currently just a couple of sheets of tin. She plans to seal it so she can install air conditioning. It will not only help her fruit from spoiling but will mean she can keep cool during these relentless hot days and nights.

Mickey now has seven family members working on the farm picking fruit and working in her shops. She stressed to me how important it is to start small. She has no desire for a big business again. She just wants enough to live and help her family. We compared the expectations of many foreigners wanting more and more to the simple needs of many Thai people.

Every day I see these small businesses run by clever, forward-thinking and hard-working women. They are what makes this place tick. Incredibly resilient and smart, Thai women are very savvy with their money. They know how to drive a good deal and never shy away from asking for a discount or better price. They're steely in their commitment to wanting more for themselves and their children. I admire the pivotal role so many Thai women play in their families and in keeping rice on the table.

While Joe and I were having an outside dinner, sitting beside a driveway at Kata on Fire Bar and Grill, a short skinny man pulled up on his motorbike. It was already overflowing with bags and boxes of rubbish hanging off it and piled high. We both wondered how anything more could be added to his load, but he went into the open-air kitchen and came out with another two big bags of bottles and cans. He's not employed by any council or recycling group. He does this so he can eat. There's a very small amount of money to be made in recycling cans, glass and cardboard. He had a headlamp on, so it was obvious he was going to be working into the night collecting from restaurants and bars and making money out of the rubbish.

I'm struck time and again by how extremely hard some people work, often in ingenious ways, to earn a living, even a small amount of money. There doesn't seem to be a sense of entitlement or expectation about what should be available or given to them. Little does this man know the role, too, he's playing in the whole recycling lifecycle.

15 April
Hills | Jungle | Tsunami

Leaving Joe to sleep, I headed out for a morning walk. There's a long concrete driveway that connects my hotel to the main road. I've noticed that, with time ceasing to matter, I tend to scuff along it in my new flip-flops and need to remind myself to lift my feet. My slowing down is happening in all sorts of ways. Where I am living is surrounded by hills and they are covered in a messy tangle of tropical plants and overrun with banana trees growing randomly at the bottom, while higher up the trees are choked beyond recognition by rambling vines. It's dense jungle, so lush and full of varying shades of green. This morning the azure sky provides a striking contrast to the luminous green as I look towards the hills. There's not a cloud in the sky, which heightens the effect. I stop and take a photo.

You don't have to go far from the urban built-up areas to see the rubber, pineapple, coconut and palm oil plantations. Phuket government officials have recently been on a massive island-wide durian-planting crusade as well. They have a target of 100,000 trees being planted to help cement their reputation as a lucrative durian-growing area. Phuket is a popular destination for thousands of Chinese tourists and they love durian. It's no coincidence that the focus is on growing that particular fruit. There's also rice growing in paddies in some of the most unexpected places, often on a small piece of land between houses. No space is wasted.

This place is full of interesting landscapes. On the west coast of the island, you'll find most of the great beaches with rocky coves and headlands. There's a stretch of coast called 'Millionaire's Mile' which winds from Kamala Bay to Patong Bay that's dotted with sprawling villas on the lush hillsides above the Andaman Sea. In comparison, the east coast tends to have smaller beaches that are covered by mangrove forests as the seabed is muddy. Kata is in the south.

While out wandering, I saw on almost every street corner down near the beach blue signs: the tsunami evacuation route and warning signs. I vividly remember Boxing Day in 2004, when a devastating tsunami struck Phuket and further north on the mainland at Khao Lak. This was caused by an earthquake off Sumatra in Indonesia. Seeing the images on TV of the mass destruction of entire towns being wiped out was confronting and many Australians lost their lives. Phuket had never dealt with such a massive natural disaster before and the death toll was horrendous.

There are also two buoys deployed out at sea to provide at least an hour's notice to those on land should this ever happen again. Hopefully the safety measures they now have in place never need to be activated. The power of the ocean and the devastation it is capable of is a little hard to comprehend when you see it at its calmest like it was today.

16 April
Together Time / New Precedent

Outside on the tiny veranda of the smoothie shop, Joe and I sat enjoying our drinks and watching the parade of locals and tourist sweep by. Such a great perch for people watching. Once we felt like it, we headed around the corner for some lunch as our plan was to spend a restful afternoon together hanging out at the beach. I'm not sure how they do it, but again the people at Red Chair had our food out on our table in under ten minutes. There's no mucking around. The waitress yells out your drinks order while she's still at your table so that arrives in two minutes and the rest follows shortly after. It's impressive.

We got talking to the staff once I ordered in Thai and found it's a family-owned restaurant. They asked how long I was staying and where I was living. I was happy to let them know I'd be one of their regulars for the next couple months.

For us, Thailand has always been a haven. It has provided much-needed respite from the real world on so many occasions. For Joe, not understanding the language, eating different food and having little control over situations or his environment would normally cause a high level of anxiety, but not here. Thai people are gentle and often softly spoken. There's never any confrontation or attitude and the peaceful surrounds insist that you kick back and just go with it.

We find ourselves doing things we love: for Joe, three-hour massages followed by a foot-scrub chaser and scuba diving every possible day; and for me, finding new delicious places to eat, chatting with the locals and perfecting the art of doing nothing.

We both really enjoy visiting the Thai elephants and can easily spend hours just watching them go about their day. We always make sure we fit in an outing or two at the Phuket Elephant Sanctuary. The elephants roam freely, interacting with each other if they feel like it. They swim, eat and wander around while we observe them from raised walkways throughout the sanctuary.

We'd love to live here for a long stint, but while we have our fur girls, it's impossible due to the strict quarantine rules at home should we want to return to Australia with them. For now, we'll enjoy the time we get to spend here and plan the next visit and the one after that.

Last night Joe said that he's had the best holiday ever this time. Big call! He promptly booked another visit for October so he can come back and do more diving. He said he couldn't leave without knowing he was coming back. I'm not sad as he has now set a very handy precedent. I'll be keeping that in mind when my time here is coming to an end.

17 April
Swimming in the Rain / Bye-Bye Husband

Joe heads home tomorrow to the most important job of all, caring for our fur girls Jasmine and Rosie. They're currently having a wonderful holiday of their own with their springer spaniel friend Harry. They sleep inside just as they do at home and very much treat their holiday accommodation as a second home. We've been so lucky to have the same wonderful pet-sitter for many years, which enables us to go away with confidence, knowing our girls are well cared for and having fun. We've been getting regular updates with photos and videos of them outside playing. That always helps when you're missing them.

On our last day together, we walked down to the beach to see if we could squeeze in one last swim. The sky was looking grey and ominous, but we went for it anyway, threw our stuff down on a sun lounge and dived straight into the warm, inviting water. Then, as expected, the sky darkened and it started to rain. Proper rain, enough for those swimming in the ocean to leave so they didn't get wet. Yep, really. They scampered as soon as it started.

This was the second time it has rained since I arrived. Once we'd had our swim, we sat out in it. I've never been so pleased to have cold raindrops fall all over me. It was just the best feeling.

With the daytime temperatures still in the high 30s and night-time temperatures lucky to get below 25 degrees, my coping strategy of having somewhere I can get wet during the day, including raindrops, and somewhere cool to sleep at night has been working well. I'm a woman in her early fifties and menopause has so far been very unkind to me. The hot flushes, night sweats, body aches and pains and insomnia have not been fun and that's just the start of my symptoms.

Once we left the beach, we had a decision to make: three hours of massage followed by dinner in our local hood, or a fancy hotel beachfront dinner. The choices while living here are sometimes a little too taxing! Well, seven margaritas later at a local restaurant and I know who thought it was one of the best decisions he'd made all day. This husband of mine has come so far on this trip, eating from street vendors, trusting my instincts around food that might not be safe to eat, living in the backstreets with me and enjoying the Thai hospitality to the max. He has truly soaked it all up, while his underwater love affair continues to grow with each dive.

There was a time when he would only eat in the hotel and wanted nothing but burgers, steak or pizza. Thankfully that came to a screeching halt after one hotel restaurant experience when he was so underwhelmed, it forced him to try the Thai flavours and out on the street. He can now eat chilli like a true Thai and enjoys most dishes, particularly when I order the local specialities – they soon become his new favourites.

He's been super supportive of me living here in my happy place. Thailand will miss you, sweetheart, and so will I. Now off you go, there are two very excited Labradors waiting for their daily carrots and my side of the bed to sleep on and I'm ready for my solo adventure to resume.

18 April
Kanom Krok / Sun-Lounge Heist / Computer Says No

Kanom krok are delicious little coconut puddings filled with all sorts of fruit or vegetables, a traditional Thai sweet that can be found at street markets or, as luck would have it, just outside someone's house close to my hotel. This street stall is on the way to Mickey's smoothie shop. I hadn't stopped before, but felt like eating them today. I began reading the labels out loud describing the fillings: corn, pumpkin, coconut and sweet potato. Hearing I could read Thai sparked a conversation with the owner, a bright, bubbly young woman in a cute floral apron. She was keen to explain to me how they're made. A mixture of coconut milk, rice flour and sugar is poured into little hot moulds and the desired filling added. A crunchy crust forms on the bottom and two of them are often sandwiched together. Six for 30 baht makes them too good to walk past.

I was soon invited to make them with her and get them out of the *krok*, the moulds. We were both laughing as I called out to people passing to come and buy them. She told me I had the job and she'd see me bright and early in the morning. I reckon I'd last ten minutes over that hotplate, but gosh we'd have a laugh. Just another wonderful Thai person making me feel so welcome in my local neighbourhood.

I've completely unpacked and spread out everywhere now that I have my room to myself.

I feel like I've got my bits and pieces just where I want them, including my clothes in little piles as I don't have any drawers. I gave Joe a pile of my clothes to take home because I overpacked. I tend to do this every time, then wonder what I was thinking. Being able to have my clothes washed so easily means I probably could have given him even more to take back.

I've had my eye on the nice comfortable sun lounges surrounding the pool. The veranda of my room has heavy wooden chairs and they're not so comfortable. Since I'm here for a long stay, I made it my mission to relocate a sun lounge from the pool. I could have asked the reception staff to help and I'm sure they would've gladly done so, but no, I had to take this on myself. So last night I waited until it was dark and lifted the lounge above my head, got into the pool and literally floated it across to my room, got out of the pool with the lounge above my head and placed it on my veranda.

This morning my efforts were rewarded as I lay on my lounge after a swim and enjoyed my *kanom krok*. I reflected on how much I was enjoying my simplified life. My thoughts drifted towards how comfortable I am allowing the day to unfold, not having activities planned or being busy for busy's sake. This is not only giving my body time to rest, but it's also giving my brain the space it was so often asking for. I'm thinking less and less about my work situation, which is a big step forward.

I went inside to check something on my laptop. The black screen of death appeared and then nothing. I couldn't reboot or recharge, so of course I thought the worst. I did some googling on my phone while reassuring myself that I could find a solution. I found the worst possible reviews on a computer-repair shop in Phuket. I eventually picked up the phone and spoke with a very helpful Frenchman out in the suburbs who encouraged me to visit his shop so he could help. In my experience there are not many computer problems that don't require a new machine these days and that's not just a coincidence, is it?

When I arrived at the shop, not only did this man look at my laptop on the spot but he also told me it was likely to be a battery issue. I think he could sense my relief and he had me wait until he got me back up and running. Then he didn't want to charge me. Honestly, the generosity is astounding. I gave him some cash and asked that he at least take his young children out for ice cream after school, to which he agreed. Talk about turning a situation around.

It was a two-hour round trip to the computer-repair shop and my regular taxi driver Khun Bow sent his very sweet and kind older brother Khun Odt to drive me there. We chatted about organic food, northeastern pineapple (better than Phuket pineapple apparently), police corruption, his kids, his extended family, his desire to travel somewhere outside of Thailand, the weather, rude tourists, Covid survival, his herbal and vegetable remedies for good health, what he had growing in his garden. So interesting and good for me. When I say 'chatted about', I mean that I was often listening hard and nodding and adding a few words when I could. It's a skill just to piece a conversation together when sometimes you only understand every second or third word. I ended up with my Thai language lesson for the day as well as a functioning laptop.

Khun Odt said he was too shy to speak English, but by the end of our trip he was using a few words. He was so humble and gentle and spoke clear, uncomplicated Thai. I'm pleased that, after such an unexpected glitch, I can now return to my simple life, where my hardest decision of the day is whether to turn left or right when I head out for dinner.

19 April
Living With Less | Education | Giving

There's a jarring, stark reality in the streets of my neighbourhood. Walking around, it's not uncommon to see piles of rubbish, building rubble, derelict buildings and dilapidated houses with people living among it all. There are also discarded, brokendown motorbikes, overgrown jungle-like gardens and just general mess. I see it every day. Thailand is seen as a developing country. When I first came here in 1989 it was called a Third-World country. So many Thai people are earning just enough to keep themselves afloat. Most work every day possible, sometimes from dawn until late into the night, and I'm guessing their local council doesn't offer a curbside hard-rubbish removal service like we get at home.

Even after all the time I've spent in this country it still astonishes and shocks me how some people live with so little here. Some live in tin sheds – I can't begin to imagine what it's like inside during summer. While I was speaking to Khun Odt in the taxi yesterday, I asked him if he had air conditioning at home. He said no, only a fan, and they put a big block of ice in front of it to produce cooler air. He said electricity is too expensive to run air conditioning all day and night. I haven't turned mine off for a second while I've been here so far and couldn't sleep without it on.

I'm lucky I can do that.

The key to getting a well-paid job in this country is education. The one thing most Thai parents want is to educate their kids for as long as they can. Thai children start school at the age of six and have six years of primary school before progressing to high school for another three years of compulsory education taking them to about the age of fifteen. If they want to sit for entrance exams to university, they must continue to study and this can be a highly competitive process.

If young people can speak English well, this increases their employment opportunities even more. Thai children start to learn English in primary school, but don't often have the chance to speak it or practice it with a native speaker, which is one reason my Thai family put their hand up to host an exchange student. They also had tutors for the kids and a normal day for them consisted of a morning tutor before breakfast, an afternoon tutor before dinner and studying until late at night. It was vastly different to what I was doing during my school years.

I've seen some obscene wealth in this country. At the other end of the scale, poverty of the cruellest kind. The middle class has certainly expanded. Many now strive to educate their children through to university and aspire to travel overseas. Being born in a country that speaks English, a language that's universally understood, gives me a huge advantage that I never appreciated until I lived here all those years ago and now often forget.

I find that, whenever I return to Thailand, I'm quickly reminded of all that we take for granted at home: the lifestyle and opportunities that we have at our disposal. Our expectations for life are generally high. Most people don't even consider there could be any other way. I know that I could easily live with less.

The accumulation of stuff can so easily take hold. Cleaning out my cupboards is not only cathartic, but every time I do it I wonder how all the stuff got there in the first place. This country provides me with a reminder of what I really need to live and what I want. There's a big difference.

Over the years I've had countless experiences here where those with less give more freely. They will quite literally do anything for you, happily sharing the little they have without expectations. It's who they are, and how they live, and so very humbling to be around.

20 April
Alpha Language School / Kruu Noi

I'd had a helpful email exchange with Alpha Language School before I left home and was encouraged by the owner to come and meet her once I was settled in Phuket. Today was the day for me to go and do just that. Her name is Kruu Noi; *kruu* means 'teacher' and *noi* means 'little', and that she is. A slight, petite Thai lady with a big, beautiful smile and long hair pulled back in a ponytail and an obvious passion for teaching.

We climbed a few flights of stairs in her multi-level school building. She took me into one of the classrooms where she started testing my Thai language. There were flashcards to test my vocabulary knowledge and some casual conversation to test my comprehension. Thankfully I didn't feel too nervous. I know the areas I want to improve and I also know my limits. Kruu Noi was excellent and concluded that I could handle an intensively paced class. I'm not convinced, but time will tell, I suppose.

I'm planning on going to school two or three times a week for the rest of my stay. This should give my skills a good boost and help answer many questions I have. More importantly, I want to keep the language study fun and carefree as I know that, once I become too serious, I invariably become self-conscious. The aim is to keep speaking, no matter what.

I find the Thai language fascinating, frustrating and freaking difficult all at once sometimes. What is very clear is that it's so important to learn to read Thai. If you can read it and understand the tone markers, you will be able to pronounce the words correctly. It's easier said than done. Written Thai doesn't place spaces between words and has no real punctuation, just to further confuse the foreigners who dare to try and learn it.

The standard English transliteration of Thai words, which I've used in this book, is often more confusing. I give you the word for island. In English it is spelt *koh*, but if you can read Thai the first letter is actually 'g' and it should be pronounced *goh*. I often hear foreigners understandably pronounce Koh Phi Phi as 'koh fee fee', but if you can read the Thai script you can tell it's actually pronounced 'goh pee pee'.

It's a daunting language, no doubt, but Thai people are always so willing to help you if you show interest. I have a few very standard responses to their surprise and praise when I speak Thai. After thanking them, I usually say something like, 'I often speak incorrectly but I try and speak every day, and Thai people are so patient with me and will try to help me improve.' If I'm feeling a little foggy in the brain, I might just say, 'I only speak a little.' They are always encouraging and enthusiastic, saying *geng mark* which means 'very skilful'.

Undoubtedly, speaking some Thai helps me live here comfortably. Being understood and able to go about my day with relative ease encourages me to keep learning. As soon as I leave the classroom, I can put it all into practice. I make heaps of mistakes, laugh at myself along the way and hope something might just find a little vacant spot in my brain and be retained. I'm looking forward to seeing how much progress I can make.

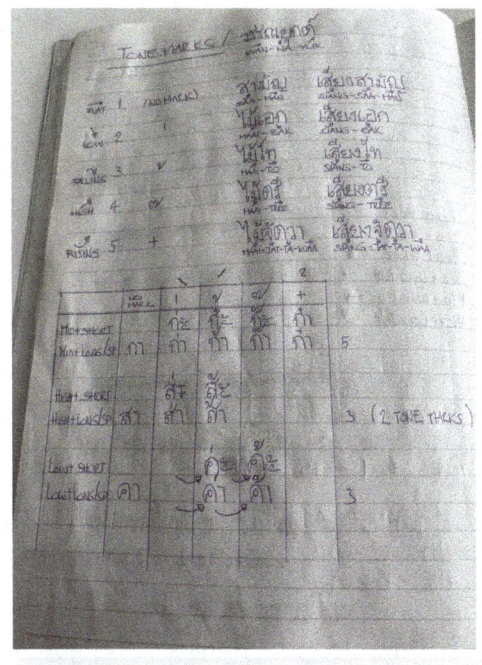

21 April

People Watching / Colourful Clutches / Khun Sak

Setting off this morning, I turned right and headed towards the beach. My weather app tells me the 'feels like' temperature is 40 degrees, which I can vouch for. I ended up at a fruit and drink stall that I've visited a couple of times and the ladies recognised me. We chatted as people of all nationalities came by the stall. Seems freshly opened coconuts are the bestseller at the moment; I won't be knocking anyone over to drink coconut water no matter how healthy it's supposed to be. It's not a flavour I like. I ordered my iced tea instead.

I sat at the stall on a rickety old swivel chair to watch the comings and goings. Soon a guy pulled up another rickety old swivel chair next to me. His first order was a beer and watermelon, the next a mojito and pineapple and the next beer only. It was about 10 a.m., but why not? Holidays are all about changing things up. There's a motorcycle hire shop attached to the fruit shop and it seems to be run by the same people.

Watching tourists wander in provided quite the entertainment. A Russian couple came to rent a bike, thoroughly inspected it for damage, had a fight with each other – because I'm now a body language expert – and he rode off while she was left to walk. Five Chinese people came to hire three motorcycles, changed to two motorcycles, changed back to three motorcycles, then two helmets for five people. They had a child with them who looked about two. They wedged him between two adults, a plastic doughnut floating ring and bags of beach stuff, and off they rode.

Then a French man asked me my opinion on the shop wanting to take his passport as security.

'There's no way I'd be giving my passport up,' I told him. 'What about a copy?'

'Oh, no, that's five thousand baht extra.'

He was clearly torn, so I suggested, 'Why don't you just hire a taxi instead?'

I checked my back to make sure there was no sign on it saying, 'Ask me anything'.

I probably won't be welcomed back to that motorcycle/fruit shop. I'm not great for business.

It's actually illegal for the motorcycle shop owners to take your passport because, strictly speaking, you should have it on you at all times. It's one of those rules like those stating that you must wear a helmet when on a motorbike, you mustn't use certain apps when hiring a taxi as those companies aren't insured and you mustn't overtake when there's oncoming traffic. All are illegal, but the general feeling is that you can pretty much do as you like so long as you don't get caught. The enforcement of the laws and rules seems sporadic at best and nothing that a healthy bundle of baht can't fix.

A Russian was killed riding a motorcycle last night, speeding, they said. I read *The Phuket News* online every day just to keep in touch with all things local and it seems there's a motorcycle death every single day. It's mostly tourists speeding or on drugs and it's such a shame to think that you might come to this beautiful place and never return to your family and friends.

I finished my drink and wandered down to the gift shop where the kind man feeds the homeless dogs and cats around the area. I've developed a bit of a crush on the cute and colourful clutch bags he sells and now I think I need one in every colour. My obsession with them seems to be pretty intense; I'm not sure how many might find their way into my suitcase by the time I'm ready to depart. What's not to love about a bright, cheerful clutch to pop your bits and pieces in? Little wonder I so easily accumulate stuff.

Tonight I went down to the beach for the sunset, but the cloud was giving us nothing and I got dumped twice by waves that were stronger than they looked. I thought that must be my signal to leave and head for dinner. I asked Khun Sak, the man in charge at Kata on Fire Bar and Grill, what I should eat. He asked me if I trusted him. Well, sure. He gave me pork *larb*, a minced meat and fresh herb salad, and massaman chicken curry: two different meats, one a spicy salad and one a curry. That's a very Thai way to eat. I've now handed over my menu selection to this helpful man as he clearly knows best. I've managed to outsource my 'what's for dinner?' dilemma very nicely.

I told him about my language school test and he's very keen to help me. He also said I should call him *Phii* Sak, 'Brother Sak', so that's what it will be.

22 April
Politicians | Kunya & Manfred

There's an election coming up in May, and the candidates are out and about with their big billboards on the backs of trucks and blaring soundtracks shouting out their promises as they drive through the streets. There was some door knocking going on by a man called Thames, as in the 'River Thames', with a whole group of party members accompanying him. I said hello and he stopped to talk. On hearing my accent, he told me he had spent eight years in Perth in Western Australia.

Curious, I asked, 'What do you stand for?'

As soon as I did that, his people started taking a video as he eagerly told me what he would fix in Phuket and how he would improve the experience for tourists.

'The reason I love this place and keep coming back is because of the Thai people,' I said. 'Look after these beautiful people and you'll be fine.'

All the nodding heads around him asked me if they could use the video for his campaign.

'Sure,' I said, 'so long as you look after the people!'

Stepping down from my soap box, I felt like sticky rice and spicy papaya salad. The shop was shut so I crossed the street and sat down instead in Kunya's coffeeshop. I ordered fried rice with chicken and diet Coke with ice in Thai and the lady taking the orders said, 'That's easy, you can speak Thai.'

There were two other foreigners in the shop and one got up and acknowledged me. I thought he must be leaving, so I said, 'Goodbye.'

'No, I'm the boss of this shop,' he said in a thick German accent and gave me his business card, which said he was Dr H. C. Manfred Florian Welker. It turned out the restaurant was run by his Thai wife and her sister. Manfred (love that name) was very chatty and started showing me photos of himself meeting all sorts of very important people. It was totally lost on me as I had no idea who they were. But I seem to have just added Manfred and Kunya to my neighbourhood must-visit list. The food alone would bring me back.

To top off my day, I also met my new neighbours at the hotel as we were out swimming at the same time. Kevin, seventy-one, and Sally Anne, sixty-three, are from Melbourne, Australia. They love Thailand and want to move here but have sixteen grandkids between them. We had a great conversation covering a huge range of topics and a few laughs. What a mix of humanity I've met today.

Tomorrow marks the halfway point of my time away. I'm nowhere near being ready to go home, but couldn't be happier knowing I'm only halfway. So far my time has gone neither slowly nor fast. I just feel like I'm enjoying each day as it comes along.

Without a doubt, I'm feeling more at ease and finding this time to be more restorative than I expected. That could well be because I hadn't acknowledged how depleted I was. It's always difficult when you're still in the thick of it to see things as they really are. When I stop and get off the treadmill of life, I'm always surprised by how empty my tank is. It would be nice if I could tune in to how

I'm feeling slightly earlier, before exhaustion arrives.

The fact that the community I'm living in is so extremely warm and friendly has no doubt helped me to settle here. It's lovely to be able to walk along the street and say hello to people. I might enjoy my solitary time, but there's a big part of me that wants to connect with the Thai people around me as well. To feel so welcomed is a gift.

My six-month visa forces me to leave the country every sixty days to then revalidate it for the next sixty days. It's weird and annoying, but it's an excuse to fly to one of my favourite places.

Singapore, I'm coming for you.

23–24 April
Singapore Luxury | Food, Glorious Food

I'm on the 19th floor of a thirty-storey, uber-luxury hotel in downtown Singapore tonight. I have a heated toilet seat, feathery, fluffy pillows, a bed that feels like it's made of marshmallows and air conditioning that's whisper-quiet. I can order food through my TV when I eventually work out how and I was greeted with a tea ceremony at check-in. It's so comfortable and so ridiculously luxurious, but I'm missing my little, humble no-frills room in Kata.

I've always loved Singapore. It's so shiny and manicured, the streets are wide and it's pleasing to the eye with a great variety of tropical plants and green spaces among the gleaming skyscrapers and British colonial buildings that all seem to be architectural marvels.

It's a serious big Asian city that doesn't seem to have much wrong with it on the shimmering surface. There are no broken footpaths, no piles of rubbish, no motorbikes being ridden by shirtless yahooing tourists, no smells of satays cooking at street stalls nor the less attractive smells that Thai streets are notorious for. Actually, it smells of nothingness. The rubbish bins are clean, it feels quiet and there's no chaos out there, and no one said hello to me while I was out today. Not one person said, 'Massage, madam?' or '*Sawadee kha*' or 'Where are you going?' or 'Taxi!' It's silent on the streets. No one is sitting outside their shop playing with their kids or eating meals together or laughing. It's hard to find a drink and, when you do, it's back to the $4 bottles of water. It really couldn't be more different to Thailand with its relaxed and somewhat light-hearted atmosphere.

I went to Gardens by the Bay, a hundred-hectare patch of newly cultivated greenery on reclaimed land in the downtown area, with soaring trees, tropical plants and flowers and aerial walkways to view the gardens. Not my first visit but I underestimated the crowds. They had a big display of tulips and an expo on Turkey, but once you've seen the rows of tulips at Table Cape in the northwest of Tasmania it's hard to top that.

Singapore is a great walking city. Pedestrians are well catered for and street signs are all in English. I decided to walk back to my hotel from the gardens via a massive air-conditioned luxury shopping centre. This place was below the Marina Bay Sands Hotel that looks very much like a giant surfboard has been placed on a couple of pylons high up in the air.

I took my time looking at the many contemporary high-rises of the business district. Many new buildings are now incorporating trees, plants and flowers on their exteriors. Hanging gardens are popular as are green spaces within these often-lifeless structures. At ground level there are plenty of beautifully landscaped gardens in unexpected areas striving to break up the steel and concrete and provide people with an oasis from the heat and hustle of the city. They do it very well.

When I got back I was keen to make sure I made the most of my luxe room, jumping straight in the shower and lathering up with the high-end shower gel. The hotel marketing blurb promised 'a shower experience akin to a spa-like retreat, the moisturising and cleansing gel leaves the skin lightly fragranced with the scent of fruits and florals'. And it did. I worked out how to order my dinner on the TV and then sat on the window seat in my luxe fluffy robe looking out.

On my second day, I went on a food tour – food, glorious food, Singapore-style. How good is it eating your way around a city and an Asian city at that? I had booked a food tour with Monica, a private guide who took me to three distinct eating precincts. I'd deliberately booked a hotel close to Chinatown, where I walked to meet Monica. Our first stop was the Chinatown Complex, a market with around seven hundred hawker stalls spread over two floors.

The place was packed with locals and curious tourists like me. Our first job was to find a seat. Monica had me sit while she went and bought an assortment of food to sample. She came back with fresh spring rolls (*popiah*) from the famous Ann Chin stall that has been making this dish since 1958. *Popiah* refers to the outer skin they make onsite from rice flour, then fill with crunchy peanuts, noodles and vegetables and roll it up. Next was carrot cake Chinese-style without a carrot in sight: steamed white radish and glutinous rice flour mixed into a cake (bland taste, soft, squishy texture), then cut into cubes, fried till crispy and cooked with an egg omelette and dark, sticky soy sauce. We finished with a small bowl of sweet green jelly-like noodles and black beans topped with shaved ice and evaporated milk. I appreciated the mouthfuls of ice as it was incredibly hot in there.

We moved to our next stop via Singapore's oldest Chinese temple, Thian Hock Keng, 'Palace of Heavenly Happiness', which stands amidst bustling bars, restaurants and cluttered souvenir shops. Built in 1839 and dedicated to Mazu, Goddess of the Sea, it's an ornate reminder of Chinatown's beginnings. Many temples around this area have now been heritage listed. The bonus was that it was air conditioned so we walked very slowly through it. I learnt from Monica that the city has plenty of air-conditioned underground walkways, which explains the empty streets. Only people like me walk around in the heat.

There was quite the queue at Maxwell Hainanese Chicken Rice, our next stop. Monica insisted it was worth it. Again, I was the keeper of the table and while waiting I struck up a conversation with a family visiting from Bali. Monica returned with chicken and a plate of fried wontons with a dipping sauce.

Monica is a Singaporean local and guiding is her full-time job. She was so interesting to chat with and answered my many questions, not only about the food I was eating but also about what it's like living and working in the city. She told me how she was hired by Amazon to do virtual tours during Covid. She would go to various spots around the city and have her visitors online with her via her iPad. It was a big hit and kept her financially afloat for two years. What a clever concept and a great way to adapt to the very weird circumstances we endured during the pandemic.

We had one more stop on our tour, so we set off walking for a couple of blocks and stopped somewhere in the financial district to try the local seafood Hokkien noodles. They were cooked in an enormous wok and it was quite a performance to watch.

I was booked on a late-afternoon flight back to Phuket, so with instructions from Monica I decided to take the train to the airport. It was spotlessly clean, fast and stress-free. I'd only ever used taxis when I'd visited the city before, but I think that will change next time.

Thanks, Singapore, you've been the perfect luxury weekend host.

25 April
Intensive Thai / Department of Immigration

I joined the intensive Thai language class this morning for the first time. It was a small class with only four other students, all guys, and a male teacher. I was all prepared to sit and listen and ease my way in. There seemed to be quite a gap between the levels of competency. But suddenly I felt slightly self-conscious when I spoke. There's one thing I haven't come here to do and that's stress over the language. It was a good class and no doubt it would stretch me, but at the end I asked to come out of the class and learn with Kruu Noi. She thinks her class will be too easy for me but that's fine by me. Easy equals fun and that's what I'm here for.

After class I asked my regular driver Khun Bow to take me to the immigration office. When I checked my passport this morning before putting it away in the hotel-room safe, I found they had stamped it incorrectly last night at the airport, giving me thirty days instead of the sixty my visa entitles me to. I didn't even think to check it at the time.

Time to put my language into full throttle; it sounds exciting, but it's not. Anyone who has dealt with Thai bureaucracy – well, to be fair, probably bureaucracy the world over –will know there will be forms and a process that leaves you scratching your head. Thai government departments love forms. I arrived at the government building to find Thai students on the information desk wanting to practice their English, so my rehearsed Thai language wasn't needed. I was directed to the visa building and when I opened the door I nearly died. It was jam-packed with foreigners of all types, sixty or more of them, waiting to be dealt with. I was close to just walking out, but as it turned out I'm glad I didn't.

The first stop was an information desk and the person in front of me was asked to fill out a form and hand over 1,000 baht. I'm not sure what expression I had on my face but the official said to me, 'Don't worry, the money isn't for me.'

'What a pity!' I said.

'Are you from Australia?'

'Yes.'

'Where in Australia?'

'Tassie.'

'I love Tasmania. I've been there five times!' This man had lived in Melbourne and worked for Westpac Bank.

When it was my turn, I explained my situation and he asked me to wait while he did some checking and returned with a form: 'Application For Correction Of Visa Stamp On Passport Or Travelling Document'. Clearly this was not the first time it had happened. He advised me to fill it in and come back in the morning as the wait time would be better. Then, asking me to follow him, he took me into the processing area and introduced a staff member who he said would look after me in the morning. I just had to ask for her.

He was beyond helpful and kind and I could feel the eyes of the other foreigners burning holes in me as he ushered me past them. Sorry, not sorry.

I honestly couldn't make this stuff up if I tried. With a wink and a warm handshake from him, I was skipping out of there in under thirty minutes. I got back in the van with Khun Bow and he was surprised at how quick I was. I explained what had happened and said, 'It was my lucky day.' He agreed.

I'll venture back in two days as I have plans tomorrow and who knows what will happen, but tonight I'm just thanking my lucky Thai stars.

26 April
Khao Lak / Khun Sa

I met my friend Khun Sa several years ago while staying in Khao Lak at The Sarojin. It's a two-hour drive from Kata and that's where I headed in Khun Bow's van today. Khun Sa works as a gardener at the hotel and used to surprise me with beautiful bunches of flowers most days during my stay. We'd chat, and although she's shy, I gradually got to learn more about her and her family.

She has a huge, generous and humble heart and today we met to have lunch together. When we were working out where to meet, I suggested she choose a café and she said she'd never eaten in a café in Khao Lak as her home is an hour and a half away by motorbike. Looking through my own life lens, it hadn't occurred to me that she wouldn't be familiar with a café. We agreed to meet at the bank because all Thai people know where the bank is.

Khun Sa cannot read or write, she can only speak Thai. We keep in touch via voice messages. This has also encouraged me to continue to practice speaking Thai. Today she told me why she had never learnt to read or write. Her parents were very poor and she only went to sixth grade in primary school, then had to start working. She never had a chance to go back to school and learn, but she's certainly made up for it in terms of the practical skills she has.

What she makes with her hands is beyond amazing.

On market days in her village she gets up at 3 a.m. to make Thai coconut sweets to sell to the locals. Her husband grinds the fresh coconut to produce the coconut milk. She said they never buy the tins of coconut milk as it's too sour. The sweets are normally all sold by 9 a.m. and then she goes about her day. If she's working at the hotel, she leaves home at 5.30 a.m. and rides to work on her motorbike. When I asked what happens when it rains, she said, 'I just wear a raincoat and get wet, but that's okay.'

Wanting her to feel comfortable, I told Khun Sa it was her pick where we would eat. We shared a simple lunch and chatted like I would with my friends at home about all things, work and life. I was pleased I only needed to look up a couple of Thai words that stumped me. She has one daughter and one very cute grandson, who is three. She had him on FaceTime during our lunch so I could talk to him. She obviously adores the little fella.

She showed me photos of all the incredible flower arrangements and decorations she had made out of pandanus and banana leaves for a wedding at the hotel on the weekend: white orchids, jasmine flowers and giant tropical leaves arranged on the beach. She had threaded little white flowers on long strands of cotton and they hung from the trees near the dunes. Hundreds of candles were also lit and placed randomly on the sand. It was simple, elegant and magical. You couldn't get a more romantic setting.

I'd written a card for her saying, 'We love you very much and think of you often.' I read it out to her and she beamed. Khun Sa had made two heart-shaped cushions by hand: one in red for me and one in blue for Joe. She gave them to me before we said goodbye.

This lady teaches me so much about what it means to make the most of what you have. Even though she has struggles in life, she also has incredible talents and she works to her strengths. I feel so incredibly lucky to have her as my friend.

27 April
Tattoos / Supernatural Powers

There's a man selling fruit from a newly built shop, who greets me with a huge smile every time I walk past. He's super cheeky and cheerful and is usually playing his guitar. I felt like mangoes and passionfruit last night, so I walked to his shop. When he asked, 'What else would you like?' I said, 'A photo of your tats!' He never wears a shirt, says it's too hot for that and I agree, and wears jeans cut off at the knee, so it's easy to see there's very little spare space anywhere on his body tattoo-free. His legs, front and back are heavily tattooed with what looks like a heap of swirly patterns. His upper body and arms are pretty similar, but with a bit more colour: red, blue, orange and green.

He got out his phone to show me a photo of how his friend tattoos him with one of those old and very sharp pen-type implements. Nothing hygienic or modern.

Thinking it was brutal, I said, 'You'd need to be drunk to do that.'

Out came the photo of all the whiskey bottles lined up and he asked, 'Do you want a tattoo from my friend?'

'I can't even imagine being drunk enough to agree to such torture.'

He's another warm, welcoming person in my street whom I enjoy seeing daily and chatting with and buying delicious fruit from. Seeing him reminded me of a tattoo festival the Thais have, which I read about. More than ten thousand people gather about an hour outside Bangkok at a large Buddhist temple called Wat Bang Phra to recharge the magic of their sacred Sak Yant tattoos.

Sak means to 'tap' or 'tattoo', and *yantra* was originally a Sanskrit word and refers to an instrument. Sak Yant are a traditional Thai form of tattoo involving sacred geometrical, animal and religious designs that are incredibly intricate and each element has a specific meaning. These tattoos are applied by hand in a very primitive way using a long metal or bamboo rod with a sterilised (hopefully) needle attached to the end. This looked very similar to what my fruit seller showed me in his photo when he was being tattooed. The end is dipped in special ink made from ingredients like charcoal. It's not uncommon for opium to be used to dull the pain.

It's believed that the tattoos etched into the skin by Buddhist monks carry magic powers, providing luck and protection; and that the supernatural powers of these tattoos require regular blessings, which is why people attend this ceremony. They pay respect to the teacher or master who originally tattooed them and this infuses new magic into every tattoo on their body. Many then enter a trance-like state, becoming their tattoo. So you have people who think they are tigers, monkeys and all sorts of other animals screaming and running towards the temple. They are met by a wall of soldiers who stop them entering and pull people out of their trance by rubbing their earlobes. It's quite the performance and not for the faint-hearted. The monks lead the people in prayer and spray them with holy water. This completes the recharging of everyone's tattoos for another year and off they go.

After my language class today, I went back to the immigration department with my completed form and high expectations. Sitting and waiting for my number to be called, I did my best not to strike up a conversation with anyone, although it was very tempting. Imagine the stories each and every one of them had as to why they were also waiting in line.

Once I got the call-up, I headed straight to the desk of the lady whom I'd been introduced to a couple days before. I handed my documents and passport to her. After much discussion with those sitting at a row of desks behind her, I was told it would take five hours to *investigate* my incorrectly stamped passport. I knew I didn't have five hours of waiting in me so asked if I could come back in a day or so and pick up my passport once the investigation was over. This was agreed. I reluctantly left my passport behind and walked out the door somewhat deflated.

When I got home, I jumped straight in the pool and then made for the Italian restaurant close by. I felt like a pizza for dinner and a Hawaiian one at that with fresh pineapple. Gosh, it was good. I got to take some home so I could have cold pizza for breakfast in the morning. Don't tell Joe. He doesn't do leftovers of any description, but I sure do.

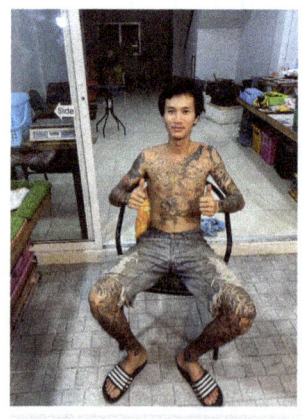

28 April
Meditation | Chasing Butterflies | Life Choices

It's a bikini and sarong kinda day. I don't plan on wearing much more than that until I'm ready to head out for lunch. I've been sleeping really well. It helps not to have anything in particular running around in my head. What a refreshing way of being. I've been a meditator for many years, but not a strict 'must sit for an hour every day' kind. There's so much talk about meditation and mindfulness. It's often pitched as an unachievable state unless practiced with strict dedication and routine. I've approached it in a far more casual way. My practice really depends on what life is dealing up at the time. For me, taking the pressure and expectation away and cutting myself some slack makes for a much deeper experience. Not overthinking it also helps and seems to sit nicely with what the whole practice is about in the first place.

I just sit quietly for as long as I can. This can often be at night until I fall asleep. I've got so much time now to dedicate to it, but I still find about thirty minutes is enough for me to feel grounded, present and at ease. It reminds me of a saying I love about chasing butterflies. Sit still and they will come. Meditation for me works in much the same way.

I left it until late afternoon to walk up and eat at Kunya's café.

Kunya loves wearing jewellery and I often spot a new piece on her. She's a slight lady with long black hair that she has had some colour added to and she wears it back in a pigtail and she adores makeup. Today she had a shimmering gold eyeshadow on, with some blush, and she looked great. I can't help but comment on how beautiful she looks each time I see her.

I found a table under a fan and Kunya was very quick to start chatting to me about the frustrations of being married to a German man. Firstly, let's just say I wouldn't cross a Thai woman, particularly one who can chop and use a knife like a master chef. Seems the intensity with which Manfred approaches life is wearing a bit thin. You can only be told so many times that everything you do isn't up to scratch before you eventually say, enough already! Kunya has reached that point.

As Kunya and I talked, Baz the builder came in for something to eat. Before long I had learned that he's from the Gold Coast in Australia, has been in Phuket for four years, is totally disillusioned with Australia and where it's headed, and has no plans to return. He met a Thai lady and fell in love. When that relationship went sour, he moved back to Queensland, hated it, sold up, moved back to Phuket, bought a hotel in Kata and fell in love again. One night he nearly died when drinking and smoking weed, but his girlfriend resuscitated him. He works illegally as the rules are that Thais need to be employed first. He's had a number of dealings with corrupt police, paid them off to get his girlfriend's sister out of jail. He can't speak a word of Thai other than 'hello' and 'thank you' and is as happy as a lark with life here. That and more was covered in about half an hour.

Off he rode on his motorcycle, no helmet. I wish him luck on so many fronts but absolutely admire his carefree attitude to life and falling in love. Wandering back to my room, I stopped to fill my locally made straw basket with bottles of water, rice cakes and M&M's. I changed straight back into my bikini and jumped in the pool. Rinse and repeat.

29 April
Stormy Show | Big Buddha

It's arrived! About midnight I was woken by an almighty clap of thunder followed by an impressive flash of lightning. It seemed like it was right on my doorstep. I pulled back my curtains and watched the show outside as there was no way I could get back to sleep while it lasted. The stormy weather was spectacular. The torrential tropical rain bucketed down. The sudden inundation of water was huge and then all of a sudden it was over.

Waking up this morning, with the sunlight streaming through my window, the weather is back to its typical clear skies and steamy 30 degrees already and on we go. I'm so happy for the garden around me that it has finally had a big drink. This first big storm has been much talked about and anticipated by all and there's plenty more on the way as we head into the rainy season. I may not be so excited should I get caught in it, but for now I'm cheering and so is all the greenery around me. The plants and shrubs are incredibly resilient. They have to be. I'm sure even the bougainvillaea looked relieved today.

Breakfast of tropical fruit dreams here today with a super side of sunshine. I'm a very big fan of passionfruit, as I've already mentioned, and here they're sweet and plump. I can eat them to my heart's content. I've also got a golden mango and a few longans, a plump berry-like tropical fruit, also known as 'dragon's eye', that's similar to lychee but with a thin brown skin that you peel to reveal translucent white flesh. I take my fruit outside and sit on my sun lounge to eat it. As I look up, I can see the Big Buddha on top of the hill in the distance keeping me company. When I walk around the streets in my neighbourhood, he's often in view, sitting up there serenely taking it all in and watching over us. I really like that.

I've been up to visit Big Buddha several times and the enormity of the structure, forty-five metres tall, and what it represents is never lost on me. It's made from white jade marble from Myanmar (formerly Burma). The Buddha is in a seated position called 'Subduing Mara', which is the most common posture with legs crossed in a meditation position and the right hand over the knee pointing towards the earth, referring to an important event in the life of the Buddha.

This story is depicted around the Big Buddha on large boards so you can take your time and read it as you wander around this imposing structure and symbol of the Buddhist faith. The story goes that the Buddha-to-be was meditating under the Bodhi Tree, the 'tree of awakening', and a powerful symbol in Buddhism. Just before he reached enlightenment, Mara the demon arrived accompanied by his armies and his three beautiful daughters. Mara's armies attacked the Buddha while his attractive young daughters tried to distract and seduce him to stop him from meditating and reaching enlightenment.

Mara can be said to embody that feeling of self-doubt which we all have inside us. The Buddha-to-be touched the Earth with his right hand, calling upon Mother Earth to be his witness. The earth goddess Phra Mae Thorani appeared in the shape of a young, beautiful woman. By wringing the water out of her long hair, she drowned the armies of Mara, allowing the Buddha to continue meditating and reach enlightenment.

I spent most of my day reading, learning some Thai and, when I felt hot, jumping in the pool and it felt just perfect.

30 April

Friendly Faces | Mixing Two Flavours | Veggie Flowers

The day after I arrived in Phuket, I had a mani-pedi and a good chat with a friendly Thai woman in one of the local massage salons. About two months ago now and yet last night while I was out walking in my neighbourhood that same lady spotted me, came and said hello and gave me a big hug. It was so lovely to see her and she was asking all sorts of questions from our one and only conversation back in February. How do Thai people do this? I'm amazed by how they're so keen for a chat and so warm and welcoming to me. I went back to the salon last week, but she was away with her family in the northeast and has only just returned. With all the foreigners that come and go, she not only remembered me but came to say hello. Little wonder I love the Thais. I'm pretty sure I have the Thai language to thank for that. I guess the novelty of someone speaking their language must stand out. I'm learning to embrace that more and more every day.

The streets are quieter now that it's no longer high season. I'm not sad about that. It's a relief not having to duck and weave people looking at their phones instead of looking at where they're going. With the crowds virtually non-existent, I enjoyed browsing in some of the shops and stopped for ice cream. I've found I like having two flavours mixed together and I felt like lemon and passionfruit. I had been trying to work out the correct way to say this in Thai. With the help of my ice cream man, I finally got it. He put two ice cream cups side by side and said, '*Duay gun*', meaning 'together', the phrase I'd been using. Then he put one inside the other and said, '*Prasop gun*', meaning 'mixed'. The penny dropped straightaway. Even more of a reason to eat ice cream when you get a free Thai language lesson with it. Oh, and the Thai word for ice cream is easy. It's *i deam*, which is ice cream said with a Thai accent.

On the way home, I called in to say hello to P'Sak at Kata on Fire. The vegetable-flower making was in full swing. They create amazing-looking flowers, used as a garnish on many of the dishes they serve, from thin slices of white radish and carrot, along with freshly picked orchids that they have growing in pots around the restaurant.

I stood and watched one of the staff creating these flowers and was so impressed. I couldn't help but ask who had taught him to do this, expecting a story about a great grandmother from the northeast who passed this skill down to all her grandchildren. He said, 'YouTube.' I had to leave as my laughter was out of control. Keeping it real around here for sure.

1 May

Pui / Renovations / My Passport Stamp

Now that the tourists have left it seems that the local people have time to create new businesses and spruce up their existing ones. There are some exciting new developments happening in my street. My laundry lady, for example, whose name is Pui (pronounced 'Booey'), is adding to her business empire. Pui has a cheerful smile on her face every time I see her. She is outgoing and, like most Thai ladies, is small in stature. She likes to wear lipstick and often has a headband holding back her coloured shoulder-length hair.

    I arrived with my washing the other night to find twinkling lights and newly potted miniature bamboo in heavy concrete pots. Pui was excited to tell me that she was going to make a new bar on her front porch so her friends, like me, can come and have a drink and a chat with her. She's beyond clever with her concepts and multi-hybrid businesses. Now you'll be able to get your washing and ironing done, buy weed (for medicinal purposes only, of course), have a cocktail or three and fill up your motorcycle with petrol all in the one place. Talk about diversification. I'm told there's a roast chicken shop owned by her in the mix as well.

Today when I dropped off my washing, the side screening wall was complete. There's no waiting on council approvals here or tradesmen that say they'll come and don't show up. There were two Burmese men on the job and it was done in a morning.

Pui checked that I liked the light colour of the wood she'd chosen combined with the fake grass. I suggested she go for the beachy, coastal look given the location, but I'm not sure that translated well. Time will tell. Pui only rents this house, but most landlords allow the tenants to enhance their place so long as they don't rip great holes in the walls when they move by taking air-conditioning units with them if they had them installed.

My guess is I'll be having a drink with Pui before the week ends at her awesome new bar. It puts a whole new spin on 'I'm just going to drop off my laundry.' And, in any case, I actually have something to celebrate: my passport stamp.

It took four forms, three round trips of forty-five minutes each way, A$120 in taxi fares and five days in total to complete. Maybe an hour of queueing and a bucketload of patience. Hindsight tells me it would've been quicker to fly back to Singapore. Thai bureaucracy is honestly next level, not just for foreigners but for the locals as well.

It's lucky I love this place and I look upon these experiences as 'personal growth and development opportunities'. One immigration drama per visit will do me, though.

2 May
Picture Postcard / Daydreaming

At the southern end of Kata Beach, I found a shady spot and decided to spend the morning there. It certainly wasn't a difficult decision and I'm calling this morning the most picture-postcard-perfect day I've had at the beach thus far. The tepid water, the small waves quietly lapping on the shore and the graduated shading of the water, going from a light emerald green in the shallows to a darker hue further out, were all wonderful. It was so worthy of the constant photos I kept taking of it.

Floating on my back in the water, I couldn't help thinking, *How could it possibly get any better than this?* The fact that I had absolutely nowhere else to be made it extra special. When I did finally get out of the water and sat on the sand, my mind turned to thoughts of how I could make this place more than just a break from the daily grind – my home away from home even for a couple of months each year. I had a great time building my pretend new life in my head. I tend to indulge in this sort of daydreaming. It doesn't mean I have to follow through, but it can often create a small opening or plant a seed.

What struck me the most was that I haven't done this kind of imagining in forever. I'm pleased that my headspace is such that

I was even able to do this. Feeling lighter, being curious and flirting with what might be possible is healthy and playful and I've missed it.

Later in the day, a bowl of soup initiated a conversation with a man from England, who told me, among many other things, that his mother was once the chef for Princess Margaret. You really could be anyone and make up anything over here. I need to remind myself to keep my cynicism in check. The man also gave me a few restaurant recommendations, having lived here for four years. The soup he was eating isn't one I'll be trying anytime soon. It was full of the inner bits of a pig and can be served with or without blood according to the Thai waitress – she seemed excited to tell me this, as if it might get me across the line in trying it.

Every day I find people who are happy to chat. One of the highlights of my stay so far are the interesting people I've met, even if the encounter is a fleeting few minutes discussing their pig-intestine soup. At home in Hobart, people are too busy, or so they say, or too cautious, and often so engrossed in their phones that you couldn't have a conversation if you wanted to anyway. Our interactions and connections with people have certainly changed and many are feeling more and more isolated and lonely. I'm afraid our online lives can only offer so much and for me they don't even come close to a real, in-person conversation.

Ask a question, have a chat, be curious – that's the advice I'm giving my solo self. Thais seem to have this within them. It seems effortless for them to say hello as you walk past around my neighbourhood. It's genuine and warm and fuzzy for all involved and it just feels so human.

3 May

Thai Time | Win Win | Sharing Struggles

We're currently learning to tell the time at my language school and Kruu Noi has given us a great explanation as to why the Thais have chosen to tell the time the way they do. I've always found telling the time in Thai difficult. Historically, there were no clocks in Thailand and the time was told by ringing a bell or beating a drum at the temple. Thai people in the villages could distinguish the difference in the sounds and this would indicate what time of day it was. The sound late at night was dull so as to not wake people.

So the Thais divide twenty-four hours into five sections and these periods corresponded to when the drum or bell would be sounded: midnight to 5 a.m.; 6 a.m. to 12 noon; 1 p.m. to 3 p.m.; 4 p.m. to 6 p.m.; and 7 p.m. to midnight. Each period of time has a different name or classifier attached to it much like we have with morning, noon, evening and midnight. This always has to accompany the number when telling the time. If a Thai person tells you the time in English, 3 o'clock to them can mean 3 p.m. or 9 p.m. in our system. Believe me, it's always a good idea to double check. They never say a quarter past the hour like we do. Minutes are said in full. For example, fifteen minutes past, apart from the half hour when you can say 'half'.

The Thai government has tried to move people over to the 24-hour clock but has failed so far. Old habits die hard and most want to keep what they have and continue to pass it on to the next generation. It seems they're comfortable with the established system. Even though it's confusing for foreigners at first, I can understand why some things should be left as they are. Just don't rely on me to accurately know what time it is.

I'm glad time largely means nothing to me at the moment. I wake when I've had enough sleep, eat when I'm hungry, rest when I'm tired, wander out and about when I feel like it. I'm largely guided by the sun most days. Such an uncomplicated and simple way to live.

This evening, I went to drop off and pick up my washing. Sweet Pui was particularly happy. She's a single mum, her ex-husband having left her when her son was six months old. It's not uncommon here for families to share the raising of kids. Her son Win Win did his primary school years with his cousin, living in Pui's sister's house a couple of hours from Phuket, so she could work. He's now twelve and ready for high school, which starts next week. He's come home to complete his education and live with his mum. Pui proudly introduced her boy to me.

Afterwards I kept walking to see Mickey and get a fruit smoothie. Mickey has been unwell this week and her kids have been running the shop. She has tendon damage in her shoulder from when she was cooking in her restaurant for many years. The doctor has told her she needs to rest, but for this lady that concept isn't an option. She made my drink and sat with me on the bench seat outside the front of her shop for a chat. There was a welcome breeze blowing. As we both struggle with the heat we loved that. Gosh, we covered some ground. Mickey spoke Thai and I spoke 'Thaiglish' and we had a great old natter. I love having the time to sit and chat with people and obviously they enjoy it as well. I suppose most customers just come and go.

We learnt that we have much in common in the way we think and see the world around us. We both find spending time in the garden relaxing. I showed Mickey pictures of all the flowers I grow throughout the year. The roses were her favourites. Her garden is full of edibles with stacks of chilli plants and an abundance of fruit trees, particularly durian. Backwards and forwards we went with our sharing of all things made by Mother Nature. It didn't matter that I didn't know every word in Thai, nor that she couldn't explain herself in English. We just made it work, you always seem to be able to do that here. Her story of hard work and determination is an absolute credit to her, but clearly that hard work has taken a toll on her body. There's no sick leave when you're self-employed here.

An hour later I thought I had better get moving, but not before calling into my local general store for more water, rice cakes and M&M's. There was more small talk with the lady who owns this shop about the weather and the fresh batch of rice cakes that had been delivered just for me. She knows how much I like them. I eat them mostly for breakfast or if I have the munchies at midnight. Her shop has lots of customers coming and going so we keep it friendly but brief.

I feel incredibly fortunate to have these ladies around me and to be able to spend time finding out about their lives, struggles and everything in between. I think these days we'd call it connecting with one another. It's not hard to relate to others when you've faced your own tough times and had to find a way through them. Knowing you're not alone in your struggles seems to provide comfort.

4 May
Frangipani | My Local Bar

Walking past a magnificent frangipani tree on the way to Kata Beach, I stop and inhale deeply *every single time*. I can tell it's old, not only because of its enormous size, but also from the number of contorted and dark scaly limbs it has. It's growing on an abandoned property that has a 'FOR SALE' sign on it. There's a wall behind it made from small terracotta-coloured bricks that could be handmade and either side of this blooming beauty is a weathered stone Buddha statue in the sitting pose. The building on the property is a mess with broken windows, the roof falling in and rubbish lying around. I've wondered what it would look like with the rubbish cleared and the building repaired or rebuilt. My main priority would be preserving and caring for this lovely ancient frangipani tree. And before I know it I start thinking about what I would do to make the place shine again and I've moved myself in. I better keep walking.

    This afternoon, once I'd finished my Thai language class, managing to bumble through telling the time, I asked my driver, whom I now call Nong Bow, or N'Bow, meaning 'little brother' (he calls me *Phii* Saow or P'Saow, meaning 'older sister'), to drop me off at Kunya's for lunch. In I went and there was Baz, the builder from the Gold Coast, again sitting up having his lunch. From the way we got on, picking up where we left off last time we met, you'd think we'd known each other for years. He was going off to buy a few more motorcycles. He already has eight and wants a few more to rent out when the tourists arrive again.

Later I had things to buy from the mini-mart and I felt like a roti for dinner. I've been buying my rotis from the same lady since I arrived and normally she's a bit busy to talk. She churns out her rotis with absolute precision. One is cooking on the hotplate while she's rolling and stretching the dough for the next. This one-woman production line is impressive. However, tonight she became my Thai teacher. I wanted two plain ones, so she taught me how to order them with nothing inside. I was thrilled. It doesn't sound like a big deal, but it's these experiences that help me so much and I appreciate the time people take.

On my walk back, I was excited to see my local corner bar was open after a few weeks of being closed. This bar is like a small open-air hut that sits on the corner of a gravel road and the main street in front of my accommodation. There's only a roof over the bar itself and the rest of the seating is out in the open. It's a simple setup and very inviting at night as the candles are lit and the music is playing. It probably only seats ten to twelve people when full and there's a Thai lady who works at the bar by herself. She's always dressed so well and often has a sequin number on or a figure-hugging dress. We regularly exchange a smile and *sawadee kha* when I sweep past, so I pulled up a stool and started to talk with her tonight.

I'd had a drink there before but not a real chance to chat with her. Her name is Khun Tuk. She comes from a rural town many hours from Phuket. The bar has been closed for a while because she's been home to see her kids; the younger ones are cared for by her mother. One is twenty-three, another sixteen and another eleven.

She told me she got married at seventeen and that she's already a grandmother as her daughter had her first child at twenty. To me she looks like she's still in her twenties herself.

She works in the bar until 1 a.m. every morning to support her family as she's a single parent. She tries hard to speak English so she can have conversations with the customers. She says hello to everyone as they stride past, but told me many people don't say hello back. So for a bit of sport we started counting how many responses she got. Her strike rate wasn't too bad, but many people do just walk on by. I encouraged her not to give up on her warm greeting as that's one reason I sat down. She put a small ceramic bowl of salted peanuts in front of me and we kept chatting.

Soon another Thai lady arrived on her motorcycle and pulled up a stool. She ordered a beer and the three of us raised our glasses for cheers all round. Turns out she owns the bar and was friendly and super keen to talk with me. She soon had me picking the music for the bar. She told me she's married to a French guy. She has an excellent command of English, but she wanted to chat to me in Thai.

Next a Thai man on a motorcycle drove up, holding a bottle of red wine with a cork in it, something I hadn't seen in a while. He was having trouble opening it and he'd come to the right spot as Khun Tuk soon had that cork out. He offered me a glass, but I was happy to stick with my mojito. He told me he sees me every day walking past his house. From what he said, I'm guessing he lives somewhere near Pui. I now have an open invitation to pop in.

It was interesting to sit for a while as people came and went. Just as I'd ordered my second mojito, a middle-aged English guy came by. He'd lived in Asia since the nineties and wasn't short on stories. He owned a condo in the area, mostly worked in Singapore, and had come back to Phuket for some fun. Yet another fascinating person to chat with.

I'd finished my second mojito and the gals were starting to talk karaoke so that was my cue to depart, and quickly. Once home, I headed straight for the pool and within two minutes it was pouring with rain. With the constant heat and humidity, I couldn't imagine anything better than a balmy evening swim in the rain.

5 May

Chicken Soup Noodles / Mr Redwine

My lunch spot today was a place I've been eyeing off for a while. A little restaurant with bamboo posts holding up a palm-leaf-thatched roof. The tables and chairs, made from large pieces of tree trunk, sanded and painted, seem to work well and add to its rustic charm. It's always full of Thais. I was keen to test again my 'eat where the locals eat' theory. I wasn't sure what was on their menu and it turns out to be just the one dish, soup noodles with either beef or chicken. You pick your noodles and your meat. I chose the chicken-and-rice-noodle combo.

My bowl arrived at my table with two big drumsticks, fresh and fried shallots on top to give it some crunch and colour. The meat had been cooked in the soup long and slow, giving it depth of flavour and making it extra delicious. With the little pots of chilli, sugar, fish sauce and fish sauce with chilli on my table, I was able to flavour my noodles just how I like them. This is one meal that Thais use chopsticks and a spoon to eat. For rice dishes they always use a fork and spoon. I enjoyed sitting among the Thais, slurping my noodles back and doing a very bad job with the chopsticks to locate the meat that had fallen off the bone and was sitting in the bottom of my bowl. I'm pleased I took a chance on somewhere new. My mantra of 'doing life differently' will keep encouraging me to do that.

I thought that eating soup in the heat might be too much for me, but it wasn't so bad. Mickey's smoothie shop is across the road so I washed everything down with an ice-cold mango and passionfruit smoothie, the perfect amount of sweet to finish off my meal. Mickey had a delivery of honey from a local man and was wondering how to sell it to the foreigners who come to her shop. I offered to put some words together in English saying where the honey is from and what trees and flowers the bees have been visiting. She was delighted by this offer of help and we'll sit together to do it in the coming days.

As I was leaving, I heard a '*Sawadee krup*' from over the road, looked across and there was Mr Redwine, the Thai man from last night. Now I know why he sees me every day. I crossed the street and asked him how he enjoyed the wine. He said he drank the whole bottle himself and was quickly drunk. I'm guessing it was given to him by a foreigner as generally Thais don't drink wine. It's expensive as it's all imported and they prefer beer and whiskey and soda.

He was sitting outside his motorbike rental shop with a female friend. I introduced myself and he told me his name was Bic. He's got a beautiful big smile and warm eyes; he said that he loves listening to me speak Thai, adding that it sounds 'so nice', which was very kind. I had wondered if he was curious to hear me speak Thai and it seems I was right. I don't mind being the weird foreigner who walks everywhere instead of riding a motorcycle and speaks Thai with an Australian accent.

I wandered home, happy to have met Mr Redwine again, to have eaten somewhere new and to be able to help Mickey. I was long overdue for a beach sunset swim. The Chinese tourists are now coming in greater numbers. They were out tonight taking photos of each other as the sun sank below the horizon. They have every single accessory for their phones and they prop them up on the sand hoping to get the perfect shot. Again, I can't help but wonder what they are doing with all these photos of themselves and what makes the perfect photo? I hope I get the chance to ask one day.

There was no time to dawdle or socialise tonight, as I was determined to beat the ominous, darkening sky. With an almighty downpour on the cusp of happening, I had to make a judgement call. I picked up my pace and my foodpanda order, which I'd placed while still at the beach, arrived at my hotel the same time I did. I'm pleased to say I was smugly tucked up inside my room eating dinner when the heavens opened. It's great when a plan comes together.

6 May
Doing Nothing | King & Country

I had a low-key day with lots of Thai language homework, lots of dipping in and out of my pool and lots of just nothing. Doing nothing and being comfortable with doing nothing is quite the art. I'm embracing it better than I thought I would. When I'm home and doing nothing, I've actually unpacked the dishwasher, put on a load of washing, wiped the bathroom sink down, filled the water bowl for our fur girls, watered my indoor plants, ordered my groceries online, put clean clothes away, found something that could do with a dust, cut fresh flowers from my garden and popped them in a vase, puffed up my scatter cushions on the lounge, done a quick vacuum, aired the doona in the sunshine and on it goes.

    I find it a bit difficult simply to sit or lie on the couch and do nothing when I'm home because, if I'm not doing all these things, then who is? I'm sure you've had similar conversations with yourself. Whereas here my nothing is just that. Sitting outside or lying on the daybed staring at the sky or with eyes closed, just me and my thoughts. Before I left home, I had friends ask me what I was going to do while I was away. I said my plan was to do lots of nothing. By their reactions I could tell that this concept was hard for them to grasp as well. I've had absolutely no desire for TV while I've been here. There are plenty of English programmes, but I have no interest. Not knowing what's going on in the world is an absolute bonus I'd never really thought about before coming away. I get what news I want online. To be honest, I've put myself on a news detox and it's working nicely.

My 'nothing' was briefly interrupted when I walked across the road for a bowl of fried rice and a pineapple smoothie at lunchtime. I will continue doing my best at this nothing state of being. I'm determined to perfect it. Having said that I haven't been watching TV, I did recline on the daybed in my room and watch the King's Coronation, Charles III that is, via my laptop. I had told my Thai friends what was happening and many of them were interested as they have their own royal family. Thais revere their royal family and it's forbidden to speak out against them in public. There are very lengthy jail terms for anyone who does.

Their current king is Vajiralongkorn. Most Thai houses have a picture of him on display and at all government buildings it's compulsory. During my initial stint here as a foreign-exchange student, Bhumibol Adulyadej (5 December 1927–13 October 2016) was the reigning monarch. Holding the throne from 1946 until his passing in 2016, he ranked as the third-longest verified reigning sovereign in world history, trailing behind only King Louis XIV and Queen Elizabeth II. His reign spanned an impressive seventy years and 126 days. He was absolutely adored by many Thai people as he'd travel to remote and poor areas around his kingdom visiting his people and providing hope. He saw the country through some very tumultuous times but was always a steady figure for Thai people to focus on.

Once the coronation was over, I ventured out for some dinner, stopping at Kata on Fire to eat chicken with cashews and

Penang curry and have P'Sak serve me. The restaurant was filling up with the same young Chinese women I'd seen at the beach yesterday. I've noticed many groups of young women out travelling together. It's heartening to see that their desire to travel is still there, maybe even more so, after years of being stuck at home during Covid.

N'Bow happened to pull up with a load of them spilling out of his van and was surprised to see me. Earlier in the day, he'd sent me a photo of his young son Boss. We talk about his family often as he drives me places. I like it that he shares his family with me. N'Bow always looks neat and tidy when I see him. Polo shirts are his thing and the other day he was wearing some very on-trend red sneakers. I told him how great he looked. He smirks rather than smiles and has a kind face, always with a smattering of stubble.

I walked home from dinner with the silvery moonlight providing ample light for me to see where I was going and jumped straight into my pool.

7 May
What I'm Missing | Walking Loop | New Friends

A brand-new café has opened on my street. I've been watching it take shape over the last couple of weeks, so I was eager to try it this morning. They've used a chocolate and black colour scheme inside which gives it a sleek modern look. I perched at the bench that runs along the front window. There were familiar food items on the menu like almond croissants and chocolate cake, alongside lots of different tea varieties and what looked and smelled like decent coffee. I could see that it's run by young people who are enthusiastic and trying hard to bring their concept together.

I had an almond croissant and a Chinese iced tea with lemon. It was good, but just like being in a café at home. There's without a doubt a market for this familiar Western food and drink, but for me it's back to the street for Thai sweets and *cha yen*. It got me thinking about what I'm missing from home foodwise. I struggled to think of one thing I'd really like to eat from home.

I found it very easy to think of what I'm not missing. I'm not missing preparing or cooking meals. I haven't cooked one since arriving and don't plan to. I don't miss grocery shopping, even if mine is done online, and I don't think I'll ever miss being asked, 'What's for dinner?' Joe has no skills in the kitchen, aside from doing tea and toast and opening a bottle of wine. He can book a restaurant and buy takeaway, but meal prep and home cooking has never been on his radar. Lucky he married me!

I can, however, think of plenty of things I will miss from here foodwise once I'm home. The variety on offer is vast. In my street alone there's obviously all sorts of Thai food, as well as Italian, Turkish, French, Indian and American burgers and fries. My choice will pretty much always be simple Thai food that the locals cook and eat. Rice and curry or noodles or fried rice or spicy salad and sticky rice – convenient, fresh and, most importantly, not made by me.

I'd scoped out a walking loop to do once I left the café. It was cloudy so I was cheering as I headed off. The first stop on my walk was a fashion boutique that had lots of tiny handbags, tiny clothes and tiny shoes. I'm not tiny so, after I chatted with the friendly staff, I stepped back out onto the footpath to continue my walk. I was offered countless discounted massages along the way. Thais believe that the first sale of the day is very important, kind of kicks things off for them. I couldn't help any of them, as even though the sun wasn't out, the humidity was and my clothes were already sticking to me.

I turned off the main street of Kata and into a side street I hadn't walked along before, and met an elderly lady selling her homemade sweets. She also had dim sum in a big silver steamer and was happy to lift the lid and talk me through what she had on offer. She told me all about what Thai people like for breakfast. My stomach wasn't ready for any of it, but I did get some sweet treats for later. I was eager to try them as they were all new to me.

I strode on, enjoying saying *'sawadee kha'* to friendly faces and looking at how people are living their lives around my local area. It was the perfect kind of walk in my mind as there were stops for food, an interesting assortment of businesses, houses and street stalls and all sorts of people going about their day. I ended up turning onto a busy main road with traffic whizzing by me and no footpath. I was ready for a drink and came across a roadside stall that sold *cha yen*. I ordered my drink in Thai and the lady serving, whom I'd never seen before, instantly wanted to be friends. She was so full of questions. I know I say it often, but the curiosity and warmth these people show towards someone they've never seen before and may never see again is never lost on me. It's hard to put into words at times.

I found out her name was also Apple – interesting to come across this name again. Soon her friend from the street stall next door came over and we were all having a great chat. They told me they desperately want to learn English, but don't know where to start. They were curious about where I'm from and how long I've been in Phuket and where I'm staying and what my favourite Thai food is. Next, they asked if they could take a photo with me. I said 'Sure' as I wiped the sweat from my forehead. They didn't seem to care that I was a hot mess. They just wanted to connect.

I can't even imagine how tedious their life must be, sitting on a dusty, busy main road in the heat waiting for customers to stop by. Both girls asked me to return to their shop tomorrow, but I said I have school. That's okay, they said, we're open until 8 p.m. I will go back and see them and also help them practice their English if I can. How could I not?

Off I walked with my *cha yen* in one hand and waving goodbye to my new friends with the other. I had a hill to walk up so I was grateful for my drink. Once at the top of the hill, I turned right and was then back in my street. Most of my street is residential with lots of small houses. The tiny house concept is nothing unusual here. Yet in the West we seem to have only just realised that a four-bedroom home isn't necessary or affordable for many. A couple of rooms here is enough as often a family will sleep in one room together and pack up their mattresses in the morning to use the space during the day to sit and watch TV in. A small kitchen and bathroom completes the house and motorbikes are parked at the front door. There's rarely a garage. Many families eat out, work very long hours and the kids go to school so they don't tend to spend large amounts of time at home. It seems to work well for them.

By this stage of my walk, I was so freaking hot I was dying to jump into my swimming pool. My cheeks were flushed and my hair was sticking to the back of my neck. A walk that might have taken an hour took more than two and I wouldn't have had it any other way. I honestly adore these wonderful, big-hearted people.

8 May
Student Again | N'Bow & His Family

I spent the morning at language school and our lesson focused on the names of the months. They're very long words based on the old Sanskrit language and are often abbreviated because no one wants to remember them, not even the Thais. I'm really enjoying being a student again. It's incredibly rewarding. Here I am in my fifties sitting in a classroom, trying to build my Thai vocabulary and sentence structure, hoping I've got enough memory space left in my often tired, woolly brain to keep adding knowledge to it and then be able to find it again when I need to. Recall is my real worry. There are times at home I've forgotten if I've turned the dishwasher on five minutes after doing so.

I'm very much going with the philosophy that when you do something you enjoy it never feels like work. And it seems to be working. My classmates are great. There are five of us who regularly attend and a few who come and go. They're all younger than me and mostly Brits, Americans or Russians. We're all trying to master this language in our own way. It's not something you can just look at once and you're good to go. Well, it's not for me. The learning process is incremental and can feel painfully slow at times. The fact that I still haven't been able to retain the months of the year proves this to me.

Times have definitely changed since I learnt my first Thai words. I had a very thick black book, *The Fundamentals of Thai Language*, which I worked through on my own while I was going to the local school in Kamphaeng Phet. I still have it. So many memories are scribbled in that book from when I'd sit in the classroom trying to learn and drift off thinking of anything else but this strange language. Now there's Google Translate, umpteen YouTube videos and language apps to help us. I've got an app that allows me to repeat the words I'm learning, and it rates how close to a native speaker I sound. I've found having a Thai voice pronounce the words invaluable. So helpful and a really smart idea.

As N'Bow drives me to and from school, he helps me with the language, repeating words for me. I pepper him with questions and he loves working out not only what I've said but also coming up with the answers in Thai and English. He often tells me not to use such formal language, but that's what we're taught at school. It's great he can give me the casual, informal, everyday version of the language and street slang as that's my preference.

We established today that he was born in May like myself. I asked him if he was having a party, but his birthday is on election day, which is a no-alcohol day. I said surely you could have a few quiet ones at home. I think he's planning to have a few friends over. He lives in a block of adjoining small houses and it sounds like all the neighbours socialise together while their kids ride bikes and play.

He told me today that his wife had just left to care for her parents in her home province. She takes their three older boys back with her as they go to school there. N'Bow then cares for Boss, their youngest, who's only three. He also has his mother living with him so she can look after the little boy while he drives his van.

N'Bow is the money earner for the whole family and this sharing of responsibilities allows him to do that.

It's beyond me how tough it must be to have your young family split apart for long periods of the year. N'Bow can't go with his wife, he has to stay in Phuket to work as he's not able to earn enough money to support the whole family in the regional areas. The tourists keep him and his family afloat.

He tells such a lovely story about why he has four children. He said having a boy first was great. When his wife fell pregnant for the second time, they were both hoping for a girl but they had twin boys. The doctor said if you have another baby it will be a girl for sure. So they tried one last time and again another boy. He laughs as he tells this story and tells me he'll never believe the doctor again. It sounds like he and his wife were hoping to have only two children as it's expensive to raise four, but I can tell he's very proud of them all as he speaks about them often. He does say that he can never just buy one of anything, he always has to buy four, otherwise there will be fights.

With the rain having just started pelting down, that might be my prompt to go for another swim in my pool and to recite the Thai months over and over and over: Morgarakom (January), Gumpapun (February), Meenarkom (March), Measaryon (April), Pritsaparkom (May)…

9 May

Missing Fruit Seller / Drunken Male Termites

The shop of my tattooed-covered fruit man has been closed for more than a week, with no sign to say when it will reopen. One minute he was there, the next not a mango in sight. I've taken it upon myself to fabricate a story to explain what has happened. I have nothing to base my wild assumptions on, but my take is that he was selling drugs and the fruit was his cover. It could've been that he didn't pay his rent, but that's far too mainstream. It's a pity. I miss his banter and his guitar playing as I walk by, and I miss buying his fruit and having him peel and cut it up for me and throw in a few extra bits and pieces for me to try.

There was progress at Pui's bar today. When I called in to pick up my freshly washed and folded clothes, she excitedly showed me the shelves for her bottles of alcohol to sit on and more side screening that has been completed. Her house shares a wall with another house and they're identical buildings. Pui wanted to make her bar space a little more private, so the screening is a good idea. Not so sure about how she will deal with the noise from her bar. At least for now it looks good. She told me that this won't be a 'girly bar', meaning a bar that offers drinks and sex like many of them do. She wants it to be a relaxing, laid-back and welcoming place where friends come together for cocktails and beers. A bit like an extension of her own home. She's bursting with enthusiasm for her new venture.

While I was out and about, I popped in to see Mickey. I wanted her to tell me about the honey. I had my notebook and pen ready to go as she gave me the main selling points. Mickey told me it's from Northern Thailand and a bit special. The flowers and blossoms the bees have been visiting belong to fruit trees. It's only available at certain times of the year and she wanted me to explain how the product could be used. Now I can put a sign together for her. She took the lid off one of the bottles and it smelled as delicious as it sounds.

Mickey seems to have a knack of knowing what her customers might like to buy. She's always adding new products to her countertop to entice an impulse purchase. It certainly works on me. Currently she has small packets of nuts as well as freeze-dried jackfruit and sun-dried bananas. She tells me they're all selling well. Her shop is across the road from a large hotel so there are plenty of tourists looking for snacks. According to Mickey the smashed avo craze has hit Kata. She's struggling to keep up with the demand for her avocados. Cafés and restaurants are buying directly from her and the fruit hardly has time to ripen before being snapped up. That must be a good way to be in a fresh food business.

I said goodbye and walked past the massage ladies who sit outside their shop, glued to their phones, always with one eye on those passing. They never miss an opportunity to ask if I feel like a massage, but today instead they eagerly asked about Joe and my fur girls Rosie and Jasmine, remembering them all by name.

I was heading for the Red Chair and found a table under a fan. I wasn't overly hungry so just ordered a chicken stir-fry with rice. There were a few insects flying around, which is not unusual for here, but gradually their numbers increased and by the time my food arrived they were dive-bombing into my drink, then my rice and then down my back and into my bra. The restaurant staff told me that when these insects arrive there will soon be rain. They were quickly swarming around the fluorescent lights and made eating unpleasant. I paid my bill as they started turning off the lights to deter the insects. I couldn't get out of there quick enough while swatting at them and keeping my mouth firmly closed.

Back past Mickey's shop I walked and she had already turned all her lights off, as had other shops. The insects were circling around the street lights. The only upside of that whole experience was that I learnt a new word, *malaeng mao*, which generally translates as 'drunk insects' and that seems to describe them well.

Back in my room, I jumped straight into the shower to get these drunken pests off me. I've since tried to find out what they are: flying male termites that drop their wings. All I can hope is that the rain arrives soon to control these critters or encourage them to go elsewhere. I never know what I'll encounter each time I step out of my room, but drunken male termites certainly weren't on my radar. Interesting that the word for 'drunk insect' has been so easy for me to remember while the month of October still hasn't stuck.

10 May

Protein Sources | No Swimming | Drain Covers

This morning, after a swim, I headed off to see my new friend Apple at the roadside drink stall. She was thrilled to see me and instantly offered me the food she was eating. It was dried smelly fish with some rice, so I declined. She introduced me to her friend who was sitting with her. They had gone to high school together and live close to one another. We got talking about the *malaeng mao* from last night while she made me a *cha yen*. They told me that many people catch these termites and eat them as they're a good source of protein, which got us laughing. I said I'd prefer chicken myself.

  I left the lovely gals and walked back home via the 7-Eleven and, while standing in front of the fridges, noticed a number of drinks with collagen added to them. There was a whole row of them and also several types of yoghurt with collagen added to it. I wondered if this was the latest attempt to encourage women to try filling out their laugh lines and crows feet?

  Before dinner tonight I went down to watch the sunset. My days continue to be on the random side and routine is still being avoided, but getting to the beach to see the sinking sun is unmissable. If that counts for routine, I'm okay with it. I'm feeling more drawn to the ocean even if it just means I sit on the sand, people watch and breathe in the salty sea air. It's agreeing with me a lot. I feel content and soothed whenever I'm there.

A first for me was seeing the shore lined with fluttering red 'NO SWIMMING' signs. Of course people were still in the water, blatantly ignoring the warnings. The waves were big, the surfers were out in force and the beach had been dramatically cut away by the tide. Lifeguards were walking up and down, blowing their whistles and signalling to the swimmers to get out of the water. With the change in the weather and choppy sea conditions, I'm happy just wandering along the footpath and then turning around and walking back along the beach.

Talking about walking on footpaths, which I seem to do a bit – the footpaths here have access points for the drains which run under the street. The other night I was out for a walk and I stepped on a drain cover and it tilted. I felt like it was going to give way. There are very few things that frighten me here, but the thought of ending up with any part of my body in a Thai drain terrifies me. I saw a drain cover tonight that had shattered into many pieces and was instantly reminded of my near miss. Let's just say I now sidestep these scary spots with absolute purpose.

11 May

Fluffy White Waves / Taxi Ride With a Smile

I wanted to see if the sea conditions had changed and to walk right to the northern end of Kata Beach. The local municipality has kindly made a new concrete path all the way –hopefully with secure concrete drain covers. All of a sudden there seem to be improvements happening in local roads and footpaths. Wouldn't happen to be an election coming, would there? I packed my beach bag, slung it over my shoulder and headed off the couple of kilometres to the northern end, where the waves were rolling in under the front row of the sun lounges. How lovely to be able to dangle your feet in the water with the tide on its way in. I found a spot in the third row and made myself comfortable.

Swimming conditions were unbelievably great. Big, full, fluffy white waves giving me endless opportunities to bounce over and under them. Happy days out in the Andaman Sea today. I stayed for most of the day, trying to squeeze the most from it. I had a few podcasts to catch up on, some music to listen to and some mindless scrolling to attend to. The only thing that encouraged me to head off was my hungry tummy and the 3 per cent battery left on my phone.

The latter important for booking a taxi to get home after some food.

I headed off down a new street for me, which fortunately, but not surprisingly, led to a row of Thai restaurants just behind the beach. I had a satisfying meal that included crispy spring rolls and sweet chilli dipping sauce. The attentive staff made sure I was near the fan, my standard request when I walk into a restaurant these days. It's a nice easy sentence in Thai and I've perfected it through consistent use.

I managed to conserve my phone battery. Within three minutes of my taxi booking being confirmed, my driver arrived and was all smiles. When I started speaking, he said, 'You can speak Thai so well *and* I can understand you!' It's our inability to nail the varying tones that often make it difficult when we foreigners try to speak Thai. Good to know my tones were on point today.

My driver didn't stop talking to take a breath from the minute he picked me up, covering everything from living in Bangkok and how crazy the traffic is to enjoying his job driving people around and the impact of the pandemic. He was particularly full of stories about being happy and making people smile. As he chatted to me, he pressed down on the heads of a couple of bouncy toys stuck to his dashboard. The heads wobbled about and it was hard not to laugh. He got me safely home and put a big smile on my face. I was still shaking my head and laughing when I put the key in the door of my room.

12 May

Solo Sisters / Rewind: 12 May 1989

Empowerment, personal achievement, self-discovery. Apparently there's a surge in women aged fifty and over who want to get out amongst it and travel solo. Who would've thought? Why wouldn't you if all this and more is on offer? It seems to me, from what I've been reading and listening to, that mature women who travel solo are currently enjoying a moment in the spotlight. There has never been a better time to join the growing numbers of us out there having the time of our lives. There's no time like the present. It's addictive, but most of all, it helps us continue to grow and boosts our confidence and reinforces our belief that so much is possible.

Travelling alone can really cause anxiety for some women, particularly for first-timers. But, as in so many aspects of life, when women are honest and open with each other about their worries and doubts, the desire to help one another comes to the fore. I'm heartened and amazed by the number of women's solo travel groups I've come across on social media. What I'm not surprised about is the support and encouragement the women in these groups provide to each other.

The stories that are shared so generously of travel and life are inspiring and sometimes heartbreaking. Women facing their fears and going for it. Some tiptoeing out of their comfort zone, doing a couple of days close to home, while others are throwing caution to the wind and going on far-flung adventures for months. You don't have to be intrepid or overly confident. You just need resolve and to want to do it. It helps knowing there are others who have felt that knot in their stomach as they wait for their flight, some who have felt pangs of guilt for booking a trip just for them, and many who have wondered how they would cope with eating dinner alone night after night while away. All they need to do is post about it and an instant bond forms with other women who can relate. As women, this support and encouragement really is our superpower, and one we should celebrate and nurture.

Women travelling on their own are everywhere. Knowing there are so many like-minded sisters cheering you on from all over the world can't help but build your confidence. The reasons women are traveling solo are as vast and varied as the countries they want to explore.

I've also been thinking about when I started to travel and what it was like for me when I was here in my teens. I opened my 1989 travel diary to read what seventeen-year-old me had to say about exploring a foreign country, sometimes on my own. I could tell from my diary entries that, after being in Thailand for two months, I was still adjusting to the heat and the culture shock.

I was offered the opportunity by a teacher at my school to go with her to Mae Sot in the province of Tak that borders with Myanmar, then called Burma. In 1988 there had been a bloody end to Burma's pro-democracy demonstrations, when three thousand students and civilians in the capital and in other cities were massacred. I said yes to the trip, knowing very little about what I might be getting myself into.

I'm still not good with winding roads and car sickness and it seems the trip that day tested me out. A couple from New Zealand also came along, and my diary tells me it was great to have an English conversation. I describe the scenery as *rather fascinating, hill tribe people, rice paddies, people walking on the side of the road with packages on their heads and dressed rather strangely and so many water buffalo being used in the fields.*

My food experience wasn't very pleasant and thankfully I can't remember the fish intestines that my diary tells me we were served. I describe it in one word: *revolting*. I do remember walking to the border and there not really being anything but barren land all around. My diary says, *I took a photo, they can just walk across the border freely. I also saw where a bomb had hit earlier and it was awful. There were refugees who have just set up camp because they had nowhere else to go. Many had young children and no clothes and very little food. It's all very third-world looking.*

I'm so thankful that my desire to travel and see life being lived differently to what I'm used to is still part of me. Reading what seventeen-year-old me did when an opportunity arose that day, saying yes and going, puts a big smile on my fifty-two-year-old face.

I laughed as I read more of that diary entry as it seems we stopped on the way back home and I got to eat delicious ice cream. A highlight of my day. My desire to travel has always been strong, but my desire to eat when travelling even stronger.

13 May

Seafood Noodles / Blue Hour / Gutsy

My time in Thailand was never meant to be busy, full or planned. Being here was more about taking the day-by-day approach and putting my needs first. Needing only to consult myself and being able to change my mind at any time, with no explanation or justification, is something I think we should all have a turn at doing. The joys of solo travel are many, but this is one of my favourites.

After a super-relaxed day pottering about, listening to music, reading and doing some language study, I thought I had better head out and find some dinner. I hadn't left my room all day and that was perfectly fine by me. I was in the mood to try a new restaurant, a family-run place in the front yard of a house that I've walked past many times. They always have a small but enticing display of fresh seafood. They mainly offer barbecued whole fish, but as I was eating alone and a whole fish might be wasted on me, I went for seafood noodles. They came with prawns, pieces of fish and squid and mussels in their shells, lightly stir-fried with bok choy tossed through. It was so fresh and just what I was in the mood for.

As usual, wanting something sweet to finish off, I found myself walking towards the beach to buy a passionfruit and coconut ice cream. I sat on the steps leading down to the beach to eat my ice cream curls. Sometimes you're just in the right place at the right time. There was a slim line of orange still on the horizon over the ocean as the sun had not long disappeared. I think I had arrived just in time to see the blue hour, that time when the twilight is so soft and the sky goes gradually from a lighter dark blue to an inky dark blue. I got my phone out to take a photo and managed to frame the shot with a few palm trees, as a reminder.

I waited until dark before making my way home. I thought I'd call into my local to see Khun Tuk. I felt like a Friday night margarita, not that I normally know what day it is. I was the only customer and we chatted away until two guys rolled up. One of them was Mr London, the well-spoken English man I'd chatted to a few nights ago. He pulled up a stool and introduced me to his newish friend Damo from Adelaide, Australia. Well, my quiet drink soon turned into quite the comedy show with these two sparring off one another with their life stories and questionable adventures. Damo had just resurfaced after five epic and enlightening days and nights in the depths of Patong, the tourist area of Phuket packed with beer bars, go-go bars, massage parlours, clubs and cabarets, where it's all about the nightlife and the selling of sex is front and centre. Let's just say there's not much he didn't do, or so the story goes.

I've found that many foreigners I speak with are here sorting through or running from mid-life jitters and/or relationship splits or are just fed up with all the expectations that life dishes up. Damo is Exhibit A. He's taking a few months off in Thailand to 'work through' his current life crisis. If he's still alive after the experience I think it will be a miracle. Judging by the way he's thrown himself headfirst into his first week, he's a man who finds it hard to say no.

The laughs were coming thick and fast and these blokes

were in for the long haul tonight. The beers and the whiskey and sodas were being consumed at a rapid pace, which was great for sweet Khun Tuk. Just the sort of customers she loves. Soon Damo morphed into the bar DJ and the tunes were pumping out for the whole neighbourhood to enjoy.

When they learnt I was living here on my own, firstly they were surprised that Joe would 'let' me do that, and secondly that I was loving being alone so much. They did express a certain level of admiration that I was 'gutsy' enough to do this. I wasn't really sure how to take this. I did let them know it wasn't 1980 and women are out travelling solo everywhere. I also pointed out that they were here on their own and it was no big deal, so why would it be for me?

My pool was calling me very loudly by this stage, so I left them to it. I don't think that will be the last I see of that duo as they're living just up the street from me. I have a sneaking suspicion they will be propping up this local bar often and continuing to embellish their already wild stories and might just be a little less surprised by women travelling solo next time I see them.

14 May

Lesson in Weed / Garlic Chicken

I had a restless sleep last night, which sometimes happens. I stayed in bed for a bit before slipping on my swimmers and getting straight into the pool. I don't think there is a more immediate and refreshing way to clear any cobwebs that might be making it hard for you to get going with the day. My swim was just what I needed. Heading out, I dropped in to see Pui and, quite unexpectedly, got a lesson in, of all things, cannabis. Pui has lots of little jars of weed lined up on a shelf with name tags on them. She ran me through them and explained the various effects each different variety has; a little like a massage menu, depending on the mood you're wishing to achieve. Pui asks her customers how they'd like to feel and she's then able to accurately recommend the right blend.

She had sold 5,000 baht worth of cannabis yesterday, all to foreign tourists. It's not every day this happens. With the average monthly wage being around 20,000 baht, little wonder she was pleased. She tells me the mark-up is good and there's plenty of money to be made in high season. She offered me my pick of the jars, but I had no desire to try it. I'm totally naive about this stuff, not having used it when I was young, and I think it stinks. I'd much rather have a decent meal or a bar of luscious chocolate than a joint.

I felt like garlic chicken made by Kunya for dinner. It's my Thai equivalent of grilled cheese on toast, one of those simple meals that just hits the spot every time, predictable and comforting and no fuss. Kunya makes it so well that I've asked for a lesson. She was excited when I asked her to teach me. I will video her making it and she's offered to show me any other dish I'd like to learn. To learn from this wonderful self-taught cook will be fantastic and hopefully I'll be able to replicate her dishes when I get back home.

Manfred has finally departed for Germany and we had a giggle about life being so much easier now. Kunya's beautiful smile was missing for days due to his intensity at times so it's great to see her relaxed and laughing again. I was her second to last customer of the night. Her last one, a Thai man who came in with no shirt on and a debilitating limp, said hello to me. Kunya served him a new dish that she's thinking of adding to her menu. It includes a bit too much organ meat for me and I'd definitely have to look up the Thai word for liver so I can make sure it's not in there. To me it looks to be a pork soup noodle dish, which she said she's been making from a very young age. The Thai man slurped it back and gave it the double thumbs up.

Once he'd finished eating, he was keen to join in our conversation with the usual questions around me being able to speak Thai. Kunya and I had him talking about himself in no time and he confided he was once a heavy drinker and smoker. He sustained a head injury from a motorbike accident, ended up not being able to work for some time and consequently lost everything, including his family. His wife took their daughter and left him. He has since given up alcohol and the smokes.

The man rides a motorcycle with one hand and has a small cart-like structure on the side that he fills with all manner of things.

He kindly wanted to give me a lift home in the cart. Thankfully by now I'm good at saying, 'No thanks, I'd rather walk,' and although I needed to repeat it, off he went in the end. I enjoyed my walk home as it was a warm evening and so many people were out and about. The streets often have a lovely, lively atmosphere and I feel like I can walk around at any time of night with confidence. I've never felt afraid walking by myself, which gives me a great sense of freedom.

15 May
Move Forward Party | BeBo

The Kingdom of Thailand has woken to a new future with the voting in of the Move Forward Party (MFP) and the rejection of the military rule they've been under for the last nine years. The MFP has only been in existence for four years and seems to appeal mostly to progressive young Thais. They will form a coalition government with another party with similar philosophies.

They've promised a minimum wage of 450 baht (A$18.95) a day, the current rate being 370 baht (A$15); a pension for people over sixty and 10,000 baht (A$430) for every citizen over sixteen to stimulate spending in the economy. They've even proposed a watering down of the harsh penalties in place of anyone being publicly critical of the Thai royal family, which is a massive and controversial change. Their leader is a forty-two-year-old man who did his higher education in the UK and his 'fun fact' is he loves Esports and Minecraft. It will be interesting to see how this new government goes about changing and hopefully enhancing this vibrant and beautiful country.

I've asked most of my Thai friends about a looming change in government and they largely seem uninterested. I think that, like elsewhere in the world, politics has proved to be disappointing and underwhelming so Thais just carry on with life. Last night I watched the TV coverage of the election result. I wanted to know not only the outcome but also if there was any hint of unrest. Thailand has a history of coups and civil unrest following elections, but this is normally confined to Bangkok. There was no sign of anything like that this time.

It was business as usual for me today with refreshing swims in the pool and the sea. Happy days all around. On my way to the beach there's a very handsome boy waiting for a cuddle. BeBo is his name and he takes a keen interest in those who pass by his door. He's eight months old and adored by his Thai mamma. This beautiful big Alaskan Malamute seems totally out of place here. He sits in front of a fan and has a big bowl of iced water to drink from, but he prefers to dig in it and splash the water all over the footpath. He's a super-playful pup and loves pats and cuddles. Twice a day he goes to the beach for a swim, which he clearly loves. He's loved by many and it's so nice to round the corner of my street and see him sitting tall at the front of his house. I can't resist stopping and making a fuss of him, but it's interesting to see that many tourists give him a wide berth, moving off the footpath to the road when they pass by him. All he wants is a pat and chat and sometimes a big cuddle. He's proving to be very useful in fulfilling my ongoing desire to have some canine company. BeBo regularly feels the love from me and I'm sure my fur girls would approve.

16 May
M&M's for Breakfast / Lazy Monday / Khun KK

Things I loved about today: eating M&M's for breakfast and fresh mango and passionfruit; the magenta orchid that decorated my pineapple smoothie at lunchtime; having two fans cool me while eating my pad Thai topped with ample crushed peanuts. I loved being tested at school on the Thai months and only tripping over June, laughing with my language classmates as we all had to stand in front of the class and tell everyone what we did on the weekend. It may sound easy but not so for some, and then leaving class to find a foreigner I'd spoken to last week at the local soup noodle shop and recommended my language school to had turned up today to give it a go.

On the way back from school, I loved listening to what N'Bow did for his birthday yesterday, seems it was a fairly quiet night with friends. I loved foodpanda delivering my dinner in twenty minutes, then my relaxing evening swim in the pool while so many people were out enjoying their holiday with drinks, food and swims. Such a nice vibe. Having my bed made for me eighty-plus nights in a row and knowing my bestie will soon be here with me was the perfect ending to the day. That's right, I've got a visitor coming to hang out with me. My friend Georgia, another first-timer to Thailand, will be with me to share in all the delights I've discovered so far. Not bad for a lazy Monday.

In other news Khun KK, as in 'kanom krok', the lady who let me make the coconut puddings with her at her roadside stall, was finally back making her treats today. She has been away and missed by me. I asked her how she was and she's one of the first Thai people to ever say to me they're not doing so well.

There was a man at her stall buying a coffee and she was talking to us both. 'Everyone thinks I've been on holidays, but it's been a very hard and sad time,' she said, explaining that her mother is old and unwell and her time away was to care for her. Her hometown is a fair distance from Phuket so she is feeling unsettled being back and away from her mother.

I really felt for her and thankfully I could talk to her in Thai and express my empathy. I thought she was wonderful to share this news with me so openly.

The man who was with us ended up saying to me, 'You're just like a Thai person.'

I responded, 'That's exactly what I want to be.'

They're just such lovely gentle souls. I will pop by again tomorrow to see how she is.

17 May
Noisy Neighbours / Name Changes

Well, it had to happen, the neighbours from hell have moved in. I think that after three months of living at a hotel I've had a pretty good run, but this lot are definitely making up for it. The accent sounds South American and they yell. The small child is in a constant state of panic and screams when in the pool. Mum has her enormous broad-brimmed hat on, a cigarette in the mouth and bikini up her bot and an arrogant air, while Dad is coughing his lungs up regularly and smoking in the pool. You get the picture. I thought I gave them the death stare in the pool yesterday, but they just waved.

This morning the room doors were banging, the music was up loud and there was more screaming. Now by all means do that at home, but when other people are trying to enjoy their holiday around you, how about some consideration? Seems not. My quiet patch of paradise has been disturbed, but at least I know it will be temporary. I was happy to be heading out to eat and going to school.

Kruu Noi told us today how Thai people are easily able to change their names and why they choose to do it. I found the conversation so interesting. I've already mentioned their love of a nickname, but now I know it's also common for Thai people to change their given names at any point in their lives if burdened by bad luck or ill health or to reflect a significant life change.

It's common for them to consult with a monk, fortune teller or other respected person in society to choose another more appropriate name. I can't imagine that. It's hard enough if you lose your wallet and need to have everything replaced, let alone a complete identity change. Then again, it could work well for those foreigners coming here to find or reinvent themselves. Surnames were only officially introduced to Thailand in the early twentieth century. I'm not sure if you've ever seen some Thai surnames but they can be quite a mouthful, e.g. Chaimongkhon or Sukpraserit. There is a reason for this. Many Thai family names are only two or three generations old, and Thai law prevents people from creating a surname that duplicates that of another family, so some had to make surnames that were longer and more complex. If two individuals share a family name, it generally means they are related.

The family I lived with as an exchange student has the surname Lamsam. This was written on my school uniform and luckily for me it was a nice easy name to pronounce. Initially I didn't know that this family name was associated with a well-known and very wealthy Thai banking family. If I said my full name to a Thai person, they would instantly say, 'Oh, very rich!' It was true that the family were related, but that had no effect on the life my Thai family lived, as far as I was aware. It was very apparent to me even then, though, that who you were connected to and the family line you came from made a very big difference in this society. It really is all in a name here, it seems.

18 May

Time to Think | Woo-Woo | Beach Seduction

By the time we're in our fifties, I believe most of us have something reasonably heavy we're carrying around with us, metaphorically speaking, that we'd benefit from being able to put down for a bit or maybe forever. Once you've lived enough of life to have dealt with disappointments, setbacks and several reality checks and come out the other end, how can you not? I'm pretty certain that's why my time away has been presenting me with benefits in ways that I'd never imagined. I also think I'll still be discovering the benefits once I'm home and for months or years to come. Although it wasn't my intention, it has helped me to reconnect with who I truly am. I think this just happens when you spend time with yourself. Letting your thoughts run off in all directions without needing or wanting to rein them back in. It just guides you towards this.

Just sitting with my thoughts, both positive and negative, and watching where they go and what they might be returning to is always interesting. This isn't necessarily about becoming all woo-woo, though I don't mind a bit of woo-woo. It's just about not being afraid of what might reveal itself. Some might call it being vulnerable with yourself.

Living with high and unrelenting levels of stress has done

all sorts of things to my well-being. It's only now that has started to ease that I can even begin to contemplate unpacking that heavy load. I knew during the very dark days of Joe's illness that I was just hanging on. Looking back, I'm not sure how I did it. Somehow I found a level of resilience and strength I didn't even know I had. The human spirit is a remarkable thing, but it's also very fragile.

Joe is also getting so much joy from seeing me happy and carefree, something he has missed over many years. I feel time is a great healer for so much in life and none more so than solitary time. What interests me the most at this point in my time away is where I want to spend my time. I've never been a massive beach gal because of the sand, and more sand, and I tend to prefer a pool, but here I'm all about the beach. It has won me over and no one is more surprised and pleased than me. I've missed not being able to finish the day with a relaxing swim in the sea while it has been a bit wild.

I feel a sense of calm and peace when I'm on the beach, even though there can sometimes be hundreds of people around. I find myself very much in my own world. It has become a place of wonder and discovery when I'm snorkelling and of rest and relaxation when I'm swimming and lounging. It appeals to all my senses: digging my feet in warm or wet sand; looking long and staring out to sea; being in awe of the how the colours of the water gradually change; tasting the salt on my lips; tuning in to the rhythm of the waves as they break; and smelling whatever food might be barbecuing at the nearest street stall. It seems to have seduced me.

19 May

Cooking With Kunya / Georgia Arrives

Today I took Kunya up on her offer to teach me how to make some of the dishes I've been enjoying eating at her café. Since it was before lunchtime, I was the only one in the café and Kunya could not have been more willing to demonstrate her prowess in the kitchen. Kunya sells this dish for 60 baht (A$2.50). I took videos while she worked. She started with *yum kai dow*, spicy salad with fried eggs. The hardest part of this dish is frying the eggs.

Yum Kai Dow

Make your salad first

- Chop up 2 tomatoes, ½ onion, 1 carrot peeled and a few springs of coriander if you like it. You want the pieces to be reasonably small, a bit like making a salsa. Put these ingredients in a mixing bowl.

Make your dressing

- Mix together sugar, fish sauce, salt, lime juice and fresh chilli. There's no measuring, it's all done by sight and feel. I love cooking like that. But roughly 1 teaspoon each of sugar and fish sauce, a pinch of salt, a good squeeze of one lime, chilli to taste. Kunya was about to put a tablespoon of fresh chilli in it when I said, 'Not that much.'

Make your eggs

- Using a wok, add a tablespoon of oil to stop the eggs from sticking. Then fry 3 eggs. You can cook them individually or at the same time depending on the size of your wok. Try to get your wok hot so you can get the edges of the egg white nice and crunchy; they cook quickly. I'm all about the crunch in most dishes. Take your eggs out of the wok and sit them on your chopping board to cool before chopping them up in a haphazard way. Don't be too delicate.

Assemble your salad

- Bring it altogether. Add the chopped eggs to the salad, pour the dressing over and lightly toss. There you have a light spicy salad. Add slices of cucumber on the side to dull the chilli.

The second dish is my favourite. Thais call this chicken garlic (gai is chicken and gratium is garlic), so every time I ask for it I get it wrong and call it garlic chicken. It's not too pungent as the garlic is cooked and sauce is added. Have your steamed jasmine rice and a few slices of cucumber ready.

Gai Gratium

The secret to this dish is only adding a very small amount of oil in the wok when cooking the chicken, as the juice from the chicken comes out and you don't want the meat to stew but stir-fry. You could add whatever veggies you like to this, but Kunya doesn't.

Cut up your chicken

- Thinly slice around 200g of chicken so it cooks quickly. Chicken thighs probably best.

Prepare your garlic

- Peel 4 garlic cloves and place them on a steady chopping board. With the flat of the knife squash them, then roughly chop.

Prepare the sauce

- Kunya adds these ingredients fairly randomly as they sit next to her wok. If you're not that confident put all the sauce ingredients in a small bowl and that will make it easier for you to add them. The sauce is key. It's 1 tablespoon each of chilli sauce, tomato sauce, sweet soy sauce and oyster sauce, 1 teaspoon of sugar, a few shakes of white pepper and a pinch of salt.

Cook your chicken

- With your wok on a reasonably low heat add your oil and the chicken. Stir-fry until the chicken turns white. Then add the garlic and continue to move these ingredients around in the wok so the garlic doesn't burn.

Add your sauce
- You need to be quick again to avoid burning the meat and garlic. Add all sauce ingredients at once and stir-fry for another minute or two. Add a few tablespoons of chicken stock if you like a bit more sauce, and you're done.
- Serve with freshly steamed jasmine rice and a few slices of cucumber. It's that simple.

My theory on eating where the locals go hasn't let me down yet. Now hopefully cooking what the locals cook will also be a winner. I really want to be able to make this when I get home, though past performance tells me I'm full of good intentions only.

Kunya is in her natural habitat in front of that wok. There are more dishes she wants to show me how to make. The ingredients are so fresh and distinctly Thai; once you start to add fish sauce, lime juice and chilli you can't go too far wrong. Kunya was chuffed to send her cooking videos to Manfred. Although he already knows what a great cook she is and I was even happier to be the one eating her creations. I walked back home with a full belly and a few potential new dinner options for home.

It wasn't long before N'Bow arrived and drove me out to the airport where Georgia was waiting for us at the arrivals exit. I have been sharing my travels and Thailand adventures with my dear friend for many years. It's hard to believe I now have her with me to experience it all firsthand for ten whole days.

I'd booked the room next to mine so we can swim together and laze around within arm's length of each other and just be near each other. Once she had unpacked and changed, we were both feeling hungry and walked a couple of minutes down the road to see P'Sak for dinner. P'Sak looked after us well with the food and hospitality and we had a chance to chat and be together. It feels so nice to have my dear friend as my neighbour for the next little while. Welcome to Thailand, Georgia!

20 May
Painted Toenails / Swimming in the Rain

Travelling solo is the bomb, but when your lovely friend pops in for a visit to share this joyous time with you, well that's the icing on top of my cake and we both love cake too! I wanted Georgia to feel confident and comfortable in getting around the neighbourhood where I live on her own. Off we went towards the main street so she could piece together all the spots she'd seen me frequenting via Instagram.

First stop was for a fruit smoothie and some fresh fruit with some people watching on the side while it poured with rain. We patiently waited it out finding plenty of things to chat and laugh about. I personally think the best way to start a holiday here is to have some pampering so our next stop was a pedicure for us both. Neon pink toes for me, sky blue for Georgia. Afterwards there was time for a swim in our pool and some relaxation before I had Georgia up and off to meet Kunya. Knowing my time with my friend is reasonably short, I've packed all our eating experiences in as a priority as that's what we mostly do when we're together.

After meeting Kunya and eating spicy seafood salad, *dtom yum* prawn soup and chicken garlic, we crossed the road to look at a shop that sells *kanom jeen*, thin, opaque, pearly-white noodles made by fermenting rice for around three days. The people who run this shop had a long, large table laid out with all the fresh veggie options. It looked so enticing it practically demanded we stop and take a photo and ask a few questions. The noodles are eaten along with a variety of curries. We watched as customers pulled up on their motorbikes, chose the curry they felt like and the veggies to go with it. It was all bagged up and off they went. What a healthy and convenient way to eat.

We went back to our hotel for a swim in the rain. Then N'Bow came to pick us up and take us to sample the night markets of Kata. It's quite a different experience travelling in his van at night. He has coloured mood lighting, gold-embossed patterns on the roof that are lit from behind and other flashy embellishments like strip lights on the floor to add a bit of atmosphere and excitement to an otherwise ordinary trip. I've seen some extraordinary fitouts in the vans over here. It seems like 'more is mandatory' is their mantra. Tonight he had the van lit in blueish-purple colours for us, which gave us both a giggle.

Our first cocktail was at a bar made from a converted old Kombi van. Cocktails, laughs, people watching with my bestie. It doesn't get better.

21 May

Friendships | 'How Much You Pay?' | Sanook with Pui

How good is it when girlfriends get together with no time limit on how long they can chat? Georgia and I can easily do a three-hour phone call and still not cover everything. We've known one another for twenty years. In that time, we've shared the exciting, wild, rocky and unpredictable rollercoaster of life. She is without doubt my steady, loyal, sensible, trustworthy, clever, kind, thoughtful, cake-loving friend. I'm incredibly grateful to have her in my life. I think female friendships are essential. Probably even more so as we get older and we start to question our lives and dare to wonder, *Is this it?*

The conversations I have with my female friends make my life so much richer. The venting, the worries, the struggles, the menopause, the imperfections, the life events, the happy days, the honesty – telling us we're mad or repeating ourselves – the adventuring together, the laughs, the tears, the questioning, the reminiscing, the what ifs, the what the hells!, the if onlys, the comparisons, the how did we get through thats?, the anticipation of what's still to come in life. And just knowing you have someone who will accept you and your often weird and ever-evolving ways and still want to hang out with you. That's true friendship to me. Oh, and to share the sheer joy of being at an age where the opinions of others don't rate. Happy vibes for sure.

This morning we walked into Kata for a massage and we were greeted like long-lost friends by the sweet staff at the salon who did our pedis the day before. They looked after us beautifully. It was a traditional Thai massage for Georgia and aromatherapy for me. We planned to go for a swim at the beach after we were all zen, but the rain had other plans. Of course, we didn't have umbrellas, but thankfully the shuttle bus from our hotel drove past, recognised me and picked us up.

Our plans to go to Phuket Town and the Sunday Walking Market soon needed to change as the rain kept coming, so I chatted with N'Bow and Plan B was to take Georgia to the undercover Naka Market with its 'genuine fakes' and food.

When we arrived, and for a bit of fun, I asked a stall seller how much a particular watch was. He tapped out on his calculator 12,000 baht, which is about A$540. I said, 'You'd have to be kidding?'

'How much you pay?' he asked and so down came the price to 10,000 baht.

I hadn't said anything and just let him do the talking. As I walked away, saying, 'I'll think about it,' down it came to 6,000 baht.

'How much you pay?' he kept saying before adding, 'My big boss coming. I need to sell this.'

'I need to compare with other shops first.'

He jumped back on the calculator and punched in 5,000 baht. I walked off and he yelled out 'Three thousand baht!' and came after me. Then I switched to Thai with a few questions and asked him not to rip me off. To say he was shocked is an understatement.

We agreed on 3,000 baht, then he blessed his whole stall with my money by tapping it all over his stock. He apologised for starting the price so high and had the cheek to say, 'If I knew you could speak Thai I would've sold it to you for two thousand baht.'

But I'm happy he's got an extra 1,000 baht from me. I wouldn't last a minute selling this stuff to people who want the cheapest price, which sometimes means quibbling over $10. I'm the worst at haggling. Just tell me a fair price and I'll pay, which isn't very helpful living here.

That was enough excitement and entertainment for us both. Georgia and I decided we'd have a picnic for dinner and headed across to the food aisles. I was hoping this would be the best way to give Georgia a taste of many of the scrumptious offerings. In the end our haul included spicy green mango salad, fresh-roasted corn on the cob, fish cakes, dried and fried pork, sticky rice, coconut custard, *kanom krok* and Portuguese tarts. N'Bow was waiting for us at the entrance to the market and drove us home.

The rain had stopped so we found a table by the main pool when we got back, spread ourselves out and went for it: a grazing dinner where you get to eat a bit of everything, the best. After our feast, we headed off to collect my washing and get some more drinking water and supplies for Georgia. We called in to see Pui, but she wasn't home.

The rain started up again and quickly got heavier so we parked up on her veranda and made ourselves comfortable on her couch and waited it out. Before long Pui and a couple of friends came home. They piled out of the car and instantly the party was on. The cold beers came out, the laughs started and never stopped. Georgia and I normally don't even drink beer, but felt it would be rude not to. Such a warm Thai welcome for my friend and they showed her that they really know how to relax and enjoy themselves. I almost forgot to collect my laundry and before everyone became too relaxed we grabbed my clean clothes and off we went.

What a day. So fabulous to see Georgia laughing, smiling and soaking up the Thai magic and everything that is *sanook* (enjoyable) here.

22 May
Bad Luck Be Gone | Phuket Noodles | Fried Bananas

I've been introducing Georgia to the local fruit and the sweet and juicy rambutans currently in season. This funny-looking, fuzzy fruit with a red leathery skin covered in soft spikes looks and tastes similar to a lychee. Georgia had been up walking kilometres and swimming at the beach before I even stirred. After our colourful breakfast of leftover coconut custard and tropical fruit, we had a quick swim in the pool and headed out on the tourist trail. Being told by the locals that it wouldn't rain, we left our umbrellas in N'Bow's van when he dropped us off at the Big Buddha. And then, predictably, it started to rain. Wandering around, we found some monks doing their morning chanting and meditation in a tin shed among building rubble. Quintessential Buddhist philosophy of just letting it be and focusing on the here and now.

By this stage, it was bucketing down, so we sought shelter under a sprawling tree. I joked to Georgia, 'Don't be surprised if N'Bow comes up with our umbrellas.' Next minute, there he was looking for us, umbrellas in hand. This shy, quiet and respectful man with the most badass tats on his arms and body has the kindest heart.

Back in the van and a lot dryer than we otherwise would've been, we continued on to Chalong Temple. We both lit candles, which was pointless in the rain, but at least the incense continued to burn. We went inside to offer our flowers and put forward our wishes to Buddha. As part of making merit you can also have your fortune told. There's a cannister of bamboo sticks that each have a number on them. You kneel on the floor and gently shake the cannister until a stick falls out. It was Number 28 for me and 5 for Georgia. We walked over to the shelves that house the fortune-telling papers, found our corresponding numbers and wandered back to the van.

Once back in the van, I had N'Bow read them to us. They only print them in Thai and my vocabulary doesn't extend this far. Mine was all 'lucky with money, health, happiness, strength', so we were all pleased with that.

Then N'Bow started reading Georgia's and said, 'No good. You have a heavy broken heart, many problems, no luck coming your way.'

I turned to her and asked, 'How did Buddha know that?'

N'Bow told Georgia she could leave that bad luck in the temple grounds. She promptly ripped up that piece of paper, got out of the van and put that bad luck in the bin.

Bad luck be gone!

I can feel only good things coming your way now, my friend, for sure.

Phuket Town was our next stop. We wandered through the pretty streets and into the ceramic shops, but little did we know it was really leading us to lunch. I felt like a bowl of noodles and googled 'best noodles in Phuket Town'. Up came Ko Yoon Phuket Noodle, five minutes' walk away.

I couldn't get my bearings or read my map. So having walked the wrong way at least twice, I was determined to find this place. And soon enough, we walked in. It felt like we were stepping back in time, into a hidden gem. The restaurant was small and cluttered; it could have easily been someone's living room. It was full of family photos, knick-knacks and ornaments, all gathering dust on the shelves that lined the walls. There were only six small tables and we were shown a menu with two dishes on it. To make things easy, we just said yes to the first option. What a good move that was. A bowl full of pork bits, crackling, fish balls, wontons, noodles, veggies and a yummy broth that we could adjust to our taste. Gosh, it was so good right from the first mouthful.

The lived-in look of this shop told us that it had been around for a very long time. We slurped back our noodles and watched a sweet little girl sitting with her grandmother filling tiny bags with chilli and fish sauce for the takeaway orders. Georgia and I looked at each other and felt lucky to be there. An older man was dishing up at the front of the shop. He was the owner and took an interest in me speaking Thai. He was surrounded by bowls full of crushed peanuts, chilli paste, chilli sauce and crunchy deep-fried shallots. These were all added into the noodle bowls to make them taste extra delicious: a spoonful of this and a dash of that.

With empty bowls and the rain not letting up, I texted our ever-reliable N'Bow, who drove his van to the door and in we got, saved again from an absolute drenching. While heading for home, I talked about fried bananas (*kluay tort*) and other Thai treats. N'Bow was part of our conversation. Before we knew it, we were parked at a roadside market while he scoured the stalls for our sweet treats. He came back empty-handed but still determined to deliver. We drove a little further. Soon we were reversing on a very busy road as, apparently, we'd just passed a fried-banana seller. N'Bow dashed off into the rain, while Georgia and I sat in the comfortable van like two princesses, laughing at how totally spoilt we felt and at how far Thai people will go to ensure we are happy. It's astounding.

N'Bow returned with a bag of *kluay tort*. They didn't even last the drive home.

23 May

Ellieephants / Relaxed Vibe

I woke to the friendly man from the hotel reception knocking furiously on my door yelling, 'Madam ellieephants!… Madam ellieephants!' It seems I got my days mixed up for our visit to the elephant sanctuary and the transport was waiting for us. Oh well, that will happen when you're feeling a tad too carefree and have a menopausal foggy brain. Georgia had already gone for a run and there was no way I could pull myself together in two minutes. I told him I would have to cancel, then called the sanctuary, who were very understanding and booked us for the following day.

After that exciting start to the day, it was all about simple pleasures for the rest of it: beach, swim, chatting, coconut ice cream, laughing, swim, people watching, chatting, pad Thai, pool swim and more laughing. I'm so pleased to see some of the stress and struggles slowly melting away for my beautiful friend as this place weaves its magic. The relaxed vibe seems to take your cares away without you even noticing. Even just taking the sharp edges off life makes a world of difference.

The weather played the game tonight so that meant we were treated to a perfect tropical sunset. We ventured a little further out of town to a new restaurant perched high up on a clifftop, with sweeping views across to Kata Beach. The ideal spot for selfies together as the sun sank below the horizon and left us with wispy pink and orange clouds. It proved to be a night made for drinking cocktails and eating a whole fish cooked simply with lemon and lime. Damo and Mr London joined us and the evening was really pleasant with lots of laughs, mainly at their expense. I'd arranged for N'Bow to come and collect us at a reasonable hour knowing we both would've had enough of the banter by then.

Later that evening I got a message from Damo. Apparently, police were stationed along the road back to town. They'd both been caught drink-driving and threatened with jail time unless they paid the fine and then some. They had told the police they would pay whatever was required but they needed to go to an ATM to get the cash. The police let them go and do that. They returned to the police with the cash, handed it over and rode home, still obviously under the influence. Only in Thailand!

24 May

Strength | Loyalty | Longevity

Take two! There was no knocking on my door this morning. I was up and ready to go to the Phuket Elephant Sanctuary with time to spare.

Elephants (*chang*) have long been an extremely important part of Thailand and its culture. They symbolise strength, loyalty and longevity and are the country's national animal. Their importance is deeply rooted in history and religion. You'll see the elephant used as a symbol throughout modern Thailand today. If you ever get the chance to be up close to these incredibly intelligent, tender and tactile animals and look them in the eye it's a very moving experience. I could spend hours just watching them, their funny behaviours and individual personalities shining through. I've been lucky enough to see them twice this visit.

Hidden away in a peaceful rainforest bordering Khao Phra Thaeo National Park, the sanctuary is home to a handful of rescued elephants. Georgia and I joined a group tour which took us up close to the elephants. We stood and watched them repeatedly thrashing the fibrous stem of the banana plant they'd been given for breakfast on the ground. It was like they were softening up their food before eating it. They did the same thing with the waxy, succulent pineapple leaves that were also on their menu. It saddens me so much to think that these incredible animals could ever suffer.

Elephants have long been used in Thailand in farming, logging, transport and tourism. There has been a significant push to stop elephants being used as performing animals in shows and slowly tourists are realising that they shouldn't ride on their backs, although this is still offered. Elephant sanctuaries are becoming more popular, offering tourists the chance to feed and observe them, instead of riding them. Feeding and observing them and just being in the presence of these magnificent creatures is all that I want to do.

The Phuket Elephant Sanctuary does amazing work rescuing elephants from a life of misery inflicted by humans – sick, injured and old elephants who've spent their entire lives working. They must buy the elephants from their owners, sometimes for as much as A$50,000, and begin the process of rehabilitating them so they can live comfortably going forward.

This caring and peaceful sanctuary is their final home. Here these gentle giants have the freedom to roam, bathe, forage and socialise, enjoying their lives and the companionship of others. It's just so reassuring to know that someone is caring for them as they age and are no longer seen as useful or income-producing. Each elephant has a human mahout or elephant keeper who possesses a special bond with them to care for them. They have bedrooms to go into in the evening and they can wander and interact with one another during the day. These elephants can eat up to 300 kilograms of food a day and they love being fed by humans when we visit. You can see that they are loved, adored and, most of all, respected by those who now have responsibility for them.

These huge, imposing mammals have complex emotional intelligence, deep feelings, compassion and self-awareness. Like humans, elephants help each other in distress and mourn the deaths of family and friends. We were told by our guide that when an elephant dies at the sanctuary due to old age, their loved ones will gently touch and caress their skull with their trunks. In addition, elephants will pause for several minutes of silence in the place where a loved one died, even many years after their death. An elephant never forgets.

I'm so glad that we've been educated to do the right thing by these animals before it's too late. They deserve our love, care and endless bananas and pineapples right to the very end.

25 May
Thai Doughnuts / Aprons & Bandannas / Scooooooop

I've been wanting to eat Thai doughnuts (*bah tong gor*) for a while. They're only available in the morning as they're eaten for breakfast, dunked in condensed milk. Yep, that's right, dunked in condensed milk.

Georgia and I went in search of these treats this morning. I had an inkling that they would be at the local market and that's exactly where we found them. We also found a few other breakfast goodies: coconut puddings wrapped in banana leaves with banana and mango inside and my old favourite, *kanom krok*. For a total of 60 baht (A$2.50), we bought ourselves a picnic feast.

We headed off to the beach, spread our sarongs down on the sand and laid out our goodies. The tide was out and the water was a stunning shade of aqua. We sat and peeled open our banana-leaf parcels, dunked our Thai doughnuts and felt pleased with our beach breakfast. We ate, swam and kept a watchful eye on a cheeky bird that had far too much confidence and interest in our food.

I'd booked us into a cooking class for the morning so we didn't have much time to loll about as Jimmy from Kata Thai

Cooking Class was coming to collect us. I've been to many cooking classes spanning all sorts of foods over the years. I love doing them, but I rarely go home and recreate the dishes, although it always seems like a great idea at the time and I take notes in great detail and with good intentions. I still can't work out what happens between the class and home and my recipe sheets getting filed with the umpteen other ones, never to be seen again.

A couple of weeks ago, as I drove past Jimmy's cooking school on the way to my language class, I spotted a large sculpture outside in the form of a Pomeranian dog with a hilariously huge chef's hat on his head. It turns out Jimmy and his wife have a couple of much-loved Pomeranians. He even has them tattooed on his arms. His wife bought the big tin masterpiece for the front garden as a surprise. I wondered if I could get the Labrador version for my front garden.

Georgia and I were soon at the cooking school with our aprons and bandannas on. Just how I imagined we would be and laughing hard at one another. I may have chosen this class partly because we'd have our bandannas and matching aprons to wear while cooking. There were six other people with us and we all looked very much the part as we began to cook.

Jimmy, who also runs the classes, is charismatic, high energy and very entertaining. He had us all chopping, scooping and tasting. He took us through all the ingredients of the dishes on our menu, introducing people to the aromatic herbs and spices like lemongrass, galangal, kaffir lime, coriander root and Thai basil. He explained the need to balance the flavours of spicy, salty and sweet with the use of palm sugar, chilli, coconut milk, lime juice and fish sauce.

Spicy prawn soup (*dtom yum goong*), Penang curry, pad Thai and sticky rice with mango were the dishes we would be cooking. We started with the sticky rice and mango as the rice has to be soaked prior to cooking. We were each allocated our own cooking station which simply consisted of a saucepan and a wok on a portable gas burner.

Once our ingredients were prepared, the cooking time was quick. When making pad Thai, Jimmy had us all in fits of laughter as he repeatedly told us to keep 'scooooooping' that food in the wok. We were all 'scooooooping' at a furious pace to keep the noodles from sticking and make sure all the other ingredients were thoroughly stir-fried through. I'm not sure if we were exhausted from all the 'scooooooping' or the laughing once we'd finished.

Afterwards the group sat down together for lunch to enjoy our mouth-watering creations. A few commented that it was the best food they'd eaten all week. They were young and might have mentioned the words 'hostel' and 'instant noodles', but to be fair it was all so delicious. We left the class with more dinner options for when we're at home and leftovers for our dinner tonight if we can find room for them.

26 May
Limestone Cliffs / Dancing on the Footpath

There is so much I love about Phang Nga Bay with its hauntingly beautiful limestone cliffs soaring high above the stretch of sugar-white sand and glassy green waters. It really is spectacular no matter what the weather – well, sort of. Just depends how much you enjoy the spray off the front of the wooden long-tail boat washing your face.

It was an early start. On the way to our boat, which was waiting for us about an hour and a half away, we stopped at Wat Suwan Kuha, a cave temple that houses an impressive fifteen-metre-long reclining golden Buddha. Often there's a monk meditating in front of the Buddha, but he wasn't there today. The area is also a haven for monkeys, crab-eating macaques, that mostly live off the bags of food the tourists purchase to feed them.

We drove on and it wasn't long before we were pulling up at the pier ready to board our long-tail boat (*ruea hang yao*). These distinctive wooden boats are synonymous with Thailand and are made entirely by hand, with techniques handed down from generation to generation. They're propelled and steered via a propeller fixed at the end of a distinctive two-metre-long pole, shaft or 'tail'. These boats are very simple in structure and comfort with plank board seats. Once the motor starts, all conversation stops. They're always adorned with colourful sashes and flowers. These are not just for decoration but rather to pay respect to and honour the water spirits and *Mae Ya Nang*, the 'Grandmother of Boats'. She is the guardian spiritual goddess of boats and the fishermen who own these boats seek protection, safe passage, a prosperous livelihood and a bountiful catch of fish from her.

We were on a private tour so it was just the two of us and our guide. The weather wasn't on our side and as the boat got going we weren't sure if it was rain or sea spray soaking us. Once you're out on the water and glimpse the dramatic limestone rock formations jutting up out of the Andaman Sea, it's easy to understand why this area has long captivated visitors and is part of a national park. Ao Phang Nga Marine National Park was declared a Ramsar site in 2002 under the Ramsar Convention, deeming it to be of 'international ecological significance'. The Ramsar convention is a global treaty focusing on the conservation and sustainable use of wetlands around the world. The area attracts thousands of tourists, many coming to see where the James Bond movie *The Man with the Golden Gun* was shot in 1974. We opted to leave the masses to their selfies and kept going to the sea-kayaking pontoon.

As you cruise around the area, you see secluded bays with small, white sandy beaches. There are more than forty mostly uninhabited islands. Describing the colour of the water as 'emerald green' doesn't seem to do it justice. They're how I imagine all deserted tropical islands should look. I've avoided sea kayaking before since I find it very hard to get in and out of the kayak from a moving pontoon, but

I was determined to give it another go to share this with Georgia.

So, somewhat gracelessly, I managed to get myself in the kayak. We were paddled around by a guide, who showed us stunning lagoons and took us into various caves, sometimes through very small openings so we had to lie on our backs to glide under the rock walls. Thais see all sorts of animals within the rock formations, and I think some of them let their imagination run a bit wild. We finished off with a walk into a cave to see the sparkling stalactites and stalagmites.

By the afternoon Georgia and I were both ready for lunch and I had the ideal location next on our schedule. As we'd enjoyed Phang Nga Bay by water, it was time to see it from a nearby hilltop. Samet Nangshe, an 800-metre-high viewpoint, provides a superb panoramic view of the bay and miles of the immense beauty spreading far around. We had a simple but delicious Thai meal, took our photos and headed for home.

Though we were exhausted by our day-long expedition, a text on the way back from the dodgy duo Damo and Mr London saw us at Khun Tuk's bar for a few G&Ts, way too many laughs and some dancing on the footpath enjoying the warm tropical evening. This is what doing life differently is all about for me – never knowing what might happen next, but being open and willing to go with it.

27–29 May

Khao Lak | FoG | Treasured Friendship

My original fiftieth birthday plan had been to be in Thailand at The Sarojin in Khao Lak, with Georgia and our husbands. Thanks to the pandemic, I was in Tasmania with my bestie and our husbands and my parents, which in the end was nowhere near second prize.

Sometimes things beyond our control have definite silver linings. Nothing was going to disrupt the fiftieth Festival of Georgia (FoG). I decided long ago that I'd take her to the hotel that I'd been raving about for a number of years and let her experience it for herself.

Joe and I first stayed at The Sarojin in 2008. Many of the staff have since become friends, including Khun Sa. They provide the most authentic and understated Thai service for those lucky enough to stay with them. They care about giving you a memorable time in a beautiful setting by the beach, providing hospitality like you never imagined existed. Any hotel that allows you to have your à la carte breakfast up until 6 p.m. every day gets my vote. I'm yet to find a more indulgent yet relaxed place to stay.

Again, as this is not really #livinglikeathai or #doinglifedifferently I won't detail our days, but I will say there were treatments at the outdoor spa while listening to the waves break on the beach in the distance, unlimited chilled glasses of bubbles with breakfast, swims in the huge turquoise-tiled main pool surrounded by sun pavilions draped in white curtains, a basket of fresh baked goods including pandanus custard pastries at breakfast, bath tubs sprinkled with rose petals and decorated with candles in our rooms, a private dinner in an open-air candlelit hut (*sala*) decorated with fresh flowers and beautiful big tropical leaves to celebrate the FoG, complete with birthday cake, swims in our plunge pool in the rain, cocktails and the most scrumptious Thai food in the breezy beachside restaurant. I even snuck in my fifty-second birthday celebrations.

To have time together with those you love is what I treasure the most these days. Georgia and I don't live anywhere near each other, so it's normally messaging or phone calls for us and we try to rendezvous once a year for a weekend together. All we need is good cake and tea and we're happy. We've now discovered we can also find that happiness together in a tropical location with a cocktail and a Thai satay stick.

I treasure you Georgia – and what your friendship brings to my life – enormously.

30 May

Coconut Milk Sweets | Bye For Now | Cherished Memories

The Sarojin bubble had to be burst sooner or later. After a few pretty soggy days, the blue sky returned and the sun shone brightly this morning just in time for my departure from Khao Lak and farewell to Georgia. While we've been staying at The Sarojin, my kind friend Khun Sa has been dropping off gifts of flowers to us both. It was lovely to see her smiling face pop up in the garden as I walked around and I was so pleased Georgia could meet her too. Before I left today she delivered some coconut milk and pandanus sweets she'd made in the early hours of the morning.

A final swim and farewelling my bestie, before getting in the van with N'Bow, who'd driven up from Phuket to pick me up and take me back to Kata. Georgia was heading for the airport a little later so she had time for some sunshine and more swimming. I squeeze out every single minute when I stay there and always reluctantly pack up and vow to return again. I think Georgia will be doing that as well. It just makes leaving slightly easier.

Arriving back in Kata mid-afternoon, I settled back into my room with a few extra decorations including a huge bunch of birthday orchids from Georgia and cards to brighten up my room. I lay on my bed for ages with that warm fuzzy feeling of having had such carefree days with a precious friend, where everything was easy and enjoyable. We made memories together that I will always cherish. We were just ourselves and that's how it should be.

True food for the soul.

31 May
Non-Routine Routine / Pampered Pooches

Slipping straight back into my non-routine routine, I pulled open the curtains in my room and let the sun stream in, looked up and said hello to Big Buddha. Then it was straight into my bikini for a morning swim in my pool. No loud neighbours. Tick. Fried rice with prawns and a pineapple smoothie at Chai Thai across the road. Tick. Pui was very pleased to see me and my washing bags. Tick. N'Bow picked me up for language school and we had our chit-chat about nothing in particular. Tick. Laughed and learned new words at school that I hope I'll be able to remember. Tick. Then home for another swim and dinner with P'Sak ordering for me. Double tick.

P'Sak looked smart tonight in his uniform. He keeps himself fit and well groomed, with short, cropped black hair and smooth, gleaming skin that looks well cared for. He always has a smile for me.

I love seeing pampered pooches whether here or at home. My fur girls ask for so little, yet provide so much. The loyalty, the company, the laughs at their antics and the cuddles just can't be beaten. There's a sweet girl at Chai Thai restaurant who has a very cute four-month-old puppy called Barn-Barn. A Shih Tzu-Pomeranian cross and she is a little bundle of white fluff, she's allowed to do zoomies around the restaurant when it's quiet. To say she's a pampered pooch is an absolute understatement, but it's so heartwarming to see how loved and cared for she is. She loves KFC chips and is more often being held by someone than walking on her own four paws.

Whenever I go into the restaurant for a meal, I ask if Barn-Barn is home. Today when I asked, the owner told me, 'She have lady period and wear Pampers nappy. She tired and sleeping.' Then he told me his daughter has her period at the same time so it's like having two daughters. They're so open and candid about this topic which is refreshing. Later in the afternoon, I saw little Barn-Barn being held by her mum complete with nappy and a little onesie to provide some privacy for her current condition. There's nothing they wouldn't do for her and she's pampered with a capital P.

When you see how many street dogs there are roaming around in Thailand and the poor conditions they are sometime subjected to, seeing those that are well cared for gives me hope that things are slowly changing. There are now many animal rescue and welfare organisations that sterilise street dogs and also provide veterinary care and new homes and lives for them. Many are rehomed overseas if quarantine rules allow it.

Without a doubt there has been a growing trend for pet ownership in Thailand with nearly 60 per cent of Thai households now having at least one animal, with dogs being the most popular. This never used to be the case and I'm so glad there has been a positive cultural shift.

1 June
Empty Nest / Lottery

Staying in the same place for a while, I'm tuning into the ebb and flow of it. In this season with intermittent rain, there's a noticeable decline in foot and road traffic. Customers are hard to come by and so some of the locals I spoke with this morning are going to Bangkok to make some money and will return in October when the tourists flock back and business picks up. They don't seem to mind. This is the seasonal work cycle for them. It was nice to be able to wish them luck and hope our paths cross again one day.

Mickey was back in her shop after a month in Bangkok, where she was settling her teenage son into rental accommodation as he's starting university. He's a lovely young man, a little shy and on the nervous side. Mickey was concerned about his ability to cope in such a frantic and high-intensity city. She had a tear when we were talking about how she felt not having him with her. I told her we call it the empty-nest syndrome. It seemed to translate well. I'm so often reminded of how similar people are in the emotions and struggles that we face in life. The human condition has no language barriers, something that's easy to forget at times.

I also passed by Pui to collect my washing, but due to the rainy weather it wasn't quite dry.

We got talking about the big lottery prize being drawn tonight with a total of 180 million baht up for grabs. I asked her what she would do if she won. 'Die of shock,' she said. We laughed and I teased her, saying I didn't want her to win because who would do my washing?

It's not uncommon at home to hear people refer to winning lotto as the answer to all life's troubles, and the dream of taking out the big prize or even a small one is certainly shared over here. Thais love the lottery. I've been told that if I'm ever stuck for conversation, I should ask people what their lucky lottery numbers are. I said goodbye to Pui and wished her luck for the draw.

So many locals were up for a chat this afternoon, all curious about where I was going and where I had been and with whom. I'm very happy that our conversations go beyond the basic pleasantries. We're sharing our opinions and snippets of our lives both good and bad, digging a bit deeper, laughing and finding that we agree on all manner of topics. There could even be a little bit of neighbourhood gossip creeping in. Little wonder my walk home takes substantially longer these days.

The friendships that I'm forming here are simple and uncomplicated and there's no overthinking on my part. I've found that it's not always easy to make new friends. Mustering the desire and the time required to get to know another person is often an issue. I think I've created many barriers: the pace of my life and a feeling of guilt that those friends I do have don't get enough attention has made me reluctant to open up with new people and establish something that may well turn out to be not to my liking.

I've noticed I'm more open and willing to share myself with others here. It's making a big difference.

2 June
Kunya Love | Kev From Wollongong | Going It Alone

I had a late lunch at Kunya's today. It felt like ages since I had seen her and it was great to see her and her sister again. They always welcome me with hugs and kisses, which isn't a very Thai thing to do but we can't help it. I find her food so comforting and nothing is ever a bother for her. She's just happy in her open-air restaurant cooking away as people pull up on their motorbikes and order from the curb or come and sit down and take their time. Her menu (I believe there's only one) has long since come apart so you end up with about four laminated pages to read if you're lucky. It's not uncommon for a page to be left behind on another table. She has many foreigners come and eat her food, and she's not only reasonably priced but quick. She doesn't offer delivery through any of the online services, but manages the orders that come her way, customer after customer.

She wears a money belt and stuffs all her cash in it, to the point where she can't zip it up at times. She only charges 60 baht for a meal, it's just too cheap, so we've come to a compromise. I give her 100 baht and that's 60 for food and 20 each for her and her sister as a tip. They think that's fantastic. I at least feel like I've paid somewhat fairly.

I was walking back home when an Australian man sitting out the front of his house caught my eye. I smiled and he asked me where I was from. I've seen this bloke sitting at his cluttered outdoor table before, but never taken much notice. It turns out he's Kevin from Wollongong, New South Wales via the mines in Perth, Western Australia. He's lived here for seven years and is now sixty-three and plans to remain here until he dies.

He bought a bar in an area of Kata that's called Spiderman Soi. If you're wondering why it's called Spiderman Soi, there's a statue of the superhero at the entrance to the laneway. It's a wide lane off the main street with rows of bars and entertainment venues and tourists gather there to find some fun. Kev told me that before Covid there were sixty bar owners and now there are only six. That I believe as I've been for a walk along that laneway and the place feels almost abandoned.

Kev isn't in the best shape. He's slightly unkempt and his teeth are yellow. When we met he was unshaven and in need of a wash. He said he didn't drink every day, just every now and then. However, the cluster of empty beer bottles on the table in front of him told a different story. He cracked open a beer and offered me one. Thanks, but no thanks. He also passed me a bowl of joints and asked me if I wanted one as if it were a bowl of beer nuts.

He told me he was writing a book and that I should drop back in and read a few chapters. He's obviously very happy with his life, but I can't help but think that he's one of so many lonely, lost souls who've dropped out of life and just live for the balmy days, cold beers and maybe the ear of a random female. I can certainly appreciate the appeal of that. I also could be totally wrong.

After an afternoon swim in the pool, I ventured out around six for my Friday night margarita with Mr London and Damo at

Tuk's bar. I wasn't there long before Pui pulled up on the side of the road on her motorbike. She had told me previously that she'd ridden past and seen me there and I encouraged her to stop next time. Pui loves red wine so it didn't take much convincing for her to come and join us.

She had a great time chatting away while Damo played DJ. Her English is great and she can easily hold a conversation and even tell jokes. Pui expects her own bar to be open in two more weeks, and then I'll be torn between turning right to visit Tuk or left to visit Pui. I know, the choices put before me these days are complicated.

After Mr London and Damo left to amp it up and party on at another location in town, Tuk, Pui and I sat talking together for a while longer. Both these women are divorced and raising their children alone. They talked very openly with me about the hardships they face and the hopes they have for their kids' futures. Tuk told me all sorts of stories about what happens late at night when she's at the bar on her own. Dealing with drunk people isn't fun. They're not all happy drunks and some of the stories were astounding and a bit scary. She's one very brave woman. I don't know how she does it. She has a few friends who sometimes keep her company if it's quiet and the staff at the hotel next door look out for her. At 1 a.m. she packs away all the alcohol, blows out the candles, pulls down the awnings, jumps on her motorbike and rides home.

My admiration continues to grow every time I learn more about the strength, courage and determination that Thai women embody while juggling life's responsibilities and raising their children on their own.

3 June

Community / Connections / Solitude

I've now been in Thailand for more than three months and I'm trying not to think of having to leave. I'm beyond grateful I get to call this place home for now. As each day passes, I'm becoming more and more attached to the people and the place and realising what's important in my life. At the moment there are constant reminders as I go about my day that a sense of belonging and community has a huge positive impact on the wellbeing of most humans, wherever you are in the world.

 I seem to be thinking about this a lot. I've questioned why and how in a reasonably short space of time I've been able to make friends here. My own self-analysis tells me it comes down to some very simple acts. I walk everywhere around my local area. People see me regularly and we greet one another all the time, which in itself creates a connection. At home I pretty much drive everywhere and rarely, if ever, will I randomly say hello to a stranger. That might happen if I'm out walking my fur girls and pass others doing the same, but it's not all that common anymore. Here in Thailand, if I'd been riding a motorbike and wearing a helmet every day (let alone driving around in a car), there's no way I would have met half the people I have.

Thai people are curious and make a genuine effort to engage with strangers, not just because they want to sell you something, but because that's who they are. They want to know why you're living in or visiting their country. Most think I'm a teacher and are surprised to learn that I'm a student of their language. And they want to hear this funny *farang* speak. People sit outside in front of their houses. They don't really have backyards. They eat and drink outside, they run their businesses from home, so the opportunity to interact with them is relatively easy. At home I drive into my driveway, use my remote control to open the garage door, drive into the garage, put the garage door down, step out of my car and walk inside. I can do that day in day out and rarely see anyone.

I've been listening to a podcast about social isolation and loneliness and the risk of premature death if this state of being is prolonged. The podcast talked about this being as serious as other well-known health concerns like heart disease and stroke. After the enforced isolation of the Covid pandemic, it seems that many people have been struggling to get back out there and form human connections again. Something that was also mentioned was the way many people now wear earbuds or headphones for a large part of the day. It basically cancels out the world around you. Even when they get home, they wander around their house listening to anything and everything and don't engage with those they live with, hence a deliberate, self-imposed isolation.

The great many benefits of our beloved companion animals and the integral part they play in people's lives didn't surprise me at all when that topic was raised. Our house feels empty and a little lifeless without our girls. When we go away on holidays, we baulk at the idea of dropping them off prematurely. It's the absolute last thing we do before heading for the airport. Returning to an empty house just feels too sad. Before I came away, I had to seriously consider how I would cope without my daily cuddles and chats with Rosie and Jasmine. I speak with them most days when Joe calls. Just being able to see them is the best.

I headed out this evening for a slow walk down to Kata Beach and further along to the northern end. There were so many people out and about enjoying themselves under the silvery moonlight. I sat alone and watched. I've also come to know that solitude doesn't equate to loneliness for me.

4 June

Birthday Colours / Happy Place

It seems to me that winter in Australia is pushing the sun lovers over here. I've noticed lots more familiar accents lately and have new neighbours who are also Australian. These young Australian guys are loud, chronic oversharers who drink beer at 10 a.m. and bomb each other in the pool. We met when I went for my swim this morning and I think they had just arrived home from their night out.

It's the Queen's birthday this weekend and the King was in Phuket today marking the occasion. Here in Thailand, the day on which you were born determines your lucky colour. When it's the King's birthday, you'll see yellow ribbons decorating schools and government buildings, and some people wear that colour out of respect. The colour for the Queen is light blue and that could be seen around the town today. Not wanting to miss out on the fun, I've looked up the day I was born on and it was a Saturday, so purple is said to be my lucky colour. Sunday it's red, Monday it's yellow, Tuesday it's pink, Wednesday it's green for daytime and grey for night (not sure why this particular day is split), Thursday it's orange, Friday it's light blue. This is all based around astrological rules that have been influenced by Hindu mythology and the colour of the God who protects the day.

I set off to do a nice big lap of my local area, calling in to buy a roti from my favourite roti maker. She remarked that I'd not been to see her in a while and asked if I was moving to live in Kata permanently. The thought may have crossed my mind more than once. I told her that if I got to eat her rotis each week that could well encourage me.

I'd love to live here on a more permanent basis, though for now I will treasure Thailand as my happy place, where I can come and reset and imagine what life might look like if I did live here again. When I do let my imagination run wild, I see days at the beach, shopping at the local fresh food market for fruit and snacks, working from home on a part-time basis, going to language school and eating out most nights. Pretty much what I'm doing now. Simple and uncomplicated days.

As I was finishing my walk, I thought I had better get some dinner and stopped to see P'Sak and order takeaway. I hadn't seen him for a while either and he remarked on how clear my Thai language was sounding. He introduced me to his friend whose name is Morning Glory – yep, the mind boggles! As I waited for my fried rice with prawns, they fed me chilled watermelon slices. We chatted and laughed about everything and nothing.

Home I went to eat and have a much-needed cool-off in the pool without a soul around. Just me and the starry night sky.

5 June
Khaow Nieow Sunkyar / N'Bow's Phone

I woke up early this morning with breakfast on my mind. That's not unusual as it's my favourite meal of the day. When I arrived at Khun KK's street stall I ordered *cha yen* and a soft bun laced with coconut, as well as *khaow niew sunkyar*, a blob of sweet sticky rice with a slice of coconut custard on top neatly wrapped into a banana-leaf parcel. There were pleasant conversations with the locals along the way as I walked by. It was a bright sunny morning and I sat outside to enjoy breakfast. N'Bow was soon waiting in the car park ready to drive me to school. He always gets out of his van and greets me with a *wai*. I do the same to him, then he opens the door for me. I knew as soon as I saw him that all wasn't right in his world. Being a reasonably reserved and shy man, he doesn't show much emotion.

Once we got going, I asked him if something was wrong. His mobile phone had stopped working, which meant no one could call to book his services and he had no business. He thought I might have been trying to contact him, which I was, so he came to my hotel early so I wouldn't be worried. I wasn't worried, but now I am on his behalf. While I'm at school he's going in search of a repair shop and I hope he can recover his phone and contacts.

I felt like we went backwards during my language lesson. I'm telling myself that you sometimes need to do that before you can move forward again. We're moving more into grammar and sentence structure and it didn't all make sense and the sentences were long and my brain hurt. I was glad to see 3 p.m. roll around and be able to get back into N'Bow's van.

When I let out a very big sigh, N'Bow asked, 'What's wrong, sister?'

I tried to explain what we'd learnt and could not even do that.

'Just study without too much pressure on yourself,' he said. 'You already know enough.'

Bless this man.

N'Bow, meanwhile, had been able to solve the mystery of his phone suddenly deciding to stop working. It had water in it. He'd found someone to look at it and they'd dried it out for him so he was back in business. He was trying to work out how this could have happened, but with a three-year-old in the house who has a fascination with his phone, maybe he had his answer.

6 June

Time Standing Still / Lured by the Ocean / Nong Nong

Time to rest and recharge and repeat endlessly to myself that I never want this life to end is giving me immense joy. Sometimes I have no idea what happens to my time. It just seems to dissolve. I know my pace has slowed considerably so that might just have something to do with it. Can't time stand still for a while? How can I hold onto these moments for just a little longer? These are the thoughts that occupy my mind these days and I have no answers other than to keep soaking it all up, moment by moment.

I had a full day of alternating between studying Thai and swimming in the pool and I might have even snuck in an afternoon nap outside on my sun lounge. With the intense heat gone, it's now bearable sitting outside for longer stretches. There's something deeply relaxing and nothing nicer than drifting off to sleep when the air is warm and not sweltering.

I eventually strolled down to the beach. The changing nature of the ocean is such a lure. You just never know what you'll get. The tide was way out today, the wind was howling and the sea was angry. The colours were muted and the frothy white waves had been replaced by dark, choppy, windswept ones. It was untidy out there.

I heard my name being called. It was Kunya and her sister coming towards me with their arms outstretched. I've never seen them outside the restaurant. They'd shut the shop and come down to the beach area for a haircut while the customers weren't around. They'd bought some mangosteen (*mungkut*) from the market and insisted on filling my bag up with them. We were all excited to see one another and then they said it was too cold and left. The temperature was about 29 degrees. They've obviously never been to a Tasmanian beach, even in summer. They both had long sleeves on. But this 'cold day' provided me with just the right amount of comfort. I was in my element.

I walked along the newly concreted footpath, not a trip hazard in sight. People were doing yoga on the beach, walking their dogs, playing soccer, running, windsurfing and enjoying the extra expanse of sand with the tide out and the water way off in the distance. Just what you'd expect people to be doing at the beach. It felt cheerful out there.

I'd arranged to meet Mr London for a quick dinner of curry and roti. He's trying to learn a little bit of Thai. We met at Kata on Fire and the staff always enjoy coming over to my table and chatting and checking that I'm using my Thai language, even if they giggle when I do. I'm used to that now and don't even bother to find out if I've said something silly. I think most of the time they're still coming to terms with the fact that there are Thai words coming out of the mouth of this middle-aged Australian woman. Either way, I'm fine with it.

Mr London wanted to practice getting the attention of the waiting staff. You use the word *nong* when you want their attention.

You can repeat it, *nong nong*, if you like. So he started off with one *nong*, then when no one came, progressed to *nong nong*, then just looked at me again as nobody responded. I tried to explain that it's all in the tone, so I said *nong kha* and over they came.

We moved to Khun Tuk's bar and after one margarita and listening to a few tunes I walked home and got straight into the pool before I went to bed. How can I hold onto these moments for just a little bit longer?

7 June
Staying Longer / Love Language

And so, I've decided to extend my stay in my happy place. I chatted with Joe about my decision and he was super excited for me. He's loving my random days and the people I've found along the way so far. It makes him happy to know that I'm content and doing something that's just for me. So while I miss him and our fur girls, it makes it even more special to be here knowing I have their support and love. Forever grateful.

I now have an extra month here. More beach time, more time at school, more Thai food to eat, more time with my new friends and more time just to continue doing this life differently. I've known for a while that I was nowhere near ready to go home. Anyway, I can't possibly leave before Pui has the grand opening of her bar. So much to look forward to and even more to be thankful for. I'm not leaving until the end of July and that makes me beyond happy. Though heaven help me, I also need to extend my visa again!

Today I read an affirmation: *At some point you just have to let go of what you thought should happen and live in what is happening.* Thank you, universe, I will do just that. It reminds me that words of affirmation are also my love language. The author and counsellor Gary Chapman wrote about his theory that everyone has a primary love language, that is a category of behaviour they most immediately respond to or associate affection with. The five love languages are: quality time; physical touch; acts of service; giving and receiving gifts; and words of affirmation.

Joe is getting better with the words of affirmation, but I must say that it's neck and neck with acts of service for me. Take the rubbish out without me asking, put the washing on and then remember to get it out and dry it and I'm one happy girl. See, it's easy when you know what makes your beloved tick, said no one!

I walked around my neighbourhood letting my friends know I was staying on longer. It really only meant something to me as they had no real idea when I was leaving. All the same, they were happy to hear I was going to be around a bit longer. I also took a selfie. I know, she who mocks and is a little bewildered by their prevalence. But I really wanted to be able to remember me on this day. Seeing what true contentment looks like.

I ended my day at the beach, sitting and staring out to sea for ages. Letting my mind wander and feeling a new and unfamiliar level of contentment that's been absent from my life for what seems like forever.

8 June

Neat & Tidy | 'You've Come Alone, Really?'

This morning I rearranged my three piles of clothes and tidied my bathroom. I like neat and tidy. It somehow makes me feel like I've got things together when maybe I don't. I'd started to mix my T-shirt and tank-top pile with my underwear pile and everyone knows you can't have that. A small amount of attention from me was all that was needed to bring some order back and I smiled to myself realising how different my life is when that's my focus for the morning.

At home my morning routine is very different. I like to rise early, sometimes before the sun. Our sunroom faces east and we look out on a vast expanse of water called the Derwent River. I've seen some truly spectacular sunrises in the almost twenty years I've lived there.

If it's not the sunrise getting me up, it's Jasmine and Rosie. They have both Joe and me well trained to let them out for a wee and then it's breakfast time for them followed by what they love the most, a carrot. Sometimes we all go back to bed. If it's a work day, I get on with my breakfast, unpack the dishwasher, shower, dress, do hair and makeup, and if I'm really organised, a load of washing might go on as I walk out the door. Sometimes there will be exercise or watering the garden. That has pretty much been my morning work routine for the last couple of decades. Thankfully I've had no commute. I live a five-minute drive from my workplace. When I lived in Sydney and commuted to work for one and a half hours each way every day, it was hell. I vowed to never do that again.

Once home from work, I try to sit with Joe for a chat, have cuddles with the girls, then it's dinner, clean up and whatever life admin needs to be done. I'm guessing that most who work full-time do something similar and it all starts to feel like a grind and a struggle. Routine is a good thing for me. Otherwise I wouldn't know which way was up, but the monotony can be mind-numbing. Covid has changed this routine somewhat with more working from home, which has been a total revelation for me. I love it.

At the moment when I wake up, I ask myself if I feel like a swim or breakfast first and the day just rolls on from there and it's wonderful. So this morning it was breakfast first. On the way to collect my washing, I chatted with Khun KK while she was making my *cha yen*. Her stall is three doors down from Pui's house. She was curious to know why I've been living here so long and how I manage to live here all by myself. Most Thai women would never contemplate going on holidays alone, never mind living overseas. When I ask why, they say they're afraid, but I'm not sure of what. There's a Thai sentence that basically means 'You've come alone, really?'

It's interesting as these women are fiercely independent in their own daily lives. They're always out and about on their motorbikes and travelling all over town to get stuff done. But for them, the idea of leaving their family and their business, let alone the expense involved, makes going away alone unthinkable.

My Thai friends mostly work seven days a week. That's just what they do. The concept of having time for yourself or putting yourself first is foreign to them. It's not that they don't want to. They just know that generating an income is their priority and taking care of others always takes precedence.

To purposely carve out time for ourselves and do things just for us can still feel a little indulgent but so worth it. For me, feeling comfortable and confident enough to be by myself gives me so many options. Solo travel has always proved to me exactly what I can do and seems to remove any self-doubt that might have been hanging around. It reinforces everything that's possible.

Khun KK also admired the fact I eat Thai food every day. I couldn't be happier eating chicken and rice for breakfast or a little parcel of sweet sticky rice. She finished making my drink. I collected my morning treats. We wished each other a happy day, had a big laugh together and I moved on to get my washing.

Pui opened her glass sliding door when she saw me and said she could hear me from her kitchen window before I arrived. She can't believe how many people say *sawadee kha* to me and how many people know who I am. Nor can I. Just another reason to stay longer if I was looking for one.

I've been building up to walk to Karon Beach, the next beach north from Kata, about five kilometres away. It wasn't so much the distance that had me hesitating, but concerns about combusting along the way. As luck would have it, the coconut ice cream man just happened to be parked at Kata Beach when I arrived. His homemade ice cream is incredibly good, not too sweet, and with an ice cream in hand and plenty of water in my bag I got going.

The walk was great, with so much grabbing my attention along the way: new spots to eat at and parts of the beach that I want to return to. Discovering new parts of this town are always a delight. It was yet another day of enjoying and appreciating the simple pleasures and feeling thankful for the opportunity to be doing this solo.

9 June
Can Do | Lifeguards | Not My Rules

Pui's dream of opening her own bar is coming true and she's beyond excited. For some reason she was waiting for the builder to come back and finish off the bar, but he kept delaying as he'd taken on a big job installing air conditioners. So like any 'can do' woman, Pui went to the second-hand shop and bought a ready-made bar. It really couldn't be more perfect. It's a heavy wooden bar that we both suspect has come from Patong, but we really have no idea. We talked about the option of painting it as it's brown. I think it looks nice the way it is.

The table and chairs, also from the second-hand shop, arrive tomorrow. I'm told she has the fake lawn ready to put down on the floor, the music is good to go and it will be an open invite to all her friends very soon. I'm buying the cocktail mixer set, so every time Pui shakes that mixer she'll think of me. She's such a dynamo. She has the perfect bubbly personality and energy level to pull this off. I see many very interesting and late evenings in her future and the prospect of getting up at 5 a.m. to fry chicken to sell to early risers, as she does now, being less attractive.

I managed a beach swim tonight, the first one in ages, since the sea was calm enough to do so. It didn't last long as the lifeguards rounded us all up and asked us to get out as they were about to finish for the day. Most of us did as asked, knowing they do a great job of looking after us. But one couple wouldn't get out of the water. The lifeguards were blowing their whistles and signalling to them to come in, but they turned their backs. I've noticed the lifeguards now film anyone who refuses to get out of the water, as they've copped criticism surrounding some recent drownings.

The whistle-blowing reached a peak and finally the couple stomped out of the water, gesturing wildly and screaming at the lifeguards. Water was kicked and people started pushing and shoving one another, including the woman. Suddenly a Thai man came running down to the shore ready for a full-on Muay Thai boxing match. This had most beachgoers watching and wondering how far this might all go.

I felt for the Thai lifeguards who were only trying to keep everyone safe. It's not in the nature of Thai people to show this level of anger and aggression in public. Thankfully things calmed down. So many holidaymakers can't swim, let alone identify a rip, yet they're willing to risk their lives each and every day. This is also true at home with many being lured to swim at our beautiful beaches. I really wish tourists would think of others while they're disobeying the rules. When someone has to be rescued – or, worse, drowns – it tarnishes the image of the place, distresses all of us who use the beach and is avoidable. I suppose I just wish people would obey the rules that are in place to protect them when they visit other countries because you'll find the locals do know best.

10 June

Language Breakthrough / Beach Club / Sisterhood

I've continued to do my online Thai lesson with my teacher Kruu Arisa while I've been here. I had a number of questions ready for her today. Lots of 'why is it like this or that?' By the end of the lesson they were all answered. I'm enjoying the learning so much; keeping my mind active with new concepts can only be a good thing. I now prefer that Kruu Arisa only uses Thai script during our lessons and that's a major leap for me. I've always liked having the safety net of the phonetics, but not anymore. I'm claiming this as a breakthrough and I'm pleased that in my fifties I still have the desire and capacity to learn. Long may it last.

After all that study and a tired brain, I was ready to have a shower and head out. I'd organised with Damo a couple of nights ago that we would go to Tann Terrace Beach Club on Karon Beach together. I'd heard many good reports about the place. Beach clubs are common in Phuket, providing a more upmarket vibe for people who have the money to spend. We arrived around 3 p.m. and it was cocktail happy hour. You really couldn't get a better location as it's directly on the beach. There are sun beds, lounges and bean bags on the sand, a DJ playing great music and often a saxophone player later in the evening. If you don't feel like swimming in the ocean, there's a pool to cool off in.

Damo and I settled in and chatted away. It's his first time living in Thailand and our conversation often revolves around him trying to understand the way the people and place work. Time went quickly and just as the sun was about to set along came a group of six women. Obviously this wasn't their first stop of the evening as the mood was very merry. We all said hello as they sat across from us on the sun lounges. They were Australians celebrating a hens night post-wedding, which is a novel approach.

There were endless rounds of cocktails coming to their table and they told us all about the wedding, which had taken place a couple of days beforehand. At 7 p.m. there was a fire show on the beach. This is very much a drawcard and the guys performing are clever and brave, with long, flaming fire sticks that they throw in the air and twirl around. They came in among the crowd to dance around the partygoers, hoping to earn a little more in tips. I had visions of a spark landing in my fluffy hair so I declined the offer of a one-on-one fire dance.

Damo and I carried on talking and at times he went over to the hens' table to mingle. It's that kind of atmosphere at the beach club where people wander around, down to the beach and back to their table. The gaggle of gals through their blur of cocktail consumption had assumed that Damo and I were a couple and became very concerned that he was neglecting me and not paying me enough attention. I reassured them that we weren't a couple and he wasn't neglecting me. It didn't seem to matter what I said, though. The sisterhood closed ranks and, before he knew it, they'd frozen him out of their conversations. He was perplexed at what he'd done wrong.

The music eventually distracted them again. As two of them stepped up on the podium close to the swimming pool to dance, one of the gals thought it might be funny to charge forward and tackle them into the water. Phones, handbags and spaghetti straps all sodden. Stunned, wet and bedraggled, they didn't stay much longer. Pity really, as it was just starting to get entertaining.

Just another random encounter. This place continues to surprise me.

11 June
Supermarket Visit / Fairy Lights

I left my curtains partly opened so the sun streaming into my room woke me up. I was in no rush to get up, then again I never am, so I lay there and contemplated my day. I always have a supermarket visit on my list of things to do when I'm in another country. Seems odd as I do my level best to avoid them at home, but in other countries I find them fascinating. I think they can tell you so much about the people that live there by what's on offer. My walk today purposely took me in the direction of a large supermarket called Makro, not one we have in Australia. It was a good couple of kilometres away.

With so many micro-food businesses here, I think this is where they must buy their supplies if they can't get them at the market. Everything was in bulk and there were so many items I would've loved to have bought, knowing I needed none of them. Also knowing my previous form with making crazy and unnecessary impulse food purchases, I had to have a stern word with myself once I was inside.

I started off in the fruit and vegetable section among the refrigerated cabinets to cool off. I particularly liked the huge variety of leafy green vegetables like morning glory, bok choy, Chinese cabbage, big bunches of fragrant Thai basil and coriander. All the vegetables looked freshly picked. Bundles of taut lemongrass and dark green kaffir lime leaves in bulk. I can only buy one stick of lemongrass at a time at home as it's hard to grow and expensive and the kaffir lime leaves I have access to are frozen and there are never more than about six leaves per packet.

I was drawn to the mushroom cabinet: there were bags and bags full of straw, white jelly fungus, shiitake mushrooms and other varieties I'd never seen before. Mushrooms are commonly used in soup and stir-fries here. We are only starting to get this sort of variety at home. The fresh baby corn caught my eye. I'd only ever seen it coming out of a can. I wandered up and down those aisles wondering how I could get five litres of coconut milk home to Australia and then asked myself why? Trays stacked twenty high with fresh eggs. I also noticed a few things from home like cheese and beef, and as expected they were expensive.

I'm not sure how long I was in there for. This is something I could never do with Joe tagging along. He doesn't share my interest in seeing new and different foods and supermarkets are a no-go zone for him at the best of times. It was dark by the time I left. I was so proud of myself that I was only tempted by the bulk M&M's!

I walked back home via Kunya's restaurant as after seeing all that food I was now hungry. Just as I was finishing my chicken garlic, Pui pulled up on the side of the road to tell me excitedly that her bar was having its grand opening in two days. I told her I'd swing by on my way home and off she went again. I did my best to go directly there. But tonight there were plenty of my sweet friends sitting outside, so I stopped to chat. Feels like a warm hug from those that I've now become so familiar with.

When I eventually arrived at Pui's, the bar tables and stools were in place on her veranda, and all the alcohol on shelves behind the bar. Menus are being printed and tomorrow new lighting will be installed and a few more finishing touches to make it just so.

She had strings of fairy lights strung around the bar and through the miniature bamboo plants she has in pots that mark the entrance. Thais do have a great love of the dreaminess of fairy lights, I've noticed. No need for a celebration of any kind for them to appear, they're up all year. I'm very partial to the festive feel of the little bud lights as well. We have them strung from tree to tree throughout our garden in the lead-up to Christmas and they are always jolly and bright.

I told Pui how proud she should be bringing this whole venture together by herself, including moving the big heavy pot plants and other clunky things around today. She told me she cried and laughed at the same time as she struggled alone, feeling tired but also satisfied that nothing could beat her. What a tenacious woman. I can't wait for Tuesday to celebrate with her.

12 June

Shoulder Knots | Cold Red Wine | Funny & Sexy

I've been very cautious about going for another Thai massage since my first one that left me feeling rather beaten up. But my shoulder felt like it needed an elbow in it. I made my way down to the massage salon to see if this was possible. I was allocated one of the older Thai ladies and she wasn't mucking around. There was no small talk as I was pummelled and kneaded. She was up on the table and on my back and into every single knot in no time. It's actually very skilful how they climb up on the table, then they use their elbows and fingers to dig and stretch every sore spot out of your body.

It's two people per massage room where I go and I was first in the room. The rooms have a Thai fabric curtain down the middle that at least gives you a certain amount of privacy in your nakedness. Maybe ten minutes into my massage a Japanese man came in and said, 'No oil, I don't like the oil.' His accent gave him away as being Japanese. I'm not sure a dry massage would be the same, and he soon relented after being reassured it was odourless. He proceeded to moan and groan in agony as his therapist got to work. At one point, she had to ask if he was okay and I'm thinking *could he just keep his noises to himself?* I mean, we're all having similar treatments but enough with the noises. It took everything I had not to burst out laughing at times. At least it diverted my attention from my own pain.

My therapist, meanwhile, found the knot in my shoulder and worked it until it was no more. At one point I had my arm up around the back of my neck and wasn't sure how that might all turn out. I'm still deciding if I feel better for having had it done. My shoulder will no doubt tell me tomorrow.

I pulled myself off the massage table, got into my bikini and headed off to the beach for a swim. I was in and out in a flash as I could see the water wasn't clean today. Such a pity. I could see bits of rubbish floating around. Thankfully this doesn't happen often. The shuttle bus from my hotel had pulled up as I reached the top of the beach steps. I rarely use this, preferring to walk, but this time I was happy to jump in the back of the truck (*song tow*) with bench seats on either side and off we went. I was in my shower with the loofah and shower gel in no time, scrubbing away, just pleased I hadn't swallowed any water today.

In the evening, after getting my mango and pineapple smoothie from Mickey, I went to Pui's. She was bathing in the glory of her bar on her own in anticipation of it opening tomorrow night. She had a red wine in hand and a big grin on her face. She said she was treating herself to a couple of glasses of wine and soon poured herself another out of a cask in the fridge. She's not fussy, so long as it's red and cold she's happy. There will be cocktails for 99 baht tomorrow as an opening night special. I have a feeling it might be standing room only in this little bar made with love and trading on such high hopes.

She told me again how pleased she is with everything she

has created but she didn't need to, I could tell. Pui thinks it has cost her 60,000 baht to set up. That's A$2,500 and you have yourself a business on your front veranda. You can't beat the will to work and the drive to earn money here. People's positive attitude and tenacity is remarkable.

Pui really has such a sense of fun about her. We often laugh together even when we have no idea what we are laughing about. Before I left she told me that she had a male customer come to buy cannabis from her. After explaining the different mixes and their effects to him, she'd said, 'If you want one that's funny and sexy, then you'll have to smoke me.' She had herself in stitches laughing when she told me.

13 – 14 June

40,443 words | 80% Thai, 20% Australian | Opening Night

When I spoke to Joe today, he told me that I'd written 40,443 words in little Insta squares since departing home in February. Capturing my days through my photos and words has become a way to ensure I'll always remember my time here. Who knew I'd have so much to say and that others would want to read it? I've loved reading the comments left by my friends. It surprises me no end how much others have enjoyed reading about my adventures and were so quickly swept up in how I was doing life differently. Joe has been copying my words from Insta into a document for me so that I have it when I get home, very kind of him. I reread what I wrote the day I departed and I could so easily sense my excitement for what was to come. I knew nothing about how this time away would unfold. I just knew I was open to and up for all that was to come my way. That's where my expectations ended.

    I can honestly say that in all my wildest dreams I could never have imagined the people I've been lucky to meet, the places I've seen, the food I've eaten and the kindest hearts that have made me feel so welcome and helped me live so happily here. Just as I wasn't aware how much I needed this break, maybe I wasn't game to let myself contemplate what my time could be like here, protecting myself should I feel underwhelmed, disappointed or if I wasn't happy. I don't have the answer and I'm not about to go looking for it, but I really could not have wished for more.

When I lived here as an exchange student, my school friends told me that I was born in the wrong country and that I was 80 per cent Thai and 20 per cent Australian. Funnily enough, one of Pui's friends has told me the same thing. Seems some things never change and that's fine by me.

I wish I had a megaphone so I could walk up the street towards Pui's bar and announce the grand opening to all. It was with a sense of excitement and joy, *sans* megaphone, that I set off to join Pui and celebrate her opening night. She had suggested we arrive after 6 p.m. as it would be slightly cooler, so that's what we did. I met Damo there as he's also now become friends with Pui.

Standing behind her bar, Pui was beaming. She was freshly showered, her skin gleaming, with her hair pulled back in a ponytail with a cream-coloured headband on. She'd chosen a cute floral sundress to wear and she had her lipstick on for the occasion. This was a big deal for her. Her big proud smile stayed with her all night.

My cocktail, a mojito, was the first one made, full of fresh limes, mint and ice. Pui had a glass of red wine and we raised our glasses, knowing what it took to make this all happen. The drinks were flowing, she was surrounded by her friends, bowls of peanuts and snacks were on top of the bar and the tunes were playing loudly.

Some of her laundry customers, all foreigners, came to collect their washing, but after a small amount of coaxing they stayed for a drink. One works in a nightclub in Patong, one works in forestry conservation and one manages a hotel just down the road.

Pui's fireman friend Pong was also there with his work colleague. They were on duty so too bad if your house was burning down, they had cocktails to drink. There were a handful of her Thai friends who run a small hotel across the street and a massage salon just up the road. It really was quite the gathering. I suppose it wouldn't be a true opening night without a signature cocktail, which was delicious, Damo dancing on the bar and the music pumping out so the whole street could enjoy it.

Pui deserves every success and I couldn't be happier for my sweet determined friend. Who would've thought I'd randomly drop my washing off to this lady – when there are any number of laundry places along the street – and we'd become friends? We both believe it was meant to be.

I gave her a little kangaroo friend to keep at her bar and remind her of me once I leave. I've assured her that this roo will keep a very close eye on her until I return next year. My roo settled in nicely among the marijuana jars.

The drinks, conversation and laughter flowed well into the night and I definitely wasn't the last to leave.

Next day, I needed to recover. I slept late and spent the day just pottering around and trying to do some Thai language homework – perhaps a bit too ambitious, all things considered. I opted not to walk up and get lunch from one of my favourite restaurants, not because I couldn't but because I'm still slightly obsessed with seeing how long it takes from placing my order until a motorcycle zooms up the long driveway of my hotel and it's in my hands. Fifteen minutes again today. It's the little things that count.

In the evening, lying on my bed in the cool of the air conditioning and listening to a podcast, I got a text message from Pui. 'Mel, can you come to my bar? I need to practice making cocktails. Free for you.'

So off I went, all in the name of work experience for Pui. She makes a mean mojito, and by 'mean', I mean generous. For me, it's all in the abundance of the limes. When I arrived, Pui told me she wanted to practice making ten different cocktails. Knowing I didn't have anywhere near the capacity for ten, I encouraged her to call a few other friends to help. She did a great job, although at one point she did say she might change to a coffee shop as shaking that cocktail shaker was harder than she realised.

We reminisced about last night and recounted a few of the funnier moments together. I so hope the happiness that I see all over Pui's face remains for a very long time.

15 June

Blue Bus | Pineapple Biscuits | Hot Dusty Mess

I've been wanting to catch the open-air blue bus for a while. For some reason I was awake this morning at 4 a.m. looking up the timetable. Seems today was the day to take myself on an adventure. Thankfully I did eventually go back to sleep until 9 a.m. These buses cost 40 baht (A$1.80) and travel all over the island, mostly transporting tourists who aren't in a rush and prefer the scenic route. The bus from Kata goes backwards and forwards to Old Phuket Town every half hour. I was running a bit late and the bus had just departed, but the speed these buses travel at meant I easily caught up to it. We hardly got out of first gear going to Karon Beach and then to the shopping mall Central. We seemed to pick up pace, but only ever so slightly, as we got closer to Old Phuket Town.

If N'Bow was driving, this trip would take about forty minutes, but the slow-burn scenic bus takes about an hour and fifteen minutes, with the joy of 86 per cent humidity engulfing you, sweat rolling down the back of your legs and a nice dusty facial included. None of this bothered me. There was a steady stream of pick-ups and drop-offs and like most I really enjoyed the ride. There was a fun factor attached to this charming method of local transport.

Apart from wanting to soak up the atmosphere of the bus, I was on a mission to go back and eat the noodles in Old Phuket Town that I had enjoyed with Georgia. As luck would have it, the bus dropped me right at the door of Ko Yoon Phuket Noodle. I walked in and went to the back of the shop and sat in exactly the same seat as before. I wanted to try the dry noodles this time so I could add my own soup and seasonings to them. In no time my bowl of noodles was placed in front of me and the owner insisted on making sure I knew how to season them to my liking, explaining the small pots of condiments in the middle of the table. My initial mouthful told me they were perfect just as they were and I didn't feel the need to add a single thing. '*Aroy laeow*,' I said. 'Already delicious'.

Your eyes don't know where to settle in this shop, there's just so much to take in. It's cluttered and unkempt, which gives it personality and interest. I don't suppose they would have time to dust and tidy; they're too busy making a living. Today the online orders were keeping them very well occupied. The owner of the shop was calling out the orders as they arrived via his phone. They were no sooner ready than a motorbike pulled up, noodles and soup were popped in the delivery box attached to the back of the bike and off they went.

I sat for a while and watched the way this restaurant ran. No one got stressed when the orders piled up. They just kept going at their own steady pace, knowing they would get to them all in good time. The people coming in to eat ranged from local office workers to tourists to Thais who probably lived around the neighbourhood, and this was part of their daily routine.

I thought it was time that I gave my table to someone else, so I said my goodbyes and told them I'd be back, to which they responded, 'You'd be very welcome.'

As I stepped out onto the streets of Old Phuket Town, I made an arbitrary choice to turn right. There's an eclectic mix of shops in this area selling everything from fabric to biscuits to herbal medicines to hardware supplies. The Phuket Old Town Fresh Market provides a focal point for people and the Chinese influence is clearly visible everywhere. It seems that many of the shops have been owned by the same families for generations judging by the age and condition of the buildings and those sitting at the front of the shops watching the world go by.

Heading down a few of the grotty narrow laneways, I stopped off at a shop run by an elderly Thai lady to buy some of my favourite pineapple jam biscuits. We had an interesting chat about these iconic Thai treats. They've been around for years and years, and I remember when I first came here we'd be given them as an after-school snack. I'm not sure what I was thinking, but I ended up with a large tin of them, maybe three kilogram's worth. I also bought a *cha yen* and a few bottles of ice-cold water for the trip home. As the bus wasn't due to leave for another twenty minutes, I went into the nearby 7-Eleven for nothing other than the chance to feel cool while waiting.

People slowly filled the bus and we were on our way. I was pleased to see that Thai people also use the bus as it's such a cheap way for them to move around. Some had crates of fruit that they'd bought from the market wedged between their feet. I assumed they were taking this fruit back to their own shops to sell.

The return trip was quick. I was a hot, dusty mess by the time the bus arrived back in Kata and my focus was on a dip in my pool. I'd enjoyed my ride. I'd seen new places and travelled through many backstreet areas I'd probably otherwise not have visited. Getting off the main roads, almost going cross-country, can be a good move sometimes. However, N'Bow with his comfy air-conditioned van has absolutely nothing to worry about.

16 June
No Red Flags / Curvy Gal / Nobody Cares

I had thought the best beach days for me might be over with the sea conditions changing so dramatically and swimming almost impossible, but I was wrong. Today the beachy goodness was in overdrive. A sense of calm had returned. The water was crystal clear again and the red flags were packed away. As I had nowhere in particular to be, it made perfect sense to spend my time at the beach, in and out of the water. With plenty of waves to float on or duck under it was a simple, soul-filling way to spend a day. While I was out in the ocean floating on my back, I actually felt more like me than I can remember feeling in a very long time. Gosh, it feels good. I feel full of joy, joyful.

    I'm what's called a curvy gal these days. The way we women see our bodies, how we talk about them, what we call them and how others are encouraged to refer to them has changed. I'm all for it. In Thailand they've never had a problem with people who are curvy. They very much expect most foreigners to be bigger than them. To be fat (*oowan*) is seen by many Thais as a sign of wealth, a sign you have enough money to feed yourself well. They see it as though you can afford to eat things like steak and hamburgers and pizza and dairy foods, which are all expensive here, nothing to do with genetics, body structure, lifestyle or that we're all just different. They will freely tell you that you're fat, not in a critical or demeaning way, but because they see you as strong and robust and fortunate to be this way.

I have an entry in the friendship book that I was given back in 1989 from all my school buddies that says: *The first time I met you, I thinked (sic) that you look like westerner much the same. When I had already know (sic) you it made me know that you are a good girl, you look like Thai although you are fat.* And that was when I was at my thinnest!

I've never seen myself as someone who could or should wear a bikini, but this trip I only packed bikinis. I was bored of my own constant negative mental chatter that has determined what I can wear to the beach for such a long time. The shame, guilt and self-loathing had to stop. If I can't wear what I feel most comfortable in at the age of fifty-two, when on earth will I be able to do it? This body of mine has carried me through the good and the bad and it's healthy, resilient and reliable, and that in itself is a blessing.

I now wear a bikini every day and enjoy wearing it. This is such an affirming shift for me. I rotate through the three sets I have and chop and change to suit my mood or depending on which one is dry. I've got some colourful sarongs that I can tie in many different ways, which are also fun to wear. I've got my rashie to wear when I swim to save my skin from burning. Finally, I'm appreciating this body that has done so much for and with me. The time for feeling comfortable and confident in what I'm wearing on the beach has arrived for me.

Funnily enough, the biggest revelation of all is that nobody else cares what you wear on the beach. They're not looking at your back rolls, your squishy cake belly in my case or your lack of thigh gap.

Everyone is too busy soaking up the perfect swimming conditions, allowing themselves to feel the warmth of the sun, hopefully feeling comfortable and relaxed and mostly looking at their phones to bother with you. And if they're Thai, they're thinking how strong you are and also how lucky you are to eat all that delicious food, which is absolutely true.

17 June

Bar Signage | United Nations | Cricket

Every single day there's something new added to Pui's bar and today it was all about signage. Earlier in the week, she'd asked my opinion on her logo. We worked on the graphics together. I suggested a few changes to help it look a little less cluttered and we changed the size of the '&' so it was the least dominant word on the sign. Pui's bar is named after her son Win Win. So her sign is round with a black background imprinted with a large cannabis leaf and a few images of cocktails and the words, 'Win Win Bar & Cannabis'. I can't wait to see it tonight when it's turned on and shining brightly.

I'd also suggested a blackboard might be good to welcome her customers and let them know she is open for business. She had that ready to go and had written on it. I asked if I could help her with her English and spelling, and she happily agreed. It's nice being able to help, even if it's just spelling the word 'cocktail' correctly, although there's something very charming about the way Thais use the English language.

I spent happy hour – 5 p.m. to 7 p.m. – at Pui's cosy new bar with Damo, enjoying a few cocktails, with much conversation and plenty of good tunes being played. It was soon time for some dinner in the main street of Kata and Sports Bar seemed like a good option.

A crowd of all sorts was there as they had come to watch cricket. Australia playing England in the Ashes. I ordered pizza, Damo a burger. We were sitting up at the bar to eat, directly in front of the big screen. It wasn't long before a New Zealand guy pulled up a stool and wanted to talk about the Ashes. Then another bloke from Australia joined in. A little later, a man from Sri Lanka joined in and then a couple from Russia were interested to learn about this strange game called cricket. To add to our United Nations, an American guy came in alone. He'd been forced out of his hotel due to a blackout and he also wanted to know about the rules of the game.

The G&Ts started to flow freely and the interest in and curiosity about this weird game of cricket grew. Damo had quite the class to teach. The game had long ended when we were asked to leave as the staff packed up around us, ready to close for the night.

That wasn't a deterrent for this motley bunch of new friends who spilled out into Spiderman Soi and continued to party into the wee hours. The bars in this lane only get busy after midnight. I had to be up early for another visa run to Malaysia, so I had one more drink and left them all to each other and thanked them for such an entertaining and unpredictable night. All thanks to the game of cricket.

18 June
Kuala Lumpur | Guilty Drug Mule

In my mind I thought I could just do a nice easy day trip to renew my visa. Quick flight from Phuket to Kuala Lumpur, in and out of Malaysia and all would be fine. I had three hours between arrival in Kuala Lumpur and departure back to Phuket. I took my laptop knowing I'd have time to kill, and saw myself browsing the shops and having a leisurely lunch.

N'Bow dropped me off at the airport and I told him I'd see him again in a few easy hours when he returned to collect me. Arriving in Kuala Lumpur, I discovered I needed to change terminals as the airline I flew in on was different to the one I was flying out on. What I didn't know was that these terminals were miles apart. I needed to take a train for fifteen minutes and I needed a ticket for that train, but first I needed to clear immigration and customs. The queue was long and moving incredibly slowly. To enter the next airport terminal, I had to do that all over again and my panic button was being pressed very hard by this stage.

Again standing in what felt like the longest, slowest-moving line ever, I waited to clear immigration and security. I was sure that I'd missed my flight. The departure board said my flight had closed. I called Joe and had him on standby to book me another flight. By this stage I was sweating like a guilty drug mule and wondering why everyone was moving and walking so slowly. It was like everything had been switched into slow-motion mode and every minute was crucial.

When I finally got through security, I had to resist the urge to bolt. I walked at a pace that didn't help the heat my body was already emitting. I stepped over people sitting on the floor and navigated around big groups as I struggled to run-walk to get to my gate. To my absolute surprise, my gate was still open. I couldn't believe my luck. I've never been so grateful for a late-departing flight. My phone was scanned and down that airbridge I limped. The flight was so empty I had a row to myself. I slumped into my seat and stared into the back of the seat in front, vowing to never do that again. Oh boy, I haven't felt stress like that in a very long time.

On my arrival back in Phuket, I spoke to the Thai official stamping my passport because the thought of going through the pain of an incorrect stamp again, let alone another trip to Malaysia, was more than I could cope with.

N'Bow was outside the airport waiting for me. My adrenaline levels had dropped, but gosh I felt immense relief getting into his van and reliving my adventures with him.

19 June

Grounded / Queen of Durian / Golden Sun

After the excitement of yesterday, I was ready for a nice quiet day. I was still feeling somewhat drained. I could have booked another flight and solved my dilemma, but sometimes I think that my ability to do all that under pressure isn't what it used to be. I got out of bed and jumped in the pool to reset myself. I was back at Chai Thai for my lunch of pad Thai and a pineapple smoothie with a pink orchid on the side of the glass before N'Bow came to collect me and I was off to school. That level of familiarity grounded me and finally I began to feel settled again.

On the way home from school, I asked N'Bow to drop me off at Mickey's shop as I felt like one of her smoothies before going back to my room. I could smell the durian as soon as I got out of the van. Mickey is the Queen of Durian. She's so proud of the durian she's now selling as it's all grown on her farm. She has nurtured these fruits and kept a watchful eye on them, waiting patiently for them to ripen, and now it's time to reap the rewards. She showed me via a video on her phone how hard they are to pick. Picture very small people who weigh nothing climbing bamboo ladders leaning against very tall trees. They cut the fruit off with a sharp knife, leaving a long tail of about four centimetres to use as a handle because the fruit is covered in spikes and can weigh between one and three kilograms. It needs to be handled with great care, nothing like picking apples or berries.

Mickey was in the process of cutting some up and putting it in the fridge. She excitedly told me it's selling so well. She's able to get top dollar for her fruit as she markets it as organic. She again offered me a piece to eat, but I just can't get past the smell. I may be '80 per cent Thai', but I'm still very happy to stick with my pineapple and passionfruit smoothies. I'd finally got my act together and made Mickey her sign to explain why the honey she sells is so special and she's thrilled. It's the simple things, isn't it?

Mickey's eldest daughter is back from Bangkok and that's also putting a huge smile on her face. Her daughter is helping her out in the shop, displaying fruit, making smoothies and finding other money-making products to sell. This afternoon she was making little bags of sweets. They're never idle here, and Mickey is never short of great ideas. She's a smart, creative businesswoman and having her family help her in the business clearly makes her happy.

To round out my day, I headed to the beach to catch the sunset. Staring at the golden ball slowly sinking below the distant horizon, leaving behind a magnificent burnt-orange glow, is really all I need to know I'm where I need to be.

20 June

Renewed Buzz | Life Appointments | Blank Pages

Kata suddenly has its high-season vibe back as there's a surfing competition coming up. On Friday, Saturday and Sunday the place will be a buzzing hive of activity. The festival crew are bumping in to set up performance stages, market stalls and the beach platform from where you'll get the best view of the surfing. Restaurants are humming, the streets feel busy with the chaos of motorcycles and cars making crossing the street a bit tricky again. People are out and about and the surfing competitors are fairly easy to spot. The atmosphere is lively and this renewed excitement in the town seems to have come at the right time after a very quiet period.

When I wasn't wandering around town, I was sitting by my pool, reading and listening to music, and once again thinking about how liberating it is living without plans, lists, schedules, routines, appointments and commitments to others. It gives you a freedom that most of us never even contemplate, let alone experience in life. I didn't know this state of being was even possible. It's not lost on me how this has come to be as I'm now so regularly reflecting on the satisfaction of doing life differently.

I started thinking about what normally fills my days and all the appointments I have just to keep me healthy: skin-cancer checks; mammograms; GP visits; dental; psychologist; optometrist and on it goes. Then you factor in your appointments with yourself to exercise, meditate and do things that you enjoy and not forgetting the layer of general life admin. Little wonder so many of us feel overwhelmed just running our own lives. I've decided when I go home to see if I can cull a few appointments. It reminds me how hardwired we are to engage in the 'doing' rather than the 'being' and how much of a conscious effort I need to make to change this. Having a break from my usual life routine has given me back not only time, but also mental space, and creating space can only ever be a good thing.

I always have a to-*do* list and rarely just sit around at home with nothing to *do*. There's always something I think I should be *doing* or I think needs *doing* whether it does or not. From week to week my diary is full of demands, and there's nothing that I love more than to turn the page for a new week and see it empty. Letting the day unfold and just doing what comes to mind is something I can't ever remember experiencing. Freeing up my life and handing my day over to the unknown feels sensational. I wonder how different my diary will look once I get home. Maximum blank pages might be my goal.

The beach was filled with even more Chinese girls at sunset trying to get the perfect shot of themselves in flimsy, long-flowing evening gowns dragging along in the water. Some had even hired professional photographers with all the fancy equipment to ensure that perfect shot was caprtured. Maybe I've missed the memo?

21 June

Antarctic Midwinter | 38 Degrees | Community

I woke up this morning knowing my original travel plans had me arriving home in Hobart, Tasmania tonight. That thought alone got me up and into the pool in a flash and then out to Khun KK to get the day started with my *cha yen* and sticky rice with sweet fried pork for breakfast. I'm still so not ready for this to be over.

What I'd normally be doing at this time of year is celebrating Antarctic Midwinter at my workplace. Tasmania is the southernmost state in Australia and Hobart the gateway to Antarctica for other nations that also have stations down there, including the French and Chinese. When the shortest and darkest day of the year has been reached and there's a move towards the light and sun returning, it's a cause for celebration. It can mentally be a much-anticipated milestone for those expeditioners wintering down on our Australian stations. They've made it through the tough dark days. We would often refer to it as Antarctic Christmas as it's celebrated with feasting and frivolity both in Antarctica and also in Hobart.

We would have a day of fun for those of us who supported the stations from Hobart. Our day started with a sombre memorial service for those who'd lost their lives in Antarctica while part of the Australian Antarctic Program. There's a memorial rock in the grounds of our office buildings and a plaque attached acknowledging each person. A wreath is laid in remembrance.

For the brave (some would say foolhardy) amongst us, there was a quick dip in the icy waters of the River Derwent followed by mulled wine and chocolate. These are on offer to those swimming when they run back to shore, teeth chattering, looking for the warmth of their towel.

A sit-down lunch for more than 150 Hobart-based staff allowed us to mingle socially with our colleagues and to see and speak with our teammates on station via video conference. Hearing about their planned activities and gourmet food offerings was always the highlight of my day. Much time and effort was put into making a midwinter video by each station. The competition between stations is fierce and I've seen many hysterically funny videos, often a result of long periods of isolation and days of darkness. It was a unique and memorable day for many of us. There's nothing I miss about it, which can be interpreted in so many ways.

Instead, here I am walking around in 38-degree heat and bright sunshine, chatting to those in my new community, the waiting staff and Barn-Barn at Chai Thai, and Jimmy from the cooking school who was out doing his daily exercise. N'Bow drove past and gave me a cute beep and I managed a wave before he was too far away. P'Sak and Morning Glory were sitting out the front of their restaurant and, as always, up for some banter and laughs, wanting to know where I was going. I had a few icy cold G&Ts down by the beach and watched a constant stream of parasailers being towed in and out by speedboat as the sun set behind them.

My midwinter's day this year ended with a lovely big cuddle and lots of pats with BeBo, who was the closest resemblance to anything remotely cold climate, being an Alaskan Malamute.

22 June

Me / Sitting on the Sand

I've been at the beach a lot these last few days and as ever found it incredibly hard to leave tonight. I seem to be in my own little contented bubble there and time stands still. It was so beautiful just sitting on the sand. I was doing nothing more than watching everything going on around me and that was enough. The surfing comp starts tomorrow and there are coloured flags fluttering on tall bamboo poles everywhere and coloured bud lights strung among the palm trees. The food stalls were busy with preparations to feed the expected crowd. There's an open invitation for everyone to come and join in the festival. It will be *sanook* here, that I can tell already.

I waited until it was dark and walked up the beach. There were people having dinner picnics, families sitting around in large groups on large bamboo mats, chatting and drinking, kids running up and down the beach and dancing to music.

The air was humid and still, which made the temperature balmy and comfortable. It was yet another one of those pinch-me moments when I wondered how on earth I got so lucky to live here. Yet it wasn't really luck. I made it happen. I booked in my leave from work, booked the airline ticket and accommodation and sorted out my life, but, most of all, I think I finally chose me.

I chose me so I could connect with my authentic self again. I chose me so I could relearn and reacquaint myself with what my needs and wants are. I chose me so I would then have more love and compassion to share with others. I chose me as I matter too. I chose me to give me time to create and rebuild the capacity in my life that has been missing. I chose me as it was time to heal.

I chose me as the time had finally come to release all that I had been holding that was really not mine to hold.

23 June

No Power / Durian Gone Viral

I walked up to drop off my washing this morning and see how Pui was feeling. I'd spoken to her yesterday and she had been so exhausted she decided to close for one night. She told me she can't do a full day of laundry work and then open her bar until midnight. Just the thought of that leaves me feeling fatigued. She said to me, 'I have no power, Mel.'

Oh, I know that feeling, my friend. Some days my batteries are nowhere near fully charged and sleep is the only solution. I encouraged her to pull back and get some help from friends before she burns herself out. Her work ethic is outstanding, but that won't help her should she grind herself into the ground with exhaustion.

This conversation reminded me of a day a couple of years ago when I sat in front of my GP explaining to her how I was feeling after supporting Joe through another very stressful period. I knew I was absolutely spent in every way and reeled off how I was feeling through tears. Without hesitation, she said, 'You're burnt out, Mel. It's little wonder with the load you're carrying in life.'

At the time I thought *but other people get burnt out, not me.* I just kept stuffing everything in because, if I stopped, then what? Reflecting on that conversation now, I realise that of course I was burnt out. I'd become used to operating with incredibly high levels of stress for long periods. It was my normal way of being. It didn't take much to trigger or upset me as my emotions were very close to the surface. Experience tells me it's really difficult to reenergise yourself when you just carry on with life, but it's even harder to quarantine yourself from life. More sleep and an awareness that I'm running on empty seem to work best for me.

I popped in to see Mickey. She has a cold so she's not going so well. Having a cold when it's hot isn't much fun. Her shop was absolutely packed with Chinese people buying her durian. They can't seem to get enough of it and she helps them pick the perfect one from her well-stocked shelves. It seems her little shop may have gone viral on a Chinese tourist website. It's now known as *the place* to get the best durian in Phuket. She told me the other day a whole busload of Chinese tourists pulled up and piled into her tiny shop that barely has space for four or five people. I would have loved to see that. She can hardly keep up with supply, but she knows only too well that she needs to make the most of this seasonal bonanza. Again, she offered me some durian to try, like I was the only one missing out on all the fun.

The streets were jam-packed for the surfing festival this afternoon. People were parking at my hotel and walking the ten minutes down to the beach. The main street was crammed with motorbikes parked side by side without a space left. The food stalls were pumping out incredible offerings, so many smells wafting around that I found it hard to choose. In the end I simply opted for my favourite coconut ice cream served inside a freshly opened coconut. I bobbed around out in the ocean for ages, content as I could ever imagine being, all on my own but not one bit lonely.

My enjoyment of this solitude hasn't necessarily come as a surprise. The longer it's just me, the more I feel at ease. I'm having great conversations with myself a fair bit, too.

24 June
Early Waves | 50% Ocean Time | Piercing

I was up and out early this morning and even missed my morning pool swim, heading straight for the beach. Surfers were out in full force when I arrived, but I'm not sure the waves got the message that there was a competition on. I sat on the sand and watched, but all I saw was surfers lying on their long boards waiting for the next wave. The waiting game got old quickly for me. Instead, I got myself into the water which was much more fun. Soft foamy waves, not great for surfing but excellent for floating around on without a care in the world.

I could hear an Australian voice close by. It was a man saying to his son that he planned to spend 50 per cent of their holiday in the ocean. Now there's a very achievable and worthy holiday goal if ever I've heard one. It must have been the first swim of their holiday as the whole family was taken with the warmth of the water. We all know how good that first swim is when you've been hanging out for your beach holiday.

Again I delayed leaving the water, but once I did I sat and listened to the commentary from the surf comp. There were a couple of cheers from the small crowd, but there was more action and noise coming from Super Surf Kata across the road where groups of people were gathered for early beers and plenty of laughs. I gave up on the surf comp after an hour or so. I think you need to be patient, or have a personal connection to a surfer, and probably knowing what makes a surf good would help. I failed on all fronts.

Heading home, I wandered through the market stalls selling all sorts of goodies and came across a jewellery stall that was also offering ear piercing. I'd been contemplating another piercing at the top of my ear. Before I was able to change my mind the needle was in and out and I was the owner of a tiny diamond-like stud. My very own Kata Surfing Competition souvenir.

I had an online language lesson in the afternoon and decided to stay close to home, even though there was entertainment to be had at the festival. I have a full day ahead tomorrow and so it was foodpanda for dinner and an early quiet night.

25 June
Phang Nga Bay / Water Goddess / Bioluminescence

Seems I've caused a bit of a stir among the staff at the hotel reception desk. There was complete disbelief this morning as I walked back past them on the way to my room with poached chicken and rice along with dried pork and sticky rice for breakfast. Plenty of chatter around how a *farang* can possibly eat what they eat. I assured them I'd much rather eat a Thai breakfast than bacon and eggs any day.

The other night while I was out watching the Ashes at Sports Bar, the American guy we befriended said he hadn't yet been to Phang Nga Bay and seen the glorious limestone cliffs. In continuing to do life differently, I recommended a tour and offered to go along with him if he needed a friend. He took me up on my offer and we were soon in a van with other tourists on our way out to the pier from which our boat was departing.

It's always interesting to be with someone as they first experience the astounding natural beauty of this bay. The massive limestone islands jutting out of the water, the calm turquoise water and the anticipation of what's ahead as we stop at our first cave. We clambered into the sea kayaks with our guide and we were soon lying on our backs as our guide carefully manoeuvred us through the small openings and out into the lagoon. 'Oh wow, wow, wooow' pretty much sums up the reaction throughout the day from my friend, and 'this is awesome' was also used often.

Kayaking is the perfect way to discover these tranquil and magical places. You really are just along for the ride as you lie back and take it all in. The sounds of nature, hearing other people laughing and enjoying themselves, the moment of awe as you leave the darkness of the caves to enter the beauty of a sunlit lagoon surrounded by cliffs. Drifting around in your kayak you can't help but feel immensely thankful that the Thai people so willingly share these beautiful places with us.

Inside the lagoon the water is clear enough for you to see the fish happily swimming around, and lizard-like water monitors are easy to spot gliding through the water then finding a sunny ledge to perch and sunbathe on. If you're really lucky you might see sea eagles and the odd brahminy kite flying overhead. If not, you will definitely hear them.

I'd always wanted to swim in these tropical blue-green waters. The tours I'd been on to date hadn't allowed time for swimming, but this one did. Jumping off the side of the boat and into the water was everything I'd always hoped it would be. I floated on my back for ages and then swam to the entrance of one of the caves and back to the boat. Blissful.

After eating our way through a gourmet buffet of scrumptious Thai foods onboard the boat, we set about making a *krathong*. This is a small, circular, floating boat made from banana stems for the base and then covered in folded banana leaves around the outside to resemble the lotus flower. A bright orange marigold flower was placed in the middle surrounded by magenta orchids. Our guide made some sweet little birds out of orchid flowers, which he perched on a swing that he'd also made and attached to our *krathong*. Candles and incense completed our offering to the Goddess of the Waters, Phra Mae Khongkha also known as Mae Khongkha, and Buddha. We were soon getting back into our kayak with our guide and I carried our precious *krathong* as we paddled towards the cave entrance.

Our Thai guide, sitting in the back of our kayak, explained the significance of the ritual we were undertaking so my friend could understand. Thai people celebrate the Loy Krathong festival – *loy* meaning 'to float' and *krathong* 'basket' or 'boat' – in the month of November. On the evening of the full moon of the twelfth month in the traditional Thai lunar calendar, they gather at the edge of waterways near them and offer these ornate little baskets that carry within them the hopes, wishes and gratitude of the individual launching them into the water. This tradition is believed to have originated from the period of the Sukhothai Kingdom (1238–1438). It's one of the most beautiful symbolic displays of a shared sense of renewed hope I've ever seen and participated in.

To be offered the opportunity to do this as darkness fell within the lagoon was both deeply moving and spiritual. We drifted in our kayak while we watched our candlelit *krathong* gently floating in the water. Others were doing the same, but we all gave each other space. As I released our *krathong* I also gave thanks and entrusted my hopes and wishes for new beginnings to Mae Khongkha.

We then headed back into the darkness of the cave and stopped to see the twinkle of the bioluminescent plankton in the water. Millions of them sparkling and lighting the water like little diamonds. I've always wanted to see this. That was a big tick against a bucket list item for me.

As we emerged from the cave, the setting sun had turned

the scattered clouds multiple shades of pink. Mae Khongkha and Mother Nature at their finest. For me there's something exquisitely special about Phang Nga Bay. Today it shone brighter than ever.

26 June
Cake | Jai | Greng Jai

I took my time to face the day after a late arrival home last night, and I went straight from bed to the swimming pool. Later I needed to sink myself into some Thai language as I had some homework to catch up on. I ended up walking up to Pui's house to get some help. We had a task to read several Thai sentences and translate them into English. There was one word that I just couldn't translate or understand even when I said it out loud. Pui laughed at the fact that this particular word had me stumped, being one of my favourite foods: cake! Instead of being the Thai word for cake, it was the English word cake written in Thai. Confusing.

I've never really been overly ambitious while learning Thai. I've only ever wanted to be able to casually chat with people, order and buy food, get from one place to another, ask for things or ask what things are. All that practical stuff that makes living in the community a little easier. It now seems I'm able to use the language to express my emotions, comment on the attributes of a person and ask others how they're feeling.

There's a word in Thai that has enabled me to do this and it's *jai*. It's a very handy word as it can have three different meanings depending upon the context in which it's used: 'heart', 'mind' or 'spirit'. This one word is most often combined with other words when describing feelings and emotions and provides a window into Thai culture and psychology. For example, *greng jai* literally means 'awe of heart'. *Greng* means 'to fear something' or 'to be afraid to act'. Combined with *jai*, 'heart' or 'mind', it means to be highly considerate and respectful of another person's feelings, situation and responsibilities. It shows a reluctance to disturb, impose or offend others and is a common character trait when talking about the concept of saving face. This concept is intrinsic to the way Thai society works.

Ordinarily a Thai person will feel *greng jai* towards someone who is of higher or equal status within their workplace or social circle. They seek to cause the least hassle for other people: to not ask for unnecessary favours or make people feel in some way obliged to help them. It's often difficult for foreigners to grasp or understand this element of the culture as we're encouraged to speak our mind and ask for what we want and seek clarity, not necessarily considering fully if this may offend another person. This Thai virtue can cause all sorts of problems when foreigners are too direct in their requests of the local people.

I find this way of being endearing. I can now tell if Thai people are being *greng jai* towards me, particularly if I give them something like money or a gift. They will normally refuse a couple of times and then finally give in. If I've given them a gift they won't open it in front of me unless I expressly ask them to. They will wait until they're at home. It's all part of the fabric of this culturally rich country.

There are more than a hundred words that have the word *jai* attached. One of the first I ever learnt was *jai dee*, meaning 'to have a good heart', and *khao jai*, meaning 'to understand'. Although in my case I more often used the opposite, *mai khao jai*, meaning 'I don't understand'.

27 June

Chut Thai | 2,000 Screaming Kids | Vivid Memories

When I walked out of my room and down the long driveway towards Chai Thai restaurant at midday, I could see the owner, dressed in Thai traditional dress, *chut Thai*, standing outside her shop. My plan was to eat lunch there, which also gave me a chance to have a chat with her about her outfit and tell her how beautiful she looked. Because she did.

Thai traditional dress is very distinctive and still to this day acknowledges the country's history. The loincloth wrap is used for both men and women and dates back to before the 1800s. There are many forms of traditional dress. What is worn will mostly depend on the occasion. Thai ladies will normally wear either a tubular, long straight skirt or knee-length billowy pants (loincloth). The pants are made from one piece of ornate fabric, which is wrapped around the lower body and pulled up between the legs to form a loose-fitting garment. On top they wear the fabric in a shawl-like wrap. A contrasting long piece of fabric is wrapped around the body twice, with the remaining fabric draped over the left shoulder. They finish their outfit off with a gold belt and other intricate and ornate pieces of gold jewellery.

Seeing her today reminded me of the first time I dressed in such an outfit. I learnt Thai dancing as one of my subjects while at school here. I enjoyed it, but didn't have the ability to bend my fingers back like the Thai girls. Much of the dance is done by moving your hands and fingers gracefully around your body. What I didn't realise was that the teachers were getting me ready to perform on stage at a school assembly, dressed in *chut Thai*.

My carefully chosen ensemble consisted of royal purple pants with a fancy gold thread through the fabric. On top I had a piece of pleated orange fabric wrapped twice around my body and draped over my shoulder, which was overlaid with a gold mesh. I had my hair in a bun, an ornate gold necklace, earrings and gold cuff on my arm. Full makeup and a flower above my ear completed my transformation.

I can still remember to this day feeling engulfed by nerves and not being able to hear the music I was dancing to due to the screaming kids when I walked on stage. Their delight and excitement was in overdrive seeing this *farang* not only dressed in Thai costume but trying her best to Thai dance, *rum Thai*.

I've found my diary entry for that day, 26 June 1989:

… very hot, put final jewellery on, everyone ordering me around in a panic, photos being taken and people staring at me, felt chaotic, I rehearsed again. Walked to the stage with my friend holding my hand, by this time I was a nervous wreck. I was jittery and my heart was pounding. I said a prayer before I went on stage as my friends had told me to. I was introduced to the stage and on I went. Well, my god they all screamed and I mean screamed. Some 2,000 kids screaming at you is enough to make anyone go weak at the knees. I couldn't hear the music and thought oh no but I carried on. I couldn't smile as my face was shaking and I wasn't conscious of what

I was doing. Every move I made they screamed with appreciation and joy. I couldn't believe it. I was finally finished and I hadn't forgotten the dance and I didn't go blank, thank god! I wai-ed and went off, but then I had to go back on stage again to receive a present and again they screamed when I was given the gift. I was so relieved when it was all over. Still shaking and it took me ages to calm down.

Reading that again, I wished I could've told that young nervous girl that these situations help build your character, and that the courage to push through when you feel so uncomfortable and full of fear will come to help you later in life. I would've also loved to have told her to relax, enjoy herself and have fun. The adoration of the students at my school lasted throughout my stay and it was something that I struggled with. I rarely had time alone and often younger female students asked for my autograph and to have their photo with me. It was very weird for this eighteen-year-old teen from country Australia.

Once I'd finished my lunch and my chat about Thai costumes and dancing, N'Bow arrived to take me to school. I was preoccupied with thinking about my exchange-student days for much of my class. Seeing that Thai costume flooded me with memories.

I hadn't been to see Kunya for more than two weeks. So when I felt hungry for dinner, I made my way to her. I was eager to see her and share my photos from Phang Nga Bay. We greeted one another with warm hugs and a *wai*. She was snacking on a small, salted fish. Seems the smell had also drawn in a local black-and-white cat that's often wandering around in her restaurant. It was sitting at Kunya's feet expectantly looking up at her plate. Kunya was eating her salted fish with handfuls of noodles, spicy dipping sauce and a crispy cabbage leaf. I stuck to my chicken garlic and fried egg salad, which was exactly what I felt like.

I enjoyed catching up on all her news and she was thrilled to see my *loy krathong* experience. She has never been to Phang Nga Bay, although she lives so close by. She's in the process of preparing her shop for the high season, adding more tables and a few menu items for *farangs* like fish 'n' chips and chicken 'n' chips. I told her to add in some salads as I'm sure they would go well in this hot climate, but added, 'I'm not a *farang* anymore. I'm a Thai so it's only ever Thai food for me.' She laughed and agreed.

28 June
Dog Rescue | Spirits | Beliefs

This morning when I reached the end of the driveway there was a dog on the busy main road. Cars were slowing down and motorbikes weaving around as this little pooch danced along, happy to be free. Terrified that I was going to see it get run over, I could barely watch what was happening. I stood still and clapped my hands, encouraging it off the road and over to me. Thank goodness it came bounding over.

I scooped up the little Chihuahua-like dog and immediately asked it where it lived. It had a collar on with a bell but that was it. As I was cradling the little dog, not knowing what to do next but also incredibly relieved that it was off the road and in my arms, an elderly Thai man came along on his motorbike with a lead and claimed the pooch, thanking me profusely. I was just thankful that it lived to see another day. Once my heart rate settled, I went off to get breakfast and go about my day.

A couple of nights ago, I stopped to have a G&T and a chat with Khun Tuk at her bar. It's quiet business-wise for her at the moment, but she still opens the bar and keeps it all looking so neat and tidy every day. She was telling me how lonely she's feeling living in Phuket with all her family two hours away on a farm where they grow rice, peanuts, corn, sugar cane and a few other vegetables. Working in Phuket she's able to earn better money and pay for the education of her kids, but there are days when you can see the sadness in her eyes.

She mentioned not being able to sleep. She told me when she was a child she would close her eyes and visions of an elderly woman came to her. Thais believe very much in ghosts and the only way she could stop these visions was to have the local Buddhist monks visit her house and provide blessings to remove the spirit. They did this and the visions stopped.

Recently, however, the visions have returned and she's been frightened by them. She told me she goes to the temple to pray and provide offerings to the spirits as a way of hopefully stopping this from happening. She had goose bumps on her arms as she told me this story and it clearly affects her. I've often heard from Thai people the real fear they have of ghosts. It interests me as I'm not a believer in them. Thais don't seem afraid of having their houses broken into at night, but any mention of a ghost and they turn to jelly.

Tonight, on my way back from yet another soothing sunset and swim, I called in to see her. Khun Tuk had a giant smile on her face. She was so keen to tell me she'd been to the temple today and the fortune-telling sticks that she shook from the canister gave her the hope she was after: that she had so many good things coming to her, including money and health, but no partner. She excitedly showed me the piece of yellow paper covered in Thai writing and seemed genuinely relieved that life was about to improve.

Of course, I really hope it does. Like so many here, Khun Tuk certainly deserves an easier life than she currently has. Longing for her children and working six days a week in a bar must be tough and tedious.

28 June

Dog Rescue / Spirits / Beliefs

This morning when I reached the end of the driveway there was a dog on the busy main road. Cars were slowing down and motorbikes weaving around as this little pooch danced along, happy to be free. Terrified that I was going to see it get run over, I could barely watch what was happening. I stood still and clapped my hands, encouraging it off the road and over to me. Thank goodness it came bounding over.

I scooped up the little Chihuahua-like dog and immediately asked it where it lived. It had a collar on with a bell but that was it. As I was cradling the little dog, not knowing what to do next but also incredibly relieved that it was off the road and in my arms, an elderly Thai man came along on his motorbike with a lead and claimed the pooch, thanking me profusely. I was just thankful that it lived to see another day. Once my heart rate settled, I went off to get breakfast and go about my day.

A couple of nights ago, I stopped to have a G&T and a chat with Khun Tuk at her bar. It's quiet business-wise for her at the moment, but she still opens the bar and keeps it all looking so neat and tidy every day. She was telling me how lonely she's feeling living in Phuket with all her family two hours away on a farm where they grow rice, peanuts, corn, sugar cane and a few other vegetables. Working in Phuket she's able to earn better money and pay for the education of her kids, but there are days when you can see the sadness in her eyes.

She mentioned not being able to sleep. She told me when she was a child she would close her eyes and visions of an elderly woman came to her. Thais believe very much in ghosts and the only way she could stop these visions was to have the local Buddhist monks visit her house and provide blessings to remove the spirit. They did this and the visions stopped.

Recently, however, the visions have returned and she's been frightened by them. She told me she goes to the temple to pray and provide offerings to the spirits as a way of hopefully stopping this from happening. She had goose bumps on her arms as she told me this story and it clearly affects her. I've often heard from Thai people the real fear they have of ghosts. It interests me as I'm not a believer in them. Thais don't seem afraid of having their houses broken into at night, but any mention of a ghost and they turn to jelly.

Tonight, on my way back from yet another soothing sunset and swim, I called in to see her. Khun Tuk had a giant smile on her face. She was so keen to tell me she'd been to the temple today and the fortune-telling sticks that she shook from the canister gave her the hope she was after: that she had so many good things coming to her, including money and health, but no partner. She excitedly showed me the piece of yellow paper covered in Thai writing and seemed genuinely relieved that life was about to improve.

Of course, I really hope it does. Like so many here, Khun Tuk certainly deserves an easier life than she currently has. Longing for her children and working six days a week in a bar must be tough and tedious.

I admire the deep spiritual and religious beliefs of some here and the obvious part these beliefs play in people's happiness and outlook on the future. Making merit by providing offerings at the temple and spending time speaking with her Buddha had totally changed Khun Tuk's outlook. Thanks to her faith, she was able to refocus and gain a renewed level of hope for her future and I guess that's what it's all about.

Similarly, when I've felt life is spinning out of control, being able to come back to what I believe in and what brings me peace certainly helps ground me and provides me with a sense of stability again. I've developed my own ways of self-soothing during some very turbulent times in my life. Everything from spending time in my garden, to rugging up and walking on the beach, meditation, sitting and patting my dogs and cooking and eating something delicious. Here it seems to be the ocean that's providing me with a feeling of steadiness, balance and soundness of mind.

I was so pleased to see this change, almost relief, in Khun Tuk today. I was touched she'd shared this insight into her beliefs with me. As I left the bar, we wished each other a peaceful sleep. Somehow I think Khun Tuk will rest easy tonight.

29 June
Brekkie Goodies / Peeling Back the Layers / Life Audit

With breakfast being my absolute favourite meal of the day, I'm so glad to have Khun KK and her husband less than a five-minute walk away. Each morning they stock their street stall full of interesting brekkie goodies, a different selection on offer each day. I'm slowly making my way through them, although I tend to find something I really like and can't go past it. I'm probably enjoying the savoury more than the sweet and anything with sticky rice is my top pick. When I asked Khun KK this morning what I should eat, she said, 'Everything is delicious because morning food needs to be so you're in a good mood for the day.' I couldn't agree more!

She opens at 5 a.m. seven days a week, having already been to the market to buy her offerings for the shop. She has a cheerful smile and greets me warmly. This couple have two young daughters who go to the local school and can sometimes be seen helping their parents in the shop. Such a sweet family. My choice for today was sticky rice and dried pork (*moo yarng*) and a little coconut pudding. I took my breakfast back to my room and sat outside on my comfy sun lounge, where I couldn't help but contemplate life. I seem to be doing this almost every day now.

I asked myself how I was feeling and was able to confirm that I still feel good, like really good. Compared to when I first arrived I'm lighter in spirit, less fuzzy in my head, content and so full of joy. This isn't some sort of surprising revelation. I haven't just suddenly woken up today and realised it. It has been building. And I now feel like it's hanging around. These feelings haven't come and gone like I expected they might. They're consistently within me.

I'm fairly confident that this gradual shift in doing life differently, day by day, little by little, has had a powerful and positive cumulative effect. Solo time, decluttering my life, a heavily reduced mental load, including not having to think about what's for dinner, lots of sleep and rest, refocusing on what matters to me, positive and interesting adventures and interactions, meeting new friends and being largely free of all my cares in an environment I love have all combined and contributed. And, of course, time – having lots of time for myself. The past four months have enabled me to peel back the layers that life has had me so tightly wrapped in. Living like you're holding your breath underwater cannot be sustained no matter how strong or stoic you think you are.

I've even dared to dream of how different my future could look going forward. I've thought more about what I want in terms of my job and I feel more and more like it's time for a change. My inner critic has found a softer voice, still there but not so loud and bossy.

Every time I come to Thailand and spend time in my happy place it encourages me to reassess, reset and remind myself of what's truly important. Being here this time has resonated with me on a deeper, more intense personal level. I've been handed so many opportunities to become more aware and appreciate this one precious life of mine. It has reinforced that this is not a practice run, nor a preview. This is the real deal. To live boldly and honestly feels right. Dare I say it, I even feel it could be life-changing.

It's not easy for me to put these feelings into words. It's almost like if I say them out loud, they will disappear. However, there are a few things I'm pretty sure of.

True happiness, or contentment as I like to call it, has nothing to do with the car you drive, the house you live in or having the best of everything. For me it's the people and animals I surround myself with. Those I love and who love me in return.

It's waking each day and feeling grounded within myself, not striving for approval from a world that doesn't even know me or my story and being unconcerned with how others might perceive me. It's finding my own muddled way through the messy un-met expectations, chaos, disappointments and grief thrown my way and being okay with not having all the answers all of the time and sometimes having no answer at all. It's the glimmers of hope, a level of reliable resilience, the wisdom so far collected and knowing this too shall pass – things that can be so easily forgotten unless we sit still and slow down long enough to again allow them to resurface.

This precious time and space to ask myself how I *really* feel and not be afraid of the answer is the ultimate gift to myself. This life audit is mostly about finding the softer, kinder, calmer me after many years of it being buried by resentment, stress and survival.

30 June
Best Pad Thai in Phuket / Chicken Feet

N'Bow and I were driving along one day when I asked him where he eats. He gave me some great local suggestions and I kicked myself that it had taken me so long to ask, as we all know the locals always know the freshest, cheapest and most delicious food spots in any town. And that was when he told me about the pad Thai shop.

Even though it looked like rain today, I set off on foot, hoping I could at least dodge the showers on my way to lunch. I'd checked the map on my phone and it seemed doable, a kilometre or so past Makro supermarket. I walked past Kunya and told her where I was going. She was shocked I was walking 'all that way'. This didn't concern me too much as Thais don't walk anywhere if they can help it. They think only poor people walk as they can't afford a motorcycle. I kept going, happy to play my part as the strange *farang*.

I noticed I wasn't taking many photos as I wandered along and wondered if I'd become used to the once unusual sights. I stopped to buy a kilo of rambutans from the back of a pick-up truck. These fruits are one of my favourites and once peeled give you this fleshy, sweet white blob with a seed in the middle that you spit out once you've sucked the fruit off it.

I checked my map a couple of times as by this stage my sweat levels were near peaking and I thought I might have already walked past it. Some of these eating spots can be so tucked away that only locals can find them. Up another hill I trudged and once I reached the top, feeling like I was about to combust, I arrived. As expected, there was absolutely nothing flash about this place, pretty much a tin shed. It was just another roadside restaurant that you could easily walk past without knowing. It was busy with plenty of Thai people eating alone, which normally means they're just grabbing something during their day, not so much eating out. Pad Thai is, after all, their equivalent to our sandwich, I'd say.

I could see that most people were going for the soup noodles. A big pot of chicken feet caught my eye and every bowl of soup had a few feet added. I stuck with my original plan of pad Thai with chicken and managed to read the menu and blackboard specials, all written in Thai. They provided free chicken broth, plain rice and water for those who wanted it. From what I could tell, the restaurant was run by a family with the parents controlling the money, drinks and sweets, while their daughters worked the woks and kept the kitchen and orders moving.

Given my state of dehydration when I arrived, water and ice on the table were such a welcome sight. I dabbed my face with a handful of the small, thin pink tissues on the table as I tried to cool off. Soon enough a big bowl arrived. The side condiments came on a plate all on their own: two juicy lime cheeks, ample bean shoots and a few dark green, chive-like stalks. I added the lot. The self-seasoning pots in the middle of the table gave me the chance to further flavour my noodles. I added peanuts and chilli flakes and mixed these thoroughly through the noodles with my chopsticks and dived in.

Having now made pad Thai twice during my cooking classes,

I have a new appreciation for how a seemingly simple dish is made. It's all about keeping the food moving and scooping it continuously to get the flavours to combine and not burn. It's quite the workout. I think a seasoned wok has a fair bit to do with adding flavour and the sauce is key. It has a tamarind base and they vigorously toss it through the noodles, making sure they're all well coated.

This restaurant in my humble opinion was deserving of its status as one of the best in Phuket. The serving size was generous and could have easily made two meals, but I scoffed it all down. It cost 60 baht for my food and 10 baht for extra water – A$3 total. I vowed to return, even if it meant asking N'Bow to drive me next time and I might even go for the chicken feet option.

1 July

Neon Lights | Saxophone | Getting My Dance On

I had been thinking about this for a while and wondering when and how I might do it. So tonight when I had a hankering for loud dance music I acted on it. I messaged N'Bow to see if he was free and could drive me to Patong, the nightclub district. I've been a couple of times on this trip already but not to go clubbing, just for shopping and a show. It's not really my scene and not somewhere I'd just hang around.

Bangla Walking Street is the heartbeat of all things nightlife in Phuket. There are umpteen bars lining both sides of the street. Some with live music, others with scantily clad girls dancing around poles, all with security on the door and most full of men.

It's teeming with life and full of the brightest neon lights. It can be slightly overwhelming when you're constantly approached to see the 'ping-pong shows' and I'd recommend a cross-body bag with one hand always on it while you're there.

I'd seen a particular nightclub on my last visit and developed a fascination for it. Armania is its name. The atmosphere they offer didn't seem at all sleazy or scary for a solo like me. It appeared a bit more upmarket and I wanted to know more. N'Bow was free and told me, 'Yes, sister, I can take you now.'

The tables near the stage come with a minimum drinking spend, but I was right at home at a table at the back and was soon sipping a G&T. The music was exactly as I hoped, thumping loud and dancy. They also had a live saxophone player on the stage blasting out the tunes. He knew how to get that dance crowd on their feet. There were acrobats doing all sorts of amazing twists and turns while hanging from the ceiling, while the club dancers randomly appeared on platforms on either side of the DJ. Do I even have to mention the incredible people-watching opportunities? I was soon getting my solo dance on…

I'd highly recommend a bit of solo clubbing. Another one of the joys of being in your fifties is not giving a toss about what people think and knowing most people don't even see you – probably helped by being in a dark, smoky place. It's so liberating and super fun once you accept it. No one bothered me and I danced like no one was watching because they weren't.

I didn't want to leave, but had sensibly booked N'Bow to pick me up before I turned into a Thai pumpkin. The traffic is crazy around this whole area with taxis, tuk-tuks and motorbikes zipping in and out and often coming from nowhere. I was very pleased to see N'Bow flash his lights at me as I stood at our agreed spot, the police box. He was very specific around where I should wait for him and I happily obliged. There are always plenty of police around here. They also have volunteer *farangs* in case people need help or get themselves into trouble.

On the way home, I asked N'Bow if he had ever been to the clubs in Patong and he hadn't. He doesn't like that part of Phuket and told me he can't see anything nice about it. He's right. It doesn't represent the Thailand I know and love so much.

If I was a local, I probably wouldn't bother with it as it's crawling with tourists and I always sense a feeling of desperation and sadness in those trying to make a living. Despite all that, disappearing for a couple of hours into a dark, smoky, pulsing, G&T-fuelled dance-music bubble and then going back to my quiet little life in Kata was immensely satisfying.

2 July

Switch Off Your Phone | Choices | Shimmering

My calves and feet have been feeling slightly tight and in need of a bit of attention. It must be all my walking, often in flip-flops, and maybe my dancing last night. Part of younger me would be so proud if it was the latter.

This morning, after my *cha yen,* I took myself off to see my local massage ladies. Straight up the stairs I went to wash my feet and into a room with a handful of reclining chairs. There were a few mats on the floor for the people having a Thai massage. The room was dimly lit, cool and had the distinct smell of tiger balm in the air. The therapist whispered her instructions to me. Her movements, as she got me ready for my massage, were gentle and kind. Once she began my massage there was silence. I closed my eyes and settled into my recliner, ready for an hour of indulgence.

My idea of a blissful massage is to sit or lie and try to leave the real world behind for an hour or two. Go within, and then emerge feeling energised, refreshed and a little less tense and tight. Deliberately finding time for calm and relaxation and maybe to silence some of the irritating chatter in my head is what I hope for.

As I was drifting off, I suddenly thought I could hear what might be a radio. I assumed the noise was coming in from the street and tried to concentrate on my breathing as all good meditators do. Eventually I couldn't keep my eyes shut any longer. When I opened them, I saw the person at the end of my row of recliners watching something on her phone, no headphones on, and then she cheered. I looked across at the only woman on the mat having a Thai massage and she had her ankle up around her head and was still managing to text on her phone.

Now, I have a very deep and committed relationship with my phone so I get it. However, if I ever feel the urge to use it while having a massage or think it's okay to disturb others with noise from it during a massage, I expect an intervention and a very stern talking to.

I believe that we still have the choice of whether to invite our phones into our lives and have the final say on when and where we use them. Even if the dopamine hit is telling us otherwise. The world won't stop for that hour you're out of contact. I know the habit and addiction is difficult to manage at times because I feel it myself. It's more the disturbing of others and lack of consideration for those around you that I object to. It's self-absorbed, selfish and just plain rude.

With my legs and feet feeling good again, but my mood slightly irritable, I walked off home to get my coral bikini on, wrapped myself in my bright, multi-coloured sarong and headed off to the beach. Another one of those sparkly, sunshiny days was waiting for me. There were kids on boogie boards riding the waves and plenty were swimming. The waves were slightly dumpy but proved to be fun to jump into and under. I had music in my ears when I was out of the water and stayed until sunset. The water shimmered as the sun went down, silver and gold, and I kept swimming until it was dark.

3 July
Unlucky in Love | Catching Customers

The Thai women that I've been so lucky to meet here have been so friendly and welcoming, so we decided that we'd gather at Pui's bar for drinks and giggles this afternoon. There were plenty of both and we chatted about all manner of topics, but for this group of gals it was mostly about the lack of romantic love in their lives. For some reason or another they've all been unlucky in love. They're all now raising their children alone, with no help at all from the fathers. It seems in Thailand it's very difficult to have any form of maintenance or child support paid, so they just get on with it and do the best they can.

The strength, devotion and love shown by each of them when it comes to their kids is wonderful. They're always showing me photos on their phones and clearly put the welfare of their kids first. Just like parents the world over, their greatest hope is to provide a life for them with opportunities that they themselves may not have been so lucky to have. Generally speaking, Thai people have a deep love and respect for their family, particularly kids and the elderly. There's never a thought about having elderly parents go into a care home. Such places don't really exist in Thailand. Culturally it's just a given that elderly parents will be taken care of by their children, and their children feel motivated and privileged to do so.

Instilling these strong values starts young. Thai children are raised to respect and appreciate first and foremost that their parents brought them into the world and cared for them as they grew into adults. P'Sak is totally devoted to his parents. He has shown me a beautiful photo of them that he keeps in his room and he goes to the temple weekly to make merit and pray for them. He sends a portion of his wage home for them and feels a deep sense of duty when it comes to their care and wellbeing. As he works away from home, his sisters do the day-to-day caring. When he talks about his parents, I can see the longing in his eyes, wishing he lived closer.

My Thai girlfriends openly shared their life stories with me. Their dreams for their future. The more they talked and the more I listened, the more clearly I realised how similar we are the world over, looking for someone to love and to be loved by in return. When they focused upon their potential to meet a new man, mainly to help solve all their money problems, I wasn't able to fully agree with their wishes. I was, however, happy to encourage them to continue doing the amazing job of raising their children on their own until they find someone truly deserving of them and their kids.

Given my renewed interest in live music, I've decided to do a bit of a music crawl along Kata Road in the remaining time I've got here. Tonight I stopped at the first bar I came to that had live music. I was enthusiastically greeted and seated and soon discovered that the entertainment consisted of a man and his guitar playing old country-and-western classics, sung with a Thai accent. It wasn't quite what I was looking for, but Wimbledon was on the TV and the people watching from my table kept me amused.

Business was slow and any man who came within a few steps

of the bar was quite literally latched onto by the female staff working there. They linked arms with the potential customer. Before the guy knew it, he was sitting on a bar stool and ordering a drink for himself and one for the bar girls. As Pui often says to me, 'I catched (sic) the customer today, Mel.' Now I know what she means.

I finished my drink and didn't feel like another, and the weather was rapidly turning nasty. We'd already had a nice big tropical downpour during the afternoon so I headed home. I had a dip in the pool, then lay in bed listening to the rain as it gradually got heavier and heavier. Another day well spent.

4 July

When Time Doesn't Matter

I've been struggling to understand how to use the word 'when' in Thai, so I asked my teacher Kruu Noi to explain it to me during our class. It turns out there are five different words that can be used to say 'when' – you see it all comes down to context or past events or if you want a specific time as the answer or if you're making a statement. As I write this it still sounds confusing in English so little wonder I was struggling to grasp it in Thai.

Now I feel slightly more justified in my inability to grasp this concept. I have a feeling there will be lots of tripping up before I get this right. Lucky I know how to say 'confusing' (*sup sorn*). I'm still enjoying my language lessons immensely. Having words and concepts explained and then being able to use them when I'm out and about is so helpful. My reading has improved and I find myself wandering around the streets reading out signs to myself. Never mind if I don't know what they mean, I just use them as an opportunity to practice.

I felt like an afternoon at the beach after all that learning. The waves were big after the stormy night we'd had, but breaking far enough out not to pound or dump me. I ended up staying until after sunset. It was one of those that just kept getting better and better long after the sun had disappeared. The clouds soaked up the final colours of the day, turning my favourite colour combination of orange and pink.

These days, there's no reason for me to ever leave the beach. There's no housework to do, no beds to be made, washing to be done, food to prepare, TV worth watching, garden to water. So I just stay and linger a little while longer. The time really doesn't matter. Talk about not a care in the world. I think I know what that truly feels like now.

I checked the weather forecast on my phone before I walked across to the Tann Beach Club for a pizza, a G&T and some dance tunes. It told me that the week ahead will be nothing short of sunny, beachy perfection. My only decision will be what time to arrive and then the setting sun will give me an indication of when I might start to think about leaving.

5 July
Beach Hawkers / Sun Lounge Men

After breakfast, I packed my flowery beach bag and walked the three kilometres or so to Karon Beach. Once there, I set myself up and went for a swim to cool off. There was a constant stream of hawkers trying to sell their wares. I was offered peanuts, sunglasses, watches, orange juice, a furry animal to hold, vapes, clothing, sarongs, jewellery, tours, parasailing, animals made from coconut shells and finally something I did want – ice cream. These people are not at all pushy and do bring a certain atmosphere to the beach. I don't know how they do this day in day out. I admire their perseverance in the heat. They get more knockbacks than sales as we who are sunning ourselves shake our heads and gesture for them to leave us alone. They push on regardless and continue doing the rounds of the beaches.

    The other people on the beach that I'm curious about are the men who rent out the sun lounges. I now know they're not all created equal. The good ones brush the sand off the lounges for you, adjust the umbrella to keep the sun off you, grab drinks and fresh coconuts for you and generally keep the area they're responsible for clean and tidy. At my spot at Karon Beach the sun lounge men even have little extras available like coat hangers for your clothes (never mind the rust on them), side tables for your phone, cold beers for sale and one of those handy small brooms I love. The latter helps you keep your lounge clean when you continually put your super-sandy feet on it.

I watched them today rustling up business on their small patch of sand, keeping an eye out for potential customers walking by and making sure the chairs were clean and out of the sun. While it was quiet, they were picking up the obscene amount of plastic that had washed up on the beach.

It's shocking to see and, as the tide went out, the true extent of the rubbish was quite unbelievable: fishing nets, plastic bottles of every type, wrappers, fishing line, rope, takeaway containers big and small and on it went. I went down and helped some other foreigners collect some of it. Surely if we all picked up five pieces of plastic or any form of rubbish instead of walking past it, which is what just about everyone does, we could keep the beach clean; though you have to ask why it's all being dumped in the sea to start with. From what I've seen, it seems that the fishing boats that rely so heavily on the ocean for their livelihood could also be the ones polluting it, which is sad.

The beach massage ladies have a permanent setup with beds under tarpaulins, and I went to them for a manicure and foot scrub. They were all aflutter when I spoke Thai with them, so many questions and so much interest. When they'd finished taking layer upon layer of skin off my feet, they were very keen for me to look at their work. I said in Thai, 'Oh, they look just like babies' feet!' They roared with laughter.

When I returned to my sun lounge, I could still hear them laughing and talking about me, wondering how this *farang* could speak to them. So sweet. Many of them were older ladies and they obviously enjoy each other's company, laughing together and doing the odd massage and foot scrub along the way. I get the sense that this part of the beach has a little community all of its own. It's proving to be somewhere I want to spend my time as I get to know these people more.

6 July
Ear Infection | Lip Balms | Herbal Inhalers

I had a somewhat disturbed sleep as my ear was blocked, and woke knowing I needed to visit the doctor. There's an international medical clinic in the middle of Kata, a ten-minute walk for me. This was my second visit. The reception staff and nurses all remembered me and were very curious about how my stay had been going. After a quick catch-up, we got down to business. When you first arrive you check in with a nurse, tell them what the problem is, they take your blood pressure and then send you straight in to see the doctor. That has been my experience to date. No waiting, no mucking around, no appointment. I can't tell you how much I appreciate this.

The doctor at this clinic is a young Thai man, with a soft and gentle manner. He wanted to speak in Thai today. I wanted to make sure I understood him so he showed me pictures as well and kept it pretty simple. With all my swimming, it seems I've got an ear infection. I knew I had water trapped in my ear, but I didn't know there was an infection as I have no pain. I left with unblocked ears, medication and a beautiful smile from the whole clinic team. It reassures me that I have somewhere to go if there is something serious that needs attention. They open from 9 a.m. till 11 p.m. every day and will even come to you. If only we had this on offer at home.

While I was out attending to my medical needs, I also called into the pharmacy close by to get more of a prescription medication I was running low on due to staying on longer. There was no need for a script. I just walked in with the box and was able to buy it over the counter. Perfect and good to know. The pharmacies here are an absolute treasure chest. So many things I'd never need, but I like knowing they're available. Most are stocked to the brim and they're everywhere. I've found that they have quite the variety of lip glosses and balms complete with SPF50, and to top it off I've found one that's tinted pink. Everything this girl could want in one little tube. I've given a number of them a test run, finding some to be too sticky, others weirdly flavoured and others again lacking staying power. Who even knew one woman needed ten lip balms in her makeup bag?

The other item that draws me into a Thai pharmacy is the humble nasal inhaler, (*yaa dom* and *yaa hom*). You'll see lots of Thais using these and I'm a fan as well. When it's oppressively hot, the vapour helps soothe a headache and any feelings of faintness. It smells fresh with its mix of herbs and flowers, and the menthol refreshes me every time; a couple of whiffs and I have a clear head and am happy. I also use what I call the 'magic green ointment', another herbal, menthol-based balm that treats everything from mozzie bites to tired muscles; importantly, too, any stinky smells that might make their way into your nostrils as you're walking the streets are quickly gone with one deep inhale. I have a tiny pot of this always at the ready.

Tonight at the beach the colour of the clouds matched my candy-pink, lip-gloss-covered lips. Pure perfection. It was dark by the time I left, and even then I wasn't ready leave.

7 July

Suffering / Courage / Cherishing the Little Things

I've been walking every day, mostly around Kata, pretty much since I arrived. Fortunately I'm able-bodied, in good health, enjoy being outside walking and I haven't really given it a second thought. Until today.

I set off for the beach around lunchtime and stopped at a place along the way for a dish of flat noodles called *lad naa*. I'd seen this shop on previous walks and had it on my foodie list. This is a popular dish among Thais. Chewy, wide white rice noodles are covered in a flavoursome, pork-based, gravy-like sauce. It's a simple dish with fermented-soybean paste the key ingredient giving extra flavour, along with soy and oyster sauce. Chinese broccoli is the only vegetable added, and because the dish originates in China there's no coconut milk, no chilli unless you add it yourself and no Thai herbs giving it a distinct Thai touch. It was just what I felt like.

With a satisfied belly full of noodles, I continued walking to Karon Beach. I was greeted by the massage ladies and the sun lounge men scurrying around and preparing my usual lounge for me. I'd promised to return for a leg-and-foot massage. So once I'd unpacked my beach bag, I wrapped my sarong around me and headed into their tent.

I was chatting away to the lady who'd done my foot scrub on a previous visit and then I saw a young girl lying in a hammock in the shade at the back of the tent. I said *sawadee kha* to her and she gave me a tiny smile. I could tell it was hard for her. From where I was standing, I could see that she was very frail, almost like a weak baby bird in a nest, cocooned by the hammock. She could hardly move.

I couldn't help but ask my massage lady, who turned out to be her mum, politely in Thai if the young girl was unwell. She told me she has a brain tumour and can't walk or feed herself and is totally dependent on her. She also told me she brings her to the massage tent every day so she can care for her. I climbed up on the bed ready for my massage with a very sad and heavy heart. My thoughts were racing trying to think of what I could possibly do to help this poor, sweet girl. I asked if there was anything the doctors could do for her and apparently there's nothing. She's dying.

At times like these I'm so grateful I can speak Thai. I chatted with her mum a little more and she was able to tell me that her dear daughter is seventeen and has been declining for the last three years. Before this happened, she was a smart girl going to school and now she lies in the hammock next to her mum so her mum can turn her and feed her and, most of all, love her. This girl only has enough strength to turn her head and swallow.

I offered my deepest sympathy and acknowledged the suffering she is obviously enduring and the courage she displays. These beautiful people have no safety net or pension system to help them survive. No allowance for caring duties. They carry on the best way they know how. I know they wouldn't be able to afford for her to spend her days in hospital as she slips away. Thankfully she's not hidden.

The way in which Thais seem to accept their lot in life is beyond my comprehension at times. These experiences, as upsetting as they are, remind me to cherish the little things in life. There's so much that I take for granted. Tonight my walk home from the beach will feel extra special.

8 July

Warm and Fuzzy | Helping Friends | Kindness Matters

Today was a day of warm and fuzzy connections with my Thai friends. Sometimes when N'Bow is busy he sends N'Odt, his older brother, to pick me up. He's also an absolute delight, a caring and considerate man and we have some great car conversations together. He speaks Thai so clearly which helps me enormously. He's so polite – he uses the polite male particle at the end of all his sentences, *krup pom*. The range of topics we cover is vast. Last week we got onto our favourite topic – food. Seems we both like very similar Thai food. N'Odt told me he has a friend who owns a *somtarm* (spicy papaya salad) restaurant in Chalong.

    I didn't feel like walking to the beach today and N'Odt came to take me. He saw me heading towards his car and he got out and presented me with bags of food. I could tell it was fresh *somtarm* by the smell of it – so delicious. He'd been to Chalong to buy it from his friend's shop for me. He waited for me to go back to my room and pop it into my fridge so I had it ready to go when I got home from the beach.

    Not surprisingly, it was pretty late by the time I returned

from the beach. I took my ready-made dinner out of the fridge, tipped the contents of each bag into a bowl and mixed. Not only did I have a sensational meal full of incredible flavours, but this *somtarm* was laced with kindness. I finished my last mouthful and recorded a video to send to N'Odt to thank him and tell him how much I appreciated his thoughtfulness. A response came bouncing back straightaway, 'You're very welcome, sister.'

Meanwhile dear Pui couldn't do enough for an Australian friend of mine who had a broken-down motorbike. She helped him get it to the mechanic and kindly gave him a motorbike of hers to use for free. There's nothing she won't do to help and when I thanked her she said, 'It's okay. We're friends and that's what friends do for each other.' I couldn't love her more.

I hadn't seen P'Sak for a couple of days and messaged him to find out where he was. He's gone back home to Buriram, a northeastern province of Thailand. He's spending time with his family and he shared with me that his father has had a stroke and his mum is unable to walk and is in a wheelchair. He sent me a video of him talking with his dear ill father, stroking his head and holding his hand. It was so touching and so sad. I appreciated him sharing that part of his life with me.

He's home to not only spend time with his family, but also to care for his parents and help on the family farm. He sent me photos of himself with the cows they raise and out working in the fields. I miss seeing him most days as I walk to the beach. I'm really pleased I'll get to see him before I leave for home.

The way these people so candidly and authentically share their lives with me fills my heart and blows me away.

9 July
Snakes | 'I Love Thailand' Tat | Lady Boys

As the rain cleared this morning, I looked up from where I was standing outside my room and could see Big Buddha still shrouded in clouds. It's so special being able to see this landmark from pretty much wherever I am around my local area. Even when I'm swimming in the ocean I look up and there he is.

Pui's friend Pong, who works for the fire brigade, told me the other day that the majority of their work isn't fire-related; in fact, they're mostly busy catching and removing snakes. I'm not sure I needed to know that, but it's too late now. I've got a particular spot at the front of my hotel where I sit and wait for my foodpanda orders to arrive once I know they're getting close. I was sitting in my spot patiently waiting for my driver today and a Russian woman, puffing on a cigarette, came up to me and asked, 'Have you seen a snake here?'

I must have looked puzzled as she then got her phone out to show me a video she'd taken of a snake around the main swimming pool. She looked at me and I looked at her. Thankfully I'm not around that pool much and now I'll never be lounging there. The good news is they're not venomous, just massive and long. I'm sorry, but a snake is a snake. At least I know who to call if I see one.

In the evening, I'd made a plan with Damo to meet up at a new bar in Spiderman Soi, as he's befriended the German owner. When I was introduced to the German, I found it hard to not stare at his array of tattoos. He has 'I love Thailand' written in Thai around his neck, which fascinated me as I read it out loud. Me too, but there will be no neck tattoo coming my way. Obviously a stubby holder or key ring wasn't enough.

His staff were all very hospitable towards us, in particular a young woman called Bambi. She got my G&T and helped herself to a whiskey and soda on my behalf. I didn't mind as I'm super curious to know how these girls come to work in these bars and the sex industry.

We started to chat and, as we were speaking in Thai to each other, I think she felt comfortable with my questions. I was honest with her about being interested in her life. Bambi comes from a very poor region in the northeast, where a large proportion of the sex workers are from. She's largely uneducated, only having finished a few years of high school. She worked in a bar in Bangkok before coming to Phuket and she calls herself a barmaid, not a sex worker. She figures she has all the skills to make a comprehensive range of cocktails, which she's super proud of. She has also taught herself a fair bit of English via watching and copying videos on YouTube. This probably explains some very interesting pronunciation and use of words.

We moved on to drink number two together. I think Bambi enjoyed speaking with someone who was not looking for anything, but simply wanted to hear her story. She told me she has a four-year-old son and his father is from the UK. Let's just say that relationship didn't go so well. Her son lives with her mother back in her hometown so he can attend school and be cared for at night. She was soon showing me photos of her boy on her phone.

I asked how she copes in a place where she has no family. It seems her workmates have become family. They provide a support network for one another while they're living away. All the girls from this bar are living in a shared house paid for by the bar owner. They live rent-free and look out for one another, often sharing meals together.

Sweet Bambi was full of more and more chat as the cheap Thai whiskey and soda boosted her confidence and her affection for me. I ended up encouraging her to go and entertain other customers as I was done drinking and she could make heaps more money from them. I was very relieved when at one point she told me she wasn't 'for sale', but unfortunately I know that if the price was right she would be. Bambi seemed happy enough, but I'm not convinced it's a life you would choose. It's a matter of survival for most. These days most women can receive an adequate education to give them greater prospects and opportunities in the work they choose to do, but there will always be some who slip through and end up in the bars.

There were also four very glamorous lady boys (*kathoeys*) working at the bar. This is what Thais have always called transsexuals or drag queens. With their skinny jeans and heels, perfect makeup and blow-waved hair, it's really difficult to tell the difference between lady boys and women these days. Thais absolutely love all things beautiful and glamourous, none more so than the lady boys. Many have smooth, clear skin and a delicate physique, and they put an enormous amount of time and effort into their appearance, so that you wouldn't look twice. It's only when they speak that you might do a double take.

I've had the chance to meet many bar girls in my solo

travels this trip, having been in situations this time around that have facilitated these conversations. Every single one of these women has intrigued me with her own unique story to tell. My curiosity gets the better of me. It's a world that I know so little about. There are many who rely on the sex industry here for their income. My feminist instincts recoil slightly, but there's a high demand that never looks like it's going to wane. They see themselves as meeting that demand and providing an income for themselves and their family. Each time I speak with these ladies, I'm left wondering if they're really being looked after. I so hope they are.

10 July
Gigolo Hub / Spontaneous Ice Cream Curls

Once the rain cleared this morning, my hunger got me out the door. I'd decided it was time I walked a little further up my street and had some Kunya love and laughter and a big serving of her Thai comfort food as a side.

I passed by Pui's house and she was out the front organising herself for a big day of laundry. While sorting washing she was eating spicy noodles that she'd just made, and she asked me to stay and eat with her as Thais love to do. I had to decline her offer as there was no way I could then eat at Kunya's restaurant. Pui is dying to cook for me so I'm sure there will be another opportunity.

Not far from Pui's place, I rounded the corner and came across a new cannabis den. It was like a pop-up with cannabis plants in pots all scattered around the cluttered tiny front garden of a house where a lady used to sell satays only a week or so ago.

A couple of Thai blokes yelled out, '*Sawadee krup…*' Then I saw a sign saying, 'Gigolo Hub'. I asked them in Thai, 'Who's the gigolo?' They burst out laughing and the banter started. They wanted me to stop in, but I said I hadn't eaten and was on the way to get food. Not many Thais will stand in the way of someone off to find food, so I got an instant leave pass. I told them I'd stop in on the way back from lunch, regretting it as soon as I said it, but I just can't say no to these wonderful friendly people and their huge smiles.

Where Kunya stands to cook in her café gives her an excellent view of who is coming her way. She looked up from her wok and instantly we were furiously waving to one another. So lovely to see her. Her sister then got in on the action. We were all laughing uncontrollably by the time I walked up the steps and into her shop.

I ordered my usual chicken garlic, helped myself to the ice and water and found a table as close to a fan as possible. The three of us had so much to catch up on and we all chatted away in Thai. Kunya cooks and talks and keeps everything running. She's a very talented multitasker. Once her customers had dwindled, she sat with me to snack on some grapes, sharing them with me. It always feels like calling in to eat with a gorgeous friend when I go there. It's relaxed and casual, the food is outstanding but not fussy, and the conversation just picks up from the last time we were together.

Eventually I left her to it as she had a few more orders coming in and I had new friends waiting for me at the cannabis den. Walking back towards them, I schemed in my head how I might be able to get past without them seeing me. Maybe they'd have gone inside or were distracted with customers, but no. As soon as they saw me, out they came and ushered me in. There were now three other foreigners sitting around the table, rolling joints, smoking bongs and drinking beer. I had to break the bad news to them that I wasn't a smoker of any kind, but they didn't seem to mind.

I sat down and was engulfed in a cloud of smoke and chatted for a while with a couple from South Africa who were teaching English in Taiwan, here on holidays for the first time. They were having a blast and keen to move to Thailand once their contract finished. The other man was Russian, I think. He told me he was selling something with coconut oil. I couldn't really understand him, but he was full of ideas about how I might like to introduce weed into my life. Probably the most unusual suggestion was crushing it and mixing it with coconut oil and putting it on bread. Thanks, but no thanks.

I no doubt impressed everyone at the table when I ordered a pineapple shake *sans* weed or rum. The Thai guys running this new microbusiness were busy making bongs from bamboo, moving their potted plants (both weed and tomato) around and keeping us all entertained. The boss had clearly sampled a fair amount of his own product as his speech was slow and he had a mellow look on his face. We talked briefly and he wanted a photo with me for some reason. I blame the novelty factor of me speaking Thai.

I left the potheads to do their thing. The situations I find myself in on a daily basis are far from predictable. I'm embracing these experiences knowing it could only really happen here. Life at home in Australia rarely presents this sort of spontaneity. Maybe I should make an effort to do something about that when I get back?

I spent the rest of the afternoon in my pool and doing some language studies. About 10 p.m., after the heat and humidity of the day had well and truly gone, I was in the mood for ice cream and knew exactly where I could get it. So I slipped a simple cotton dress over my now dry bikini and off I went. Ten minutes later, I had a bowl of lemon and passionfruit ice cream curls in my hand. What's not to love about doing this life differently here?

11 July
Sunrise Offerings & Blessings / Fourteen More Days

If you're ever out and about just on sunrise here you'll see Buddhist monks in their saffron robes, with bare feet, walking around the streets with a large bowl in their hands collecting food from local people wishing to make merit. Lay Buddhists offer the food to pay their respect and in return the monks provide a blessing and their wisdom. It's a very important morning ritual for many Thais. I always make these offerings each time I visit Thailand. I like the ritual of it and the giving of sustenance to others. At sunrise I headed out to do just that. I walked to a street vendor about twenty minutes away to buy the food that I wanted to give. Having been out doing this before when our TP friends were here, I knew where the monks would pass by while doing their rounds.

When I arrived, I could see the monks in the distance, so I had time to have a look at all the delicious foods on offer. I chose based on what I would like to be eating myself, which today was sticky rice parcels wrapped in banana leaves, rotis, a couple of poached chicken and rice boxes, a few small bags of yellow curry, a handful of random sweets that looked yummy and bottles of water.

Once I was happy with my offering, I stood and waited with a group of other people who had started to gather. We all took our shoes off. It's important to appear lower than a monk when you meet them. That's why you'll see them sitting up on a platform in the temple while everyone else sits on the floor.

It wasn't long before the monks reached us. As the first one approached, he opened the lid on his alms bowl (*bart*) and I placed my food inside it. The alms bowl is a significant possession for a Buddhist monk. He had a basic saffron-coloured shoulder bag for the bottles of water and any excess food. Everyone in my group did the same. Then we stood in silence with our heads bowed, eyes closed and our hands clasped together, the same as a *wai*, while the monk recited a blessing on us all before continuing on his way.

There's no fuss attached to this ritual, called *duk bart*. It's silent and sacred for those receiving the blessing and it's believed to bring happiness and a peaceful life. No eye contact is made. The more a person gives without asking for or expecting anything in return, the more they are thought to become rich in the larger sense of the word.

Monks don't prepare their own food, so they rely solely on the offerings from their community. They take the food back to the temple and share it among themselves around 8 a.m. They must eat before midday each day as after that time they're forbidden to eat until sunrise the next day. Thai Buddhists believe that the spirit lives on in another form after death, and that the food they offer to the monks is passed on to the spirits of ancestors, which is why it's so important to choose delicious offerings. I'd been wondering not only about the alms bowl but also about what other possessions a monk has. After making a few breakfast purchases for myself, I wandered home feeling lighter in spirit and made it my job to find out more. It seems these begging bowls have quite the story that I'd never been aware of before.

'Baan Bart' is the name of a neighbourhood in Bangkok where locals have been handcrafting alms bowls since the 1700s. It means 'Bowl House'. It's located in the narrow side street near the Saket Temple, Wat Saket. I read about these bowls being crafted from raw steel using only hands and a hammer. This ancient method is still used today by these people. Eight pieces of steel are used to make a bowl, representing the eight spokes on the Buddhist Wheel of Dharma, which represent the Noble Eightfold Path, a central teaching of Buddhism. The seams are fused together to give a distinctive pattern. You can see some bowls left in their natural state having only been polished, giving them a clean metal finish, while others are coated with layers of black lacquer.

I've put this location on my must-visit list next time I'm in Bangkok. I also found it interesting to read about the possessions that a monk has. The bare necessities are usually a robe, holy water bowl, monk manual, bath towel, umbrella, sandals, mosquito net and blanket. Little wonder they can devote themselves solely to their practice with such few material needs or distractions around them.

I do find the Buddhist way of living appealing. This period of living with simpler needs, enjoying simpler days, having simpler decisions to make and looking at life in a simpler way has reinforced my feeling that life doesn't have to be so complex.

'I only have fourteen days left here,' I just whispered to myself. I'm in complete denial that my special time is so close to ending.

12 July

Greener Green | Bluer Blue | Soft Sea | Sans Selfie

It was a cracking morning today. Blue sky with the odd wispy cloud and Big Buddha was in full view as I walked up to get my *cha yen*. The green jungle around me looked greener and the blue of the sky bluer. I knew that after school today I was headed straight for a sun lounge on the beach. N'Bow was busy so he sent N'Odt to drive me to school, which was lovely as we always have plenty to catch up on. N'Bow had been telling me about his favourite fried bananas shop last week and said he'd been to buy them for me a couple of times, but the shop was either shut or sold out. Today when I got in the car, N'Odt handed me a brown paper bag of still-warm fried bananas with a big smile and kind greetings from N'Bow. Honestly, these two know how to make a girl smile.

We got talking about these particular fried bananas as I shoved one into my mouth. N'Odt told me they were perfect. The banana was just ripe enough, not underripe which makes them chalky, or overripe which makes them mushy. He told me the batter had the right amount of sweetness in it and the crunch was spot on. Seems not all fried bananas are created equal. I didn't know that these were the elements of a superior fried banana, but I'm glad I do now. I'd give them a ten out of ten just based on the thoughtfulness surrounding the purchase of them for me and the taste. I think N'Bow and N'Odt are onto something.

Once we reached my school, I told N'Odt that I'd be sharing my prized bananas with my class buddies, and he produced another bag that had been sitting on the passenger seat. Fried bananas for everyone, it seemed. Their kindness is next level.

In class, while munching on fried bananas, I learnt another Thai word expression, *narm jai*, which literally means 'to give water from your heart'. Thais say it means to be considerate and caring towards other people. When N'Odt picked me up from school, I was able to use my new expression straightaway to thank him. I then sent N'Bow a thank you message with *narm jai* in it as well. With all the people that I've met here, there will be no shortage of opportunities to use *narm jai mark* – *mark* meaning 'very' – because it's just who they are and how they go about life.

Kruu Noi refers to N'Bow and N'Odt as my bodyguards as they take care of me. They're always outside the school before I'm due to finish, never let me down, make a point of running around the front of the car to open and close the door for me. Now they're feeding me. I may never leave this place.

After school, with my beach bag over my shoulder and my headphones on, I trundled off on my well-beaten path to the beach. I haven't been wearing my headphones while walking, preferring just to take in the sounds around me, but today I had the music cranked up loud. I could be kidding myself, but I think it helped me lift my feet and pick up the pace as I walked along.

Despite being full to the brim with fried bananas, I stopped for a bowl of ice cream curls. Knowing my time is fast closing in on me, I will spare no opportunity to eat these. Today's flavour selection was mango and coconut. That was eaten even before I stepped on the sand. My usual sun lounge was vacant, and the sun lounge boys looked pleased they could offer it to me. They stayed and chatted and helped me lay out my towel before going off to get my big bottle of chilled water without a word from me. Bless them.

The sea was much softer, with gentler waves. It was easy for me to float on my back without getting a mouth full of water. As usual I did nothing more than go in and out of the water. In between I had my music in my ears and my eyes on the happenings of the beach. I spoke to the beach massage ladies, who told me they'd had a busy day with a constant stream of customers, which made all of us smile.

Those wispy clouds that I'd seen this morning were still around at sunset, turning pink and some closer to the horizon a bright orange. The parasailing was in great demand. It brought a smile to my face watching the bright, rainbow-patterned sail gliding across the sky in front of me every few minutes. I couldn't help but think what a spectacular evening to be up there doing that.

The social-media-obsessed females posing for shots were out and about. I've had to stop myself questioning how you find yourself a guy who is willing to photograph you from *every single angle, every single head tilt, every single splash or pretend frolic* in the water and on it goes because obviously they exist. I've moved on to wondering if anyone – apart from those around my age and older – even knows the sun is setting let alone sits to admire it?

What's happened to those spontaneous dodgy shots where no one is looking at the camera or your hair is crazy or the sun has totally blown out your shot and you're not pouting but just smiling because you're loving life? I find these shots are the ones I stop and reminisce over as the memories of that moment in time comes flooding back. They're my most loved photos.

I created my Instagram account on 2 January 2012. I now have more than 7,300 photos, and as I scroll back through my grid, the absence of the staged selfie is very evident. Those I do have are from the last couple of months when I've been alone. I wanted a few of myself, particularly when I'd just got out of the surf and was feeling great. They captured the happy smile on my face which is what I wanted most.

I wandered home via the Kata Night Market and headed straight for the sticky rice and mango stall. My pace was pretty brisk, without the help of my headphones, as I walked back to my room in anticipation of indulging in one of my favourite Thai sweets for dinner.

13 July
Kata Temple | Thai Gold | Kitchen Utensils

Moments after I sat down in the restaurant across the road from Kunya's café (as she was closed), the rain started and the streets were quickly flooded. The sheer volume of water would make any drainage system struggle and this one did. I ordered *somtarm*, sticky rice and barbeque chicken and happily watched the rain continue to fall like it was never going to end. But after about thirty minutes, as suddenly as it started, it completely stopped.

My plan for today was to visit Kata Temple. It's not a place usually frequented by tourists and I'd asked N'Bow where it was because when I tried to find it previously, I failed. This time I had my directions, and a couple of kilometres later I was walking up a long steep driveway and into the temple grounds. Set back from the road and nestled amid lush jungle, the place had a lovely sense of serenity. I sat for a while on a bench under one of the sprawling trees to cool off and take it all in.

In front of me was the ornate and beautiful temple (*wat*), covered in the distinctive Thai patterns and painted in glistening gold. I was looking at the ordination hall, where new monks are ordained, and other important ceremonies take place. There's always one altar with one Buddha image in this building. On either side of the steps leading to the entrance, there was the distinctive *naga,* a mythical serpent-like creature that according to legend sheltered the Buddha while he was meditating. It's very common in temple architecture to see *nagas* used as decorative features for staircases.

I wandered around the temple grounds for a little while and, as I was leaving, I happened to see a ginger tabby cat lying beside a rooster on the steps of another building. An odd couple completely at ease with one another and, in my mind, most likely friends – live and let live in action. I was happy to have spent some time at the temple this morning and sent N'Bow a photo so he knew I'd finally found it as I knew he'd also be pleased.

Heading back, I stopped at a couple of interesting places. The first was a Thai gold shop (*raan tong*). Gold in Thai is *tong* and shop is *raan*. They sell the bright yellow gold, which I'm told is 96.5 per cent gold or 23 karat. These shops act much like banks in that Thai people commonly buy and sell gold as an investment. It often helps ease the temptation of spending all your cash. They sell gold bars and gold jewellery but rarely with gemstones, just gold.

These shops, usually red inside and out, are absolutely overflowing with gold. An interesting fact that I learnt today was the measurement for the weight of gold is baht, the same word as the unit of money. Something to be aware of should I ever be in the market for the odd bar of gold in the future. Being clear on what baht you're referring to might be quite important.

I called in to a shop that was so jam-packed with stock that it was hard not to trip over while shuffling sideways down the aisles. The stock was on the floor, crammed on the shelves in high piles and chaotic in its placement with a thick coating of dust over all of it. I had a brilliant time rummaging around. I'd been on the lookout for a few Thai kitchen utensils for Georgia. We'd used the very versatile flat-bottom soup spoons and a stir-fry scoop during the cooking class with Jimmy and we both wanted to have these for our cooking adventures at home. Jimmy had told me there were no shops in Kata selling these utensils, but I wasn't so sure. This shop looked to me like it had everything you'd ever need in your Thai kitchen. You'd just have to find it in among random things like nuts and bolts, showerheads, ironing boards, fans and plastic containers. There were baskets to cook sticky rice in, ceramics of every description, glassware, woks, pots, steamers, chopping blocks and the cooking utensils I was after.

The owner was very curious about me speaking Thai and wanted to call her friend on FaceTime so I could talk to her. I made the excuse of it being so hot I needed to get home quickly, and off I trotted with my utensils, busting to tell Georgia. By the time I got home, I was quickly in the pool as the level of humidity seemed to have soared after the rain. I opted for a quiet night in with a food delivery from a local restaurant that does a very luscious red duck curry and rice.

14 July
Yar Kit Mark | Hints of Apricot | Frugal Living

With my brain feeling fresh this morning after a deep and long sleep, I decided to start the day off with some Thai language. I'm much better in the morning, particularly if I'm trying to learn new concepts. Getting things to sink in and then stay isn't anywhere as easy as it once was. I've been doing a self-paced online course purely on Thai grammar and tone markers. I gave myself a very generous deadline to complete it knowing there wasn't anything to be gained by making it a chore. I ticked off the last module of the course this morning. It always feels good to finish something these days. Now let's see what my recall is like in a week or so.

Feeling pleased with myself and with the rain having stopped, I swam in my pool, played music, lounged, snoozed, ordered lunch online, read and chatted to my friends at home. I tried not to think about leaving, planned my return here in my head as I really don't know what's possible just yet, and of course reflected on how much goodness has come my way since arriving all those months ago.

It was then time for me to get out of my head as the sunset wasn't far off. Time seemed to slip by very fast today. I put on a dry bikini, one of my cotton sundresses, filled my beach bag, slid into my trusty flip-flops and headed off. The ocean swim was just what I needed to clear some of the cobwebs and racing thoughts. The Thais have a great expression they use for such circumstances, *yar kit mark*, which means 'don't think too much'. It's another favourite for me.

I was at Kata Beach as the sky turned a pinkish-mauve with hints of apricot. The clouds, massive and fluffy, hung low in the sky. They went from white to a soft grey and provided just the right amount of drama to make this one of the best sunsets I've seen for a while. I took a video and sent it to Joe.

I called in to see if P'Sak was back at work having returned from Buriram, and he was. Seeing him was the absolute highlight of my day and I gave him a big hug. We had missed one another very much, but had kept in touch via messages and photos that he had been sending of his farm adventures. There was much to catch up on. He had tears in his eyes when he spoke about leaving his dear parents and coming back to Phuket.

I hadn't been to the restaurant while he was away as it's not the same for me. The other staff are all delightful, but the care he shows and the fact that he orders my dinner for me can't be topped. I put him to work straightaway and he chose me a delicious dish of stir-fried prawns and asparagus, so good, simple and fresh, and another tick off the menu.

I've had some really interesting conversations with P'Sak, including how he lives on his monthly wage of 18,000 baht (A$770), for which he works six days a week from 10 a.m. until anywhere between 10 p.m. and midnight. He rents a room with three of his friends and they all have a small corner to live in. For this he pays 1,500 baht a month, which he's very pleased with. His petrol for his motorbike is 1,500 baht a month, he eats most of his meals at work for free and he tries to send 5,000 to 6,000 baht home each month. Hospitality staff rely heavily on tips to boost what they earn. His wage and conditions are typical of so many people in Thailand. Suffice to say, he's not living the high life. He's frugal and focused and he finds all sorts of clever ways to keep his expenses at a minimum. This insight into how he lives gives me an added level of appreciation for how he goes about his life and once again highlights what I take for granted in my own life.

15 July
The Metro | Upscale Clubbing | Freddie Mercury

In 1990, after returning from my exchange-student year in Thailand, I moved from my home in Albury, New South Wales to Melbourne, Victoria. I lived in Richmond, an inner-city suburb, and would drive my little red Honda Civic into the city around 11 p.m. on a Friday or Saturday night. I'd park outside the Metro Nightclub, go inside and listen to the music and dance on my own. I wasn't interested in drinking much. I just loved the loud dance tunes and being in a place where the rest of the world was shut out for a couple of hours. It seemed to provide an escape from the chaos of the city and I felt very grown up at the time. When I'd had enough, I'd get back in my car and drive home.

Fast forward three decades and in Phuket my desire for such an outing seems to have been reignited. I think being on my own has felt much like my younger days when I was single and carefree. Joe can't deal with loud noise and has hearing difficulties from his deployment, not to mention his anxiety in crowds, so this has never been something we'd do together. As my time here has progressed, I've been able to give myself permission to do as I please. My mantra of 'doing life differently' can be once again thanked for that. Probably the only real difference now is the cheeky nap in the afternoon I need to help get me to the starting line at 10 p.m., and sending Joe a video message when I arrive at and depart from the nightclub, so he knows I'm okay.

I washed and blow-dried my hair, which is very rare at the moment, put on some sparkly earrings and a bright lip gloss and headed off alone to the Armania nightclub. I was ready for some dance music, entertainment and a few G&Ts. Apparently, I'm not just clubbing anymore but 'upscale clubbing', according to their marketing blurb! I found my preferred table and promptly ordered my drink and food in Thai with my attentive waitress. Immediately I had a new friend. We spoke for a bit and when my drink arrived she so sweetly asked if I'd buy her a drink. How could I refuse?

The huge claret-red velvet curtains leading into the nightclub were still drawn so I had a bit of time to kill. The main bar, Bar Funk, is connected to the club and they had acrobatics going on and the people watching both in the bar and out on the street easily kept me fascinated while I waited for the curtains to be drawn back.

The choice of clubs in Patong is staggering. But I think I've found the one for me. The DJ soon had it pumping. The beat and vibrations of the music pulsed throughout the room and my body. This was before the saxophone player appeared. I was in my element. The place filled quickly and the strobing lights alternated colours regularly. Later in the night, a Turkish couple asked to share my table. The woman told me her husband wasn't a dancer, so we gals danced together like we were besties and he kept the table for us.

I was sitting close to the entrance of the balcony level, the VIP area, where for a pretty hefty price and a minimum alcohol spend, you can book a spot complete with couches and dance the night away with your friends overlooking the main dancefloor. I started making up all sorts of stories in my head about the groups of people as they headed up the stairs. My G&T consumption at this point might have fuelled my imagination as well.

I hadn't booked N'Bow to pick me up this time but thought I'd wing it with a taxi when I felt I'd had enough. I said goodbye to my Turkish friends and headed towards where I knew I would find one. On the way there was a live band playing at another open-air venue and what looked like the Thai version of Freddie Mercury. I had to satisfy my curiosity. After one passionfruit mojito and a couple of great Queen songs with 'Freddie' doing an excellent job, I knew I was ready to head home.

16 July

Low Profile | Indigo & Peach | Duck Crackling

My early-morning arrival home saw me sleeping late and then napping again during the day. I think I could confidently say today was a recovery day after all that upscale clubbing. Ordinarily I'm not a night owl. I need my sleep to function well, so sleep I did. I kept a very low profile during the day, but was ready for a swim and a sunset by about 5.30 p.m. Down I went to the beach with as little as possible in my bag as I didn't feel like carrying anything too heavy. I'd normally carry water with me, but I stopped to buy it along the way tonight and carried one towel instead of two. Clearly my energy levels needed replenishing.

I'm never not glad that I've made the trek to the beach for the sunset. I sat with my feet in the sand for a while instead of heading straight into the water. There was one cluster of clouds in the sky, directly over where the sun was setting on the horizon. So as day turned into night and the sky became a deep, rich indigo, the clouds turned a gorgeous shimmer of peach and in turn so did the reflection on the water. Absolutely too good to miss. I waited until it was dark before I left and went walking along the shoreline. The hopefuls with their metal detectors were out scouring the sand. I bet they find some interesting stuff, like my prescription sunglasses that

I wore in the surf and had promptly knocked off my face by a rogue angry wave, never to be seen again.

I called in to have dinner with P'Sak and he had something he wanted me to try. He asked me if I liked duck, which I do. Out came a duck salad which was a total flavour bomb. Not only were there juicy pieces of duck, there were also a number of different fragrant herbs, dried chilli, duck crackling, crunchy fried kaffir lime leaves and shaved red onion, all dressed in a spicy lime dressing. The salad came with crisp cabbage leaves and sticks of cucumber. You spooned the salad into the cabbage leaves, topped it with cucumber and ate it. Incredible.

I told P'Sak about my nightclubbing adventures. I invited him to come with me when I next go, not expecting him to say yes, but he jumped at the chance. He's never been to any nightclubs in Patong while living here. So we made a date for Tuesday. I said to him that I'd be the local showing him around and he could be the *farang*. The grin that appeared on his face was priceless.

17 July
Final Week / Cards / New Plans

I can't quite believe that I'm heading into my final week in Thailand. I've been trying hard to ignore the fact that my time is about to end. I'm still so not ready to leave. I've been sitting and writing some cards to my amazing Thai friends today to express my sincere thanks for all that they have done for me. There have been so many Thai people and the odd foreigner who have made my time incredibly memorable and meaningful. They've helped me live so easily here by driving me around, washing my clothes, feeding me the most delicious foods, teaching me the Thai language, introducing me to many new aspects of living like a Thai and allowing me to be part of their lives and showing me how life can be done differently. Being around people who live completely differently to me has been the reminder I've needed to look closely at my own life. Sure, a house and a car is necessary where I live, but I might just be culling my wardrobe and my overflowing cupboards knowing I don't need all that stuff and digging a little deeper into how I go about life.

I'd like to think that when I return home, I will continue to walk and lounge around for hours and keep my stress levels at a minimum and buy ice cream on a whim, but only time will tell. The ingrained habits of home are hard to shake and that's one of the main reasons I came away in the first place. Being here, unshackled from the daily grind, has enabled me to do life differently. I'm very curious to see how I carry this forward into the future.

I'm so pleased that my language skills are now at a level where I can write something from my heart to thank these people and know I've got it right. I've delighted in reflecting on all the goodness that has come my way and thanking my friends for so generously giving that to me, mostly unintentionally because that's who they are. They've undoubtedly been warm and wonderful humans to me.

On each card I've been able to say, 'Looking forward to seeing you again next year.' We all know there's only one way to keep the dream alive and that's to make another plan. I don't know exactly what that plan will look like yet, but it will take shape once I'm home and I have time to reassess where I'm at. I'm already predicting that my ability to feel settled at home will be very average.

Living here has been the tonic I didn't know I needed. How could I have known it would play out and come together piece by piece as it has? What I did know was that I desperately needed a change. I couldn't just keep settling for what I had because it felt safe or I didn't have the energy to do it any other way. In all the discomfort, uncertainties and parts of my life that for so long I couldn't quite make sense of, now seem to have come together and feel in many ways remarkably timely.

Living simply and with kindness in a culture that values respect and fun really agrees with me.

18 July
No Cooking / Coconut Cake / Clubbing With P'Sak

I haven't cooked one single meal since I've been here. I haven't even boiled water to make instant noodles or a cup of tea. I have cut up fruit if that counts, but I don't think it does. When I'm at home I don't mind cooking and if I put in some effort the results can be okay. But the monotony of the evening meal and even thinking about 'what's for dinner', let alone making sure I have the ingredients to make it, has for some time been grinding me to a halt.

For five whole glorious months, there's been no grocery shopping list, no feeling guilty about throwing out limp broccoli or saggy spring onions because I haven't managed to incorporate them into our meals in time, no unpacking of grocery bags or heaving them up our stairs. This lengthy break from doing any of it seems to have been what I needed. Adding this back into my day is not something I'm looking forward to. We might be eating out for a bit when I first get back, which won't be a bad thing.

Having freshly made food available all day and most of the night is an absolute treat. Being able to eat what you feel like and not what's in the back of the fridge is even better. If I lived here permanently, I know I'd do minimal cooking. Why would you when others can make it so well and cheaply and it can be in your hands in fifteen minutes and ready to scoff?

I'm also here to tell you that white rice isn't the enemy. Thai people believe that if you have one serving of rice with your meal you'll always feel full. It sustains many millions of people here and around the world. I think they could be right. Like many women my age, I've been on my fair share of diets, eating plans, restricted eating, fasting, keto and on it goes. I've managed to maintain none of it. Finally, I've found that if I just relax, eat when I'm hungry and not define foods as either good or bad I'm so much better off in every way. It has taken me years to finally allow myself to do this. The diet industry and culture has so much to answer for.

This morning I wandered up to get my *cha yen* and spoke with Khun KK about her daughter's cold. I will miss my friendly morning chats that accompany my tea. There were showers on and off today, but it made no difference to the time I spent in my pool. In fact as soon as it started raining, in I got. When I got out, I saw a message from N'Bow. 'Are you at your hotel, sister?' Well, yes I was. He wanted to come around to see me with a special cake. Okay, then! I dried off and soon enough a photo of him waiting at the front of my hotel popped up on my phone. Out I went and he handed me a box, telling me that his friend was in Trang province today and he asked him to buy this special cake for me. You can't get it in Phuket. I got him to open the box and explain the cake to me. It looked similar to a sponge cake with a creamy coconut icing and top layer of freshly shredded coconut.

So generous and thoughtful of him and he was so pleased that I was excited by it. I'll be sharing this with my friends along the street, but not before I have multiple slices and of course a slice for breakfast in the morning.

I checked in with P'Sak during the day to see if he was still keen to come nightclubbing. He told me how he was counting down the hours until he finished work at 10 p.m. I was also looking forward to having him venture out with me for my last night of clubbing. I fitted in a nap, though he of course couldn't, and I booked a taxi to pick me up and arrive at his house at 10.30 p.m.

When he got into the taxi, he had a huge smile on his face in anticipation of our night out and experiencing something thrillingly new. He was dressed smartly in a striped, short-sleeve cotton shirt and long shorts. Bangla Road in Patong was unusually quiet due to the rain coming and going, but the bar girls were still all out trying to earn a dollar. I guided us through the street and into Armania. P'Sak stood and stared for ages when we entered, just taking it all in.

There's no way P'Sak would spend money at a place like this and it's mainly geared towards tourists as are the prices. It was by no means expensive, but with so little disposable income this would seem very indulgent for the average Thai person. It was my thank you gift to P'Sak for playing his part in freeing me from the 'what's for dinner?' dilemma, even though he couldn't quite understand what my problem was. Unsurprisingly, it doesn't translate well over here.

I ordered our drinks, beer for him and G&T for me. We both sat for a bit, dancing in our chairs and watching the crowd build on the dancefloor. Three beers later and we were dancing together and having a great time. All the entertainment of the acrobats and club dancers enthralled P'Sak. I asked him if he wanted another beer and he hesitated, then said yes. After five beers, he said to me, 'I drunk.' It was 1 a.m. and he had started work at 10 a.m. the previous day so, being the responsible 'local', I suggested we wrap it up and head home.

We easily found a taxi and I spoke Thai while he laughed at me, but by this stage my Thai was way better than his. Within ten minutes of us getting in the car, I heard his first snore.

20 July

Girl, Not Monkey / The Whole Street Knows You, Madam

I woke up to a couple of messages from P'Sak thanking me for the fun we had last night while out at the nightclub. I scrolled through the photos I'd taken on my phone and there were some great memories among them. Two friends laughing and smiling, most with an overlay of either red or blue thanks to the fancy lighting.

How can today be my last day at Alpha Language School? I've enjoyed these classes so much with Kru Noi and my study friends. She has made learning interesting and opened up many aspects of Thai culture that have long been a mystery to me. We've had so many giggles along the way while trying to learn this crazy language. None more so than today when one of the students tried to say that she has a friend who is a girl. Instead she said, 'I have a friend who is a monkey.' To be fair, the words are quite similar. She had no idea what she'd done until we finally composed ourselves and told her.

We've all come to the class with varying levels of Thai and different expectations and we've helped one another. Learning a language is a great leveller and even more so as you get older. I'll miss my classes and the opportunity to use my brain in a different way. It's reassuring to know I still can. We had a shorter class today, then all went for lunch at a restaurant within walking distance of the school. Kru Noi presented me with a lovely gift of tea and a notebook, and we gathered around to take a photo of the group. Finding a supportive and enjoyable place to keep improving my language skills was high on my list when I first arrived. That has certainly been achieved, but I will always be a student of the Thai language.

I came home and reluctantly opened one of my suitcases, thinking I had better start packing a few things. My language study books went in first and clothes that I won't be wearing in the next couple of days. I know I can only tackle this bit by bit, so that was enough for the day. I'd been talking to Pui about taking her out for an Italian meal before I leave as it's her favourite food and the red wine that goes along with it agrees with her. Tonight was our night to eat together so I walked up to her house to collect her and we walked to the end of our street. There's a good Italian restaurant that we both wanted to go to, but as we approached it we could see it was closed.

Pui had heard me talk about the Tann Beach Club so without hesitation I ordered a taxi and off we went. Like P'Sak, Pui hadn't been out in Phuket much. She was excited and impressed to see what was behind the concrete wall she often drives past. The club's beachfront bar and restaurant with tables and couches among the palm trees on its beachfront terrace was full of people, creating a great atmosphere. We ordered drinks and pizzas and sat and chatted and laughed until they arrived. I gave Pui the card I had written for her which made her cry. She has been beyond generous and kind to me right from the first day I met her. It was so important to me that

I could thank her in her language.

I've never met a more determined and hardworking woman with such a huge heart and beautiful smile. She reminded me of so many funny stories tonight, her favourite being the morning she opened her kitchen window and could hear me talking and laughing while I waited for my *cha yen* to be made. I don't think she'll ever forget that. She's still cheeky enough to call me madam and thinks it's remarkable how 'the whole street knows you, madam'.

For someone who lost everything when the pandemic hit and devastated much of the country, her progress and determination to claw her way back, having moved to Kata only eight months ago, is a credit to her tenacity. Watching her open her bar and try and create another income stream for herself and her son has been awe-inspiring. We didn't stay late tonight as Pui was going home to do more laundry. Well, of course she was.

I truly believe that it's the people you meet when you travel, particularly when you travel solo, that leave the most lasting impression. Meeting Pui has reaffirmed that for me.

21 July

N'Bow | Raspberry & Passionfruit | Salt Water

This man! N'Bow, my driver, my bodyguard, my Thai teacher, my younger brother, the father of four young boys, the giver of coconut cake and fried bananas, has never said no to taking me all over the place. He picked me up in the early hours from clubbing, stops the traffic so I can cross the road, has a wonderful older brother N'Odt and, most importantly, is my friend. As with all the incredible Thai people I've met on this trip, it was just by chance that we became friends. I ordered a taxi via an app when I was staying in Karon four months ago and he picked me up. I ordered another taxi and he came again and remembered me. He offered me his direct contact details, which I saved in my phone just in case. I'd had plenty of drivers do this so thought nothing of it. Then I started school and needed a regular, reliable and safe driver so I sent N'Bow a message and the rest is history.

He's shy, polite, softly spoken and incredibly respectful and has those pretty impressive tats on his arms. It's only in the past week or so he's felt okay to stop referring to me as madam when he talks to his son Boss. We've spent hours and hours together while driving in his van, talking about everything and nothing. I'll miss his kind, considerate and caring nature and, of course, being driven everywhere. I think I've paid all his kids' expenses for the year with my taxi fares, or at least I hope I have. He calls me his older sister and I call him my younger brother. I gave him his card yesterday when he picked me up for school. He read it while he was waiting for me and told me how clever I was writing it all in Thai when I got back in the van and he reassured me that I hadn't made any mistakes. I'm unbelievably fortunate to have met N'Bow. He's one amazing human. He will be the last one I say goodbye to when I leave as he'll take me to the airport. I wouldn't want it any other way.

I've been doing a great job of having a bowl of ice cream curls every day this past week, knowing they will shortly be a thing of the past. As I headed off to the beach tonight, I called past the ice cream stand and ordered raspberry and passionfruit. I'm not sure why it took me this long to order this combo, so delicious. I swam until late at the beach and wandered along it in the dark. For a change there was little colour in the sky at sunset, just an inky dark blue with a few scattered grey clouds. I only passed a handful of people as I walked as most holidaymakers had moved on to their night adventures by this time. Those of us who were out had the warm tropical air and the sound of the waves crashing on the beach all to ourselves.

I honestly never expected to spend quite so much time at the beach. I've gradually felt more and more drawn to spend as much time as possible there. The number of times I've begrudgingly got out of the water, in the fading daylight, then needed to reassure myself that I'd be able to return tomorrow, has increased substantially in the last month or two. So many blissful hours of calm, lost in my thoughts, sitting solo on the sand with nowhere else I needed to be.

Completely at ease and so soothing for my soul.

How I'll miss my sunset swims and the stunning colours I've seen while watching another well-lived day sink away. My photo reel is full of my beach time. I already know just how incredibly special this place has been and will always be to me. I can without question recommend the healing benefits of the ocean. As Isak Dinesen once said, 'The cure for anything is salt water: tears, sweat or the sea.'

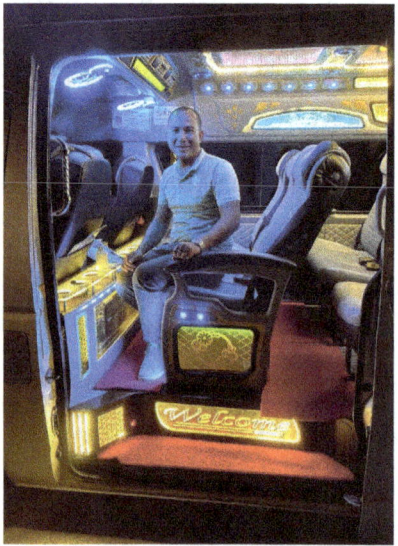

22 July
Packing | Kunya Kisses | Not Letting Go Yet

The packing took a more serious turn today after I went and got my *cha yen* and soft coconut bun for breakfast. I have one bag already full and have no idea why I have so much stuff. I've been given a number of presents by my Thai friends and I'm now giving away all my supplies like hand creams, mozzie spray, aloe vera gel, water and my big tin of pineapple biscuits. Not sure what I was thinking buying such a quantity.

Despite not being a souvenir buyer, I've accumulated a very healthy pile of those cute little clutch bags: some with pom-poms on them; some with neon pink, yellow and orange patterns; but most with big, hot-pink-and-red-embroidered flowers on them that will make fabulous presents. The rest will live with me; each time I take one out, they'll put a smile on my face as I'm reminded of these happy times.

After I walked to Pui and gave her a heap of odds and ends, which she was very pleased to take off my hands, I kept going to see Mickey. I had walked past her shop so many times lately and it was always full of customers. Today it wasn't, so we had a great catch-up sitting at the front of her shop together while I had a pineapple and passionfruit smoothie. No one makes smoothies like Mickey. I continued on my way to visit Kunya and had to have my favourite chicken garlic dish. I gave Kunya her card and watched her read it. She read it out loud so her sister could hear and I got a big kiss from both ladies.

I asked Kunya if she will be in her restaurant when I come back next year. She tells me she has a ten-year plan to be in this same spot and I was very pleased to hear that. We'll keep in touch in the meantime with regular messages and photos. Kunya is another delightful person who has welcomed me here, fed me so well, shared her skills with me, laughed so many times with me and she has definitely helped make my time fun and memorable. I told her I would be back on Sunday for one last meal with her. She wants to make something special. I told her that's okay, but I still need to eat chicken garlic one last time. I hope we can all sit together and eat, chat and laugh. That I'd love.

The local Italian restaurant was open tonight so I whisked Pui away from her laundry for some Parma ham, olives, pasta and red wine. We sat at the front of the restaurant and watched the traffic whiz by. Pui told me more about her life when she worked with an Italian man and that's how she developed her love of Italian cuisine. She also told me about her hopes and dreams for her son. 'Just want him have a happy life, Mel.'

We walked home together and I let her get back to work while I went for a swim in the pool and did a bit more procrastinating around my packing. Seems I've really moved into my room and felt so comfortable it's sad to be pulling it all apart. I got a message from P'Sak asking if we could possibly go clubbing one last time tomorrow night. Well, I didn't need to be asked twice! I'm more than pleased to be squeezing every last drop from this experience including one last dance.

I'd like to say that before I went to sleep tonight I had a long hard think about returning home and what it might be like, but I still can't really turn my mind to it. Until I fly off the island, I'm still here and can't – or won't – let go of any of it.

 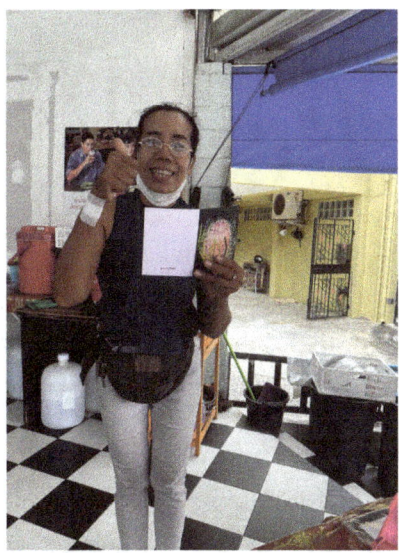

23 July

Monsoon Clouds / Curtains of Rain / One Last Dance

Today being my second-last full day in Kata, I had chicken and rice for breakfast and a sticky rice parcel with coconut custard in it and a *cha yen*. I told Khun KK that I would be coming for my breakfast right until the day my flight leaves. She asked what I was going to do when I returned home and if Joe had missed me. I told her I'd be going back to work to save my money for another trip to Thailand and, yes, Joe was missing me and it would be so nice to see him again. She liked that.

Even though I could see a storm approaching, I went to the beach for a mid-morning swim. In keeping with my desire to eat ice cream curls every day before leaving, today's flavour was passionfruit and lemon. The sky had turned all shades of dark grey and green as the massive monsoon clouds formed. I could see the rain way out to sea while I was in swimming, so I knew it was only a matter of time before it arrived. As much as I'm in awe of the bright colours on a sunny day at the beach, the sky was so dramatic and moody I couldn't stop taking photos of it. It changed rapidly as the storm raced towards us and so many people, including me, stayed in swimming until the lightning blazed across the darkening sky.

And then it arrived, the rain pelting down, almost in curtains. I joined a huddle of beachgoers under a tarpaulin, waiting it out. There's such an intensity to these monsoonal storms: thunder and lightning and torrents of water. And then, just when there were rivers forming between my feet, it stopped. The surfers were back out on their boards in no time. Knowing where the runoff from the overflowing drains ends up, that was my swimming done for the day.

I messaged N'Bow to see if he was free to pick me up. Despite being under cover, I was still pretty soaked. N'Bow was home with Boss, who was frightened by the storm, so they both came out to collect me and get me home safely. The rain didn't let up much, so it was a perfect afternoon for me to sit quietly in my room and read when I wasn't scrolling on my phone. I also knew I'd need a power nap before picking up P'Sak. He'd messaged to say he was finishing early due to the rain and the lack of customers, so I booked a taxi for 10 p.m.

It got to about 9.30 p.m. and he texted saying, 'Let's cancel, too much rain.' I said, 'You can if you like, but I'm still going.' Quick as a flash, he replied, 'Me too!' I knew he was being considerate (that's *greng jai* in action) as Thais never let the weather bother them and I have an umbrella. I picked him up and, when we got out of the taxi in Patong, we stepped into rivers of water. Luckily, we were both wearing flip-flops.

We'd spoken in the taxi about trying a couple of other clubs, but Armania was our first stop as we both love it. It was one great song after another. The sax player was in top form and the DJ had all of us with our hands in the air in a flash. We danced and laughed and took funny silly selfies together just like all the twenty-somethings do.

P'Sak said he was drunk after just three beers this time, but he managed to keep it together as we were determined to see another club. This next nightclub had a totally different vibe, a small room with a bit more rap music going on and shisha being smoked on almost every table. We were quickly befriended by a Thai girl with plaited pigtails and sunglasses and wearing something that looked like a school uniform. She asked P'Sak if I was his girlfriend. I said, 'Yes, yes, I am!' He was totally confused until I explained that otherwise the next question would have been, 'Could you buy me a drink?' and we would've struggled to leave.

One drink each and we moved on, but we both knew as soon as we heard the techno rap they were playing at the next club that it wasn't our scene. We like music we can dance to, not just stand and shake our heads up and down to. As there was no point having a drink, we looked at one another and headed for the door. It was 2.30 a.m. and, after the fun we'd already had, we agreed to wrap up the night.

P'Sak had again lost his English language skills, so we sat in the back of the taxi chatting away in Thai like two old friends, already reminiscing and laughing about our adventure.

That's probably my nightclubbing career over for the next twenty years, but I've had an absolute ball.

24 July

Bye For Now / Missing You Already

I wrote myself a list yesterday, the first in five months. I was afraid that I might forget or miss something or someone on my last day in Kata. I clearly didn't trust myself. My morning ritual, not routine, started the day off: pulling the curtains back to let the sun in and saying good morning to Big Buddha. It was a sparkling morning and the glistening blue pool looked very inviting. I walked down the driveway that had become so familiar, looking up into that lush green jungle that surrounds me. After the downpour of rain overnight, everything felt more humid than normal but also looked even lusher and greener.

It felt like I was experiencing everything in slow motion, wanting to savour each moment as much as I could. I figured that my brain was trying to slow time down, knowing this wouldn't be happening tomorrow. I think this is what those in the know call 'being in the moment'. I chose a *cha yen* and *kanom krok* filled with fresh shredded coconut for breakfast. This morning Khun KK was interested to know when I planned to return and if I might forget how to speak Thai. Both questions I'm pretty curious about myself, but I have no answers to them just yet.

I walked to town passing that handsome boy BeBo. He was

watching everyone walking past but not bothering to lift his head – he's seen it all before. I've loved playing with him each time I walk past and, most of all, his cuddles are the best. He's just a big softie.

My favourite clutch and tote bag shop was my next stop. The cats were having a fantastic time when I arrived. One decided to do zoomies inside the shop and knocked over a tall stack of bowls made from coconut shells. Very amusing. I got talking to the owner and he told me one of the cats was at the vet. Each time I've been in there and bought something I've always given him extra money to feed the stray cats and dogs that he kindly cares for, and this time was no different. He's very aware that my love for a bright pink bag and a floral clutch is deep. I gathered my final purchases and placed them on his counter. He went into his back room and came out with a cute neon-pink mini-pouch and gave it to me. Off I went with a spring in my step and a big smile because he's such a great human and those dogs and cats are in such good hands.

Looking down at my brightly painted pink toenails always makes me smile so a fresh pedicure before leaving was also on my list. I've continued to come to the same salon since I first arrived and always receive a warm welcome. There were so many questions today about what I've been doing and where I've been and this time much disappointment that I was leaving. They too encouraged me to keep speaking Thai and want to see me next year. I assured them I'd be back and the first thing I'd do is call in for a pedicure and massage. They're such lovely ladies who do a great job for such a small amount of money.

Once that was ticked off my list, I knew I wasn't leaving without one final ice cream. I went with my favourite flavours of lemon and passionfruit again. As my ice cream was being made the power went off, so the curls couldn't be curled. I didn't care as I knew it would still taste delicious. Thank you, curly ice cream, for satisfying my sweet cravings time and again. I wish you were available at home, but then again, maybe it's best you're not.

I felt my clubbing until dawn catching up with me, so I headed back to my room. A relaxing swim, more packing and time to lie outside, absorb the peace and quiet and regroup was what I needed. My sun-lounging time has been so vital and provided me with some of my best pondering opportunities. To sit solo in silence and stare into the sky, to just be, to let my mind wander and sometimes doze off has been incredibly beneficial and blissful.

The afternoon seemed to be getting away from me and I still had a few things on my list. I'd been in touch with Damo and we'd said our goodbyes. He's still got another month to go before he decides if he'll head for home. Mr London returned to the UK a couple of weeks ago for some family commitments. The three-way WhatsApp messages have been given a very good workout since.

Off I went to see Kunya for a late lunch, stopping en route to say goodbye to Mr Redwine and his girlfriend, the sweetest people who've been nothing but curious and kind towards me. They wished me *chork dee* (good luck) as I did them. I gave Mickey a wave as I passed by and promised to return.

As I continued up the road, Kunya spotted me long before I arrived. The crazy waving started and was followed by the laughing and big smiles. First was my chicken garlic, but Kunya also wanted to make me her special dish, which turned out to be *dtom yum pla*, a spicy soup full of fresh fish and veggies, ginger, garlic and herbs. It was spicy but not too spicy, which she knows is how I like it. Apparently, it's full of things to keep me well and give me strength and it felt like a big warm hug from my friend Kunya. I did have to draw the line when she wanted me to eat a chunk of raw ginger. I've got a flight to catch tomorrow with no room for a grumbling belly.

My chats with Kunya and her sister and the silly banter we've had together have been the best. Kunya is a natural in her minimal kitchen and I've never seen her stressed, even with a full restaurant. She's welcoming to all and loves feeding people. She will have her new menu next time I visit, but I already know what I'm ordering whether it's on the menu or not. There were hugs and kisses and promises to keep in touch all round before my taxi came to collect me to take me to the beach one last time.

It was a such a different-looking beach to yesterday. The tide was way out so it felt like a hike from the towel to the water, but so worth it. I swam and ducked and dived in and out of the waves like a dolphin or at least that's what I hoped I looked like. At last, I dragged myself back to my towel.

Sitting on the sand, I recorded myself a little video that I intend to play when life at home becomes a bit dull and the daily grind begins to creep back in. I talked about how I was feeling within myself and how grateful I was for the time I've had. So fortunate in every way. I also said how much I love this place and that I think it loves me. I may have made myself cry. Finally, I actually said, 'I suppose I better toddle on home to Joe and my fur girls.'

As I was sitting there talking to myself and waiting for the sun to set, a small dog, with no encouragement at all, came trotting over and sat beside me. She asked for belly rubs, then went back to her mum, then came back and sat on my feet, then went back to her mum. She was so cute and must've known I needed the comfort of a canine because they just know these things.

It was all about the blue hues tonight as the sun set. From the palest baby blue right through to a deep, dark denim. Again, it was beautiful to watch the colours change and remind myself of all the goodness my beach time has given me over the months.

The simplicity of going for a swim, sitting on the sand and sinking my feet into it, watching the sunset, swimming in the rain, walking along the shoreline and just being there. Without a doubt the best soul food there is.

I slowly packed my things and flung my trusty beach bag over my shoulder and headed home. I brightened up my mood for a moment by stopping to buy my tenth tube of lip gloss and putting it on my lips straightaway. The obsession is real.

In no great hurry to get home, I walked to where it all began, the first hotel, Kata Poolside Resort, which I remembered so randomly choosing while I was still in Hobart, knowing nothing more than that I wanted to be able to walk to the beach and have air conditioning in my room. As I stood there, I felt like capturing the sights and sounds of the evening on video. There's always so much activity and life in this area and tonight was no different. I pressed the record button on my phone and was panning towards the road when Pui swerved off it with her son on the back of her motorbike and said, 'Hello, madam!' Honestly, that gal and her timing. She pulled over and we both laughed very hard and she asked, 'Where are you going?' I asked her the same question.

It's these random little encounters with all sorts of people, occurring every single day, that have enriched my time here beyond my imagination. People stopping to say hello, beeping and waving, yelling out to me – they just want to connect at every opportunity, much like they did thirty-four years ago. But this time I've loved it.

I told Pui I was going home for a shower, then to have dinner at Kata on Fire with P'Sak, then to her place for a drink and a goodbye. Off we went, me shaking my head and smiling that Pui was now part of my video for home.

Showered with full fluffy hair and my bright and cheerful

jellybean dress on, I went off to have P'Sak order dinner for me one last time. I was amused when two of the female staff at the restaurant told me I looked like Barbie from the movie. Now I've heard some strange stuff here, but Barbie, are you kidding me? I went with it and now I need to see the movie. I wasn't overly hungry after my lunch with Kunya. So with the approval of P'Sak it was the fresh asparagus and prawns for me again. I gave P'Sak his card and the wide grin on his face said it all. So many of the staff came to my table to say goodbye.

It was getting late so I thought I'd better get moving. Before leaving, I felt like I could eat a small sticky rice with mango. I asked P'Sak and off he went to the kitchen. What was soon delivered almost left me in tears. A large plate with thin slices of mango arranged in the shape of a love heart with the inside of the heart full of white and green (Thais like to colour their rice for a bit of variety) sticky rice. A magenta orchid made it just so. I was already feeling the love, but now I was totally engulfed by it. P'Sak poured the coconut milk over it for me and was so chuffed that he'd been able to surprise me and that I loved it. Talk about making a girl feel special.

I felt very sad saying goodbye to my clubbing friend. We had tears in our eyes. He's the most gentle and caring soul you could ever hope to meet and I've been lucky enough to do just that. I promised him that, when I return next year, we will be hitting the clubs together for sure.

I arrived at Pui's place carrying my leftover sticky rice and mango in a box for her. It was very late and my emotions were close to the surface. We had a drink together and one of her neighbours joined us. I hadn't managed to see Khun Tuk to say goodbye as when I walked past she'd been very busy with customers. I asked Pui to do this for me as they're now friends. Pui said she wanted to come to the airport with me tomorrow and send me off. With that, I finished my drink and left to complete my packing, or culling as it turned out to be.

My heart was so full, but also heavy.

25 July
Unsettled Heart / Tears & More Tears

I woke to my alarm and the sun was already streaming in as I'd deliberately not fully closed my curtains. As has been the case all week, my heart was glad but also sad. They have a saying in Thai, *mai sabai jai*, which translates as 'unsettled heart'.

N'Bow had made arrangements to visit N'Odt after dropping me off at the airport so Pui wouldn't be able to come along. He felt terrible about it, but I explained that a long goodbye would be even harder, so it was for the best. With my bags finally closed, I looked around my room, out to my pool and up to Big Buddha and asked that he look after my friends until I return and I smiled. Room 241 has been my base for 'doing life differently' and allowed me to feel safe, secure, happy and rested. And the air conditioning never missed a beat.

With my bags loaded by N'Bow, we drove up to Pui's place so I could see her and say goodbye. She was waiting out the front for me and came with me as I got my final *cha yen* and said my goodbyes to the lovely Khun KK and her husband. Khun KK was so kind, telling me the street won't be the same without me in it. N'Bow, Pui and I huddled together and took one last photo.

Saying goodbye to Pui was awful. We've become so close and

loved one another right from the start. There were lots of tears, but we know we'll see one another again. She's a Thai woman wanting to embrace all that is Western and I'm a Westerner wanting to live like a Thai. I've promised her that I will bring her over to Australia for a visit in the future and we can eat pasta, olives and bread and drink red wine together. But, more importantly, I'll see her in Kata again.

Although I was upset leaving Pui, N'Bow and I soon started chatting as we always do and I pulled myself together. He told me how much he's loved the last four months with me and how he'll miss me. I tried to say the same, but the knot in my throat and the tears streaming down my face didn't make it easy. Pulling up at the airport departure point, N'Bow got my bags from the van. We *wai*-ed one another and I gave him a big hug. My eyes were overflowing with tears and I couldn't speak. I just turned and walked towards check-in and he got back in his van and drove off.

Feeling overwhelmed by the love and kindness, I sat in the airport lounge and felt lost and untethered. I had to find the bathroom to restock my tissue supply. I moved myself to a comfortable chair in the corner and spoke to dear Joe on the phone once I could string a sentence together. He knew it would be hard for me to say goodbye. Then the messages from Pui, N'Bow and P'Sak started popping up on my phone.

25–26 July
Singapore—Melbourne—Hobart / Home Sweet Home

I lay on the bed in my teeny-tiny hotel room in the middle of Chinatown in Singapore trying to process everything. My emotions were still too raw and I couldn't. The only thought that comforted me was knowing I'd be sleeping in my own bed the next night with my favourite human of all, my husband, and with our fur gals snuggled in beside us. More tears came almost from nowhere, a mixture of happy and sad ones. Eventually sleep came my way.

Arriving back at Changi Airport in the early hours of the morning, I did my best to miss my flight home, dragging my feet to the departure gate with just enough time before it closed. I was lucky enough to be in fancy-pants, lie-flat-bed class, with so much space, comfort and excellent food and drink it makes you wish your flight would take longer so you can indulge and enjoy it all. Being in my own little bubble on the plane was perfect. My fragile emotions were still bubbling away so close to the surface. I tried not to think about saying goodbye to my friends as I knew my eyes would soon fill again. I diverted my thoughts towards making my Thai friends and Kata part of my world going forward.

My three dearest loves greeted me at the airport. Two of them offered me their paws and were very keen to kiss my chin, the other preferred a long, tight hug and a kiss on the lips. I struggled to believe I was home, though the unpacking signalled that something had finished. But then Joe handed me a bundle of about 145 pages secured with a very large bulldog clip. He'd collected all my thoughts, experiences, adventures, musings, laughs, reflections, observations and stories from my Instagram squares. I had no idea I'd written that much, but I was so glad I had.

Thailand had provided me with the opportunity to live my best life and given me time and space to do something so incredibly necessary and special for myself. Doing more of what brings you joy and giving yourself permission to do this one precious life differently can never be underestimated and it's never too late.

I will always be immensely grateful for and cherish what 'doing life differently' has shown and given me. That mantra, those three simple words, has changed my life in so many ways. Some obvious and others that are yet to be realised.

My happy place and its wonderful people have humbled me once again. For me this is just the beginning. *Korp khun mark kha prateet thai* – Thank you very much, Thailand.

Now, I wonder how long before I'm asked, 'What's for dinner?'

Epilogue

I knew I would be unsettled when I got home. What I didn't know was to what extent or how deeply I'd yearn for my life back in Kata. All those friends and family I met up with on my return who asked me if I was glad to be home got the same response: 'No, I just want to go back.' This yearning didn't fade but got stronger and stronger. This was no reflection on those at home whom I'd not seen in a while or my life at home. It had everything to do with the level of contentment and pure joy that I had grown to love while away. Letting that go, having convinced myself long ago that such goodness was for others, was my biggest hurdle.

My initial instinct was to sell up, downsize and go back to Phuket. Joe was all for it and it's certainly not off the table as a possibility in the future, but we would never leave without Jasmine and Rosie. I was constantly thinking of and missing my friends, the beach, the sunsets, the food, the pool swims. Pretty much everything. My garden was still hibernating when I returned with most of the trees still bare and leafless. Everything looked so bleak compared to the lush tropical jungle of Kata. Thankfully there were daffodils, rhododendrons and hellebores flowering. They did their best to provide some colour and cheerfulness. My waratahs were also close to coming alive and putting on a spectacular show in my backyard, which is always welcome.

Then I started writing this book. Again, I didn't really know why I was doing this or what was involved other than tidying up what I'd already written. I always wanted to keep my musings and had envisioned the pages Joe had printed for me being spiral-bound and put on our coffee table so I could flick through them until it was time to find them a spot in the sideboard with all our other keepsakes. I had a few people encouraging me to give writing a go while I was away. One in particular, my lovely friend Maeve O'Meara, said, 'It's time, Mel, you're fifty-two and it's time for you to shine. People want to read something real and genuine.'

Before I knew it, I was researching self-publishing websites and signing up for an online writers' boot camp in the US. Off I went, bouncing from one thing to another with no plan, reading and researching, happy at being taken on yet another ride into unknown territory and just watching it all unfold. Naively I thought I had most of the words I would need for a book and it would just be a matter of 'touching them up' and adding a bit here and there. I soon learnt that what I had written for Instagram needed a little more if it was to be used in a book. I have had a couple of nasty bouts of imposter syndrome that I have had to counsel myself out of and keep pushing forward.

I set about rewriting and polishing what I had already written and luckily the words just poured out of me. I'd look at my photos and Instagram and be instantly transported back remembering what I ate, whom I chatted with and how I felt. My experience was sitting within me so vividly even I was surprised. I've really enjoyed the process of writing. My desire to sit and write for countless hours, giving so much of myself to my book, is probably what has amazed me the most.

It has been wonderful to retrace my steps and share my experience more broadly and permanently in these pages. It has helped me to not only relive, but also to keep alive, my treasured adventure. I now don't feel like I have to let it go. This lived experience is very much part of who I am and my story.

Writing this six months after my return, hardly a day has gone by that I've not communicated in some way with my friends in Kata. We message one another and I have regular video calls with Pui, in some cases multiple times a day. She will often send me a photo of the Big Buddha while she's having her morning coffee as she can see it from her house. She likes me to know what sort of day it is over there. She also knows how much I liked looking up at him from my room.

The day I left Kata, Pui's older brother had a stroke. I got a message from her telling me she had driven the five hours to her hometown in three, so I knew it was serious. He had two very costly operations and, even then, the family were unsure if he'd survive. After more than a month in hospital, he went home with his wife caring for him. He's still unable to care for himself. He can now eat a little, having survived on rice porridge for months, and he's starting to walk. It's incredible when at times all hope was lost for him.

Pui has been through an unbelievable amount of hardship since I left, not only this but so much more. I've felt increasingly helpless. There's almost another book waiting to be written solely about her trials and tribulations. Low season was difficult for her. There were many days with no income at all, making life very tricky when there's rent and expenses to pay. She sold her TV, one motorbike and a computer and I'm actually not sure what else. She remained positive that high season would resolve this situation and the cash would start to flow again but it didn't eventuate. She continued to do her laundry work in the morning, then work in her bar from the afternoon into the night. It meant she was often surviving on a couple of hours' sleep as she would sit up into the early hours waiting for customers to stop in for a drink. She was happy to stay up to 'catch the customer', so as to avoid having her power cut off, although that still happened.

She fell off her motorbike three times, injuring herself. The last time she told me she was lucky a truck didn't run her over. A kind bystander pulled her off the road, thank goodness. It seems that every time she gets her head slightly above water something else happens. Her washing machine breaks down, her landlord decides to increase her rent just because he can, the police pay her a visit because they saw a foreigner sitting at her bar smoking cannabis. She was threatened with a three-month suspension of her licence or a very hefty fine. She paid the 20,000 baht and there went her savings and her ability to pay rent. Soon after, her beloved bar – that she was so proud of and had put everything into – closed.

I have watched this woman question her own existence at times. Then the next day she would tell me, 'I can pass this, Mel. Don't worry, everything I can pass. I'm strong.' I'm left wondering how can life be so cruel to those who have so little and work so incredibly hard just to survive? There have been many days when we've just cried or laughed together because there was little else we could do.

I know Pui is strong, resilient, clever and everything else, but she has also been asking her Buddha why her life is so hard. The other day she told me she had been asking for too much from him so now she would stop and just accept life as it is. I told her that maybe she had exhausted all her luck and it was time to just be calm.

This reminded me of a time when Pui had promised Buddha

ninety-one boiled eggs if a particular request she had made came to fruition. It did. Up she went to the temple with her ninety-one boiled eggs and sent me the photo. I suggested that she may need to do that again. One thing I am confident of is that her faith guides her and she will always return to it when life seems impossible.

Watching Pui struggle from afar motivated me to think hard about how I could help her. What could I do from home that could possibly provide an income stream for her that didn't require her to wash and iron for hours on end only to be paid a maximum of 50 baht or A$2.15 per kilo?

My idea was to create an online shop for us both to work together in. I would train and upskill Pui in loading the products on the site, updating the site and responding to emails, once I'd trained myself! She would source our stock, negotiate a good price for us and send it to me to sell. I already knew I wanted to sell the bright, cheerful clutch bags that I'd become very partial to. I had given many to my friends as presents and they loved them as much as I did.

The online store brightblossombags.com was born in February 2024. It's now giving Pui an income of 100–200 baht (A$4–8) per bag sold. More importantly, it has restored her dignity, self-belief and ability to provide for herself and her son. When our shop went live, I asked Pui to log on. She was in tears as she said to me in disbelief, 'Mel, I never believe that I would have online shop! I feel hopeful for my future.'

Not long after, while messaging Pui, I noticed that the Thai spelling of her name was different. When I asked her about it, she told me she had changed her name. She was ready to have a new life and a fortune teller had allocated her a new name that she feels is far more suited to her. She's still Pui but feels like her life is now taking a different, more positive path.

P'Sak was starting a study course when I left Kata as he wanted to get his licence to be a tour guide. Studying seven days a week for a month and then going to work each evening, he achieved it. He would send me photos of the presentations that his teachers were delivering in English so I could read what they were being taught. He has since finished work at Kata on Fire and has started his tour guiding. He will be an excellent ambassador for his country. I've already started compiling a list of places I would like him to take me to when I return and he's all for it.

Just before Christmas, his father passed away. He was distraught. He included me in all the ceremony around his father's funeral via regular photos and explanations. A traditional Thai funeral was not something that I was familiar with and I felt very privileged to be included in this deeply sad and private time in his life. He sent me a photo of his elderly mother four days after her husband passed away, sorting a mountain of cucumbers that had been harvested from their farm. She was out in the heat packaging them up to send to the market. Just remarkable.

I regularly send N'Bow messages asking him to deliver me a bag of fried bananas or for him to ask N'Odt to send over some *somtarm*. I downloaded the Thai keyboard to my phone a month or so before I left, feeling I was ready to take the plunge. We only communicate in Thai when we message each other, so it's been fun to make lots of mistakes and have him laugh at my messages. He also sends me video messages telling me about the weather and where he's going for the day. It's always great to hear his familiar voice again. I get random photos of Boss riding his bike or eating his dinner. His whole family had a bout of illness that really had them all struggling for over a month. It was stressful as no work equals no income.

Kunya sent me a photo of her new menu. Very fancy and

a bit too professional for my Kunya, I must say. Maybe by the time I see her next it will be back to being a number of separate pages spread among the tables in her café. She's doing well and is busy most days, but like everyone, somewhat disappointed with high season as the tourist numbers seem a little lower. She will no doubt be okay as she has built up quite the local following with her great food for a very reasonable price. The last time I heard from her she told me that Manfred might be in Germany for some time as he's not well.

I tell them all how much I miss them and they return the sentiment. We've used all the emojis there are with crying faces, love hearts and sad faces to express how we feel, but life must go on and so it does.

While away I came to the conclusion that it was time for me to find another workplace. The decision wasn't that hard in the end. I've since joined a brand-new team of people working on different subject matter, but still within the Commonwealth Government. The learning curve has been incredibly steep. The truth is my heart and mind have been elsewhere and probably always will be.

I'm heading back to Phuket towards the end of 2024, knowing that it will be a very different experience for me once again. I'm okay with that as there's still so much I want to discover. In the meantime, one thing that will never change and has only intensified is the love and commitment I have for my Thai friends, my happy place and doing life differently.

Oh, before I go, you might be curious to know how my 'what's for dinner?' dilemma has played out. Well, there have been a few more cheese-and-biscuit dinners, toasted sandwiches, platters made from fridge bits and takeaway pizzas. The break from it certainly did help. I have not re-embraced it with gusto and given the choice I'd be giving my foodpanda app a very good workout.

Thank You – Korp Khun Kha

Having absolutely no idea what I was in for when I set about writing this book, I am extremely fortunate to have had incredible support from many. I now know there's no way I could've done it without them.

To my husband Joe, your unwavering support and patience while I've been writing this memoir has been nothing short of incredible. I've largely been absent from our family and you've been so understanding, even solving the 'what's for dinner?' dilemma at times! You've been a sensible sounding board and have always reassured and encouraged me when I got the wobbles. You probably know the words in this book better than I do as you've read and reread pages upon pages when I wasn't sure if I'd properly captured what I was trying to say. Your help with proofreading, correcting my punctuation and grammar, although annoying for you, has been invaluable to me.

I love you sweetheart now and forever.

To my editor Jennifer Barclay, apart from your great editing credentials, I selected you because you had your lovely fur girl Lisa in your profile photo. How could I not! I nervously sent off my first draft not even knowing if it would be worth pursuing and you encouraged me to go for it. You've asked so many great questions and provided the path to enable me to dig a bit deeper, share more broadly and look closely at how this time away has shaped me and ultimately changed me. Thank you for walking beside me as I've tried to make this book the best it can be. Big pats to Lisa, too!

To my copy editor, proofreading guru Ian Smith, you absolutely saved the day. Your careful and considered approach to my words and the final polishing you provided was invaluable. My heartfelt thanks.

To my book cover designer Hazel Lam, who created my fabulous book cover from a stack of my favourite photos from my time away, my desire for hot pink to feature and some words around what the book was about. You absolutely nailed it. I knew instantly when I saw your design that my words would be very happy living inside that cover. So incredibly talented you are. Thank you.

To my wonderful friend Maeve O'Meara, who lit the spark and has continued to embolden me. Your belief in my words and your wisdom that others might also enjoy them has provided me with the purpose I needed to complete this book. Thank you doesn't even come close in expressing how much I appreciate you.

And last, but definitely not least, a huge thank you to all of my lovely, loyal Instagram friends and followers who have inspired, encouraged and remained interested in my adventure and have continued to look forward to reading this book. You've kept me going when it started to feel too hard. Immensely grateful always.

About the Author

Mel lives in Hobart, Tasmania with her husband Joe and their two much-loved Labradors, Jasmine and Rosie.

Her love of and fascination for all things Thai began in 1989 when she first lived there for twelve months as an exchange student. Since then, Thailand has remained a constant presence in her life, serving as a backdrop for holidays, university studies, and a brief professional stint as a Thai-speaking graduate at a major insurance company.

She learnt to speak the language while attending high school during her first visit and has chipped away at it over many years. When it all comes together, she can now read, write and speak the Thai language.

The combination of food and travel, making and eating plain cake with a cup of tea, growing flowers and the resulting big beautiful bunches that end up scattered inside her home, cuddles and chats with her Jasmine and Rosie and the colour pink – the brighter the better – all make her smile.

A surprise author, taking a leap into the unfamiliar world of self-publishing, Mel had no idea she had a book in her.

www.doinglifedifferently.com.au

Bright Blossom Bags

BAGS BLOOMING WITH COLOUR & KINDNESS

vibrant clutches & totes that spread smiles & style

We'd love you to visit our little shop.

All our bags come sprinkled with happy vibes.
We believe that when women help
other women, magic happens!

All our bags are made in Thailand.

www.brightblossombags.com
IG @brightblossombags_
FB – Bright Blossom Bags

www.ingramcontent.com/pod-product-compliance
Lightning Source LLC
Chambersburg PA
CBHW051932290426
44110CB00015B/1953